CITY OF DETROIT.

REVISED ORDINANCE OF 1863.

ORDINANCES

OF

THE CITY OF DETROIT,

REVISED AND PUBLISHED

BY ORDER OF THE COMMON COUNCIL.

DETROIT:
WALKER, BARNS & CO., PRINTERS TO THE CITY,
Free Press Office, Nos. 18 and 20 Woodbridge St.

1864.

NOTE.

The changes which have been made in the municipal law since the latest Compilation of the Ordinances, that of 1859, sufficiently justify the action of the Common Council directing the present Revision. The number and extent of such changes may be inferred from the fact that less than forty of the one hundred chapters of this Compilation were contained in that of 1859.

In the Revision of 1855, the plan was adopted of collating the Ordinances under separate titles, according to their subjects. The same method was pursued in the Revision of 1859. It has been deemed advisable to adhere to this plan, in the present work, as far as was practicable. While, therefore, it has been necessary, in this Revision, to introduce new titles, the order of the titles is nearly the same as in the previous Compilations. But the arrangement of the chapters, under the several titles, is different from any heretofore adopted.

For convenience of historical reference, the compiler has thought proper to indicate, at the beginning of each chapter, whether it was contained in the Compilation of 1859, or is an entirely new Ordinance, enacted since that Revision. The date of every amendment is also given, at the end of the section amended.

DETROIT, December 24, 1863.

TITLES.

CONTENTS.

TITLE I.

OF THE CITY OFFICERS.

TITLE II.

OF TAXES AND ASSESSMENTS.

TITLE III.

OF STREETS, SIDE-WALKS AND PUBLIC PLACES.

TITLE IV.

OF THE DETROIT RIVER, FERRIES, AND WHARVES.

TITLE V.

OF DRAINS AND SEWERS.

TITLE VI.

OF MARKETS AND SALES.

TITLE VII.

OF THE PUBLIC HEALTH.

TITLE VIII.

OF THE PUBLIC PEACE.

TITLE IX.

OF THE RECORDER'S COURT, AND THE PUNISHMENT OF OFFENDERS.

TITLE X.

OF THE PREVENTION AND EXTINGUISHMENT OF FIRES.

TITLE XI.

OF RESTRAINING ANIMALS.

TITLE XII.

OF HACKS, DRAYS, AND PORTERS.

TITLE XIII.

OF PLACES OF AMUSEMENT AND RECREATION.

TITLE XIV.

OF THE SUPPORT OF THE POOR.

TITLE XV.

OF STREET RAILWAYS.

TITLE XVI.

MISCELLANEOUS.

REVISED ORDINANCES

OF

THE CITY OF DETROIT.

TITLE I.

OF THE CITY OFFICERS.

CHAPTER I.

OF THE CITY ATTORNEY.

[Chapter One of Compiled Ordinances of 1859.]

SECTION 1. The City Attorney shall have the charge of, and conduct, all the law business of the Corporation, and of all the Boards, Officers, Departments, and Committees thereof, and all other law business in which the City shall be interested, when so ordered by the Common Council, and shall draw all leases, deeds, contracts and ordinances of the City. General powers and duties.

SEC. 2. He shall keep his office in such place as may be designated and provided by the City, and shall execute bonds to the Corporation in the amount of two thousand dollars. Office.

SEC. 3. He shall, in writing, advise the Common Council, all Boards of the City, and their Officers and Committees, respectively, and the chief officer of any department or bureau of the City government, upon all matters which may be submitted to him for his opinion. To advise Council and officers.

SEC. 4. He shall certify to the correctness of the form of all official bonds, deeds, leases and contracts of any kind, in which the To certify to bonds, deeds, leases, etc.

City is interested, before the same shall be accepted or adopted by the Common Council, or any officer of the Corporation.

To prepare drafts of bills.

SEC. 5. He shall, when required by the Common Council, prepare the draft of any bill to be presented by the Corporation of the City to the Legislature for passage, with a proper memorial.

To prosecute and defend actions for and against City.

SEC. 6. He shall prosecute and defend all actions which may be brought by or against the Corporation, or any Board or Officer thereof.

To institute actions for rents, license fees and penalties.

SEC. 7. He shall institute actions against all persons owing the Corporation for rents and licenses, or who may have incurred any penalty or forfeiture, under the Charter and Ordinances, or by reason of the breach of the condition of any official bond.

To file statement and pay over moneys.

SEC. 8 He shall, once in every quarter, file a written statement, under oath, with the Controller, stating the nature and amount of any debt due to the Corporation, recovered by him, the person against whom, and the tribunal before which it was recovered, and the time when he recovered the same; and he shall, at the time of making said statement, pay all sums so recovered to the City Treasurer, who shall give him a voucher therefor, a copy of which he shall file with the Controller.

To make report.

SEC. 9. He shall, on the first Tuesday in January, in each year, report to the Common Council, the titles and nature of all actions prosecuted or defended by him during the preceding year, and what actions are pending, what determined, and how, and such other information, concerning the law business of the City, as he deems proper.

To keep register.

SEC. 10. He shall keep in proper books, to be provided for the purpose, a register of all actions prosecuted or defended by him, and of all proceedings had therein; a list of all contracts, bonds, and other papers certified to by him, and copies of all opinions which he shall give upon any point submitted to him.

Disbursements, statement of.

SEC. 11. He shall, at the expiration of every three months, during his term of office, furnish the Controller with a sworn statement of all the disbursements, which he may have made in conducting the law business of the City, for the amount of which the Controller shall draw his warrant upon the Treasurer.

Additional counsel.

SEC. 12. He shall, when he deems it necessary, in the trial or argument of causes of importance, in which the City may be a party, or interested, request such additional counsel or aid as he may designate: *Provided,* That he shall, in all cases, inform the Common Council whom he wishes to employ, and shall employ no one without their consent.

SEC. 13. He shall, without special direction from the Common Council, institute all actions for rents, penalties, forfeitures, and license moneys, for all trespasses and injuries upon, and to the property of the City, or any Board thereof. To commence actions.

SEC. 14. He shall examine all tax and assessment rolls before their confirmation, and make such alterations in the form thereof, as may be necessary to their legality. To examine tax rolls, etc.

SEC. 15. All the principal officers of the City shall, from time to time, place in the hands of the Attorney, for his action, all claims for debt, money, or damages done to the City, which may arise in, or grow out of, the office and business under their charge; and whenever suit is commenced against the Corporation, the officer on whom process is served, shall deliver the same to him. To receive claims from officers.

CHAPTER II.

OF THE CITY COUNSELOR.

[Ordinance approved December 21, 1861.]

SECTION 1. It shall be the duty of the Counselor to give to the Common Council, any Committee thereof, the Mayor, Controller, or any Board of the Corporation, when requested, his legal counsel and opinion on all legal questions arising under, or concerning the Charter, or any Ordinance of the Corporation, and on all legal questions and subjects in which said Corporation shall be legally interested. Counselor to give his legal opinion to Common Council, Committees, and Heads of Departments.

SEC. 2. The legal opinions of the Counselor shall be given in writing. When they are reported to the Common Council, they shall be printed and published, as part of the proceedings of the meeting of said Council, at which they are reported; and when they are reported to any Committee of such Council, to the Mayor or any Board of the Corporation, they shall be filed by such Committee, Mayor or Board, in the office of the City Clerk. Opinions to be in writing. When printed and filed.

When he shall appear as attorney and counsel.

SEC. 3. He shall appear as attorney and counsel in behalf of the Corporation in all suits, prosecutions or proceedings, which shall be brought in any Circuit Court, or in the Supreme Court of this State, or in any United States Court, by or against said Corporation, or any Board thereof, or which, when thus brought, shall be removed, in any mode whatever, from such Circuit Court, into the Supreme Court, and, as the case may require, shall prosecute or defend therein, to the termination thereof.

When as associate counsel.

SEC. 4. He shall also, on the request of the Attorney, appear and act as his associate counsel in the Recorder's Court, in all suits, prosecutions or proceedings brought in said Court, by or against the Corporation, or any Board thereof, or brought under the provisions of the Charter, entitled "Chapter 7, Opening, altering and closing streets;" and shall also, on the request of the Attorney, appear and act as his associate counsel in the Supreme Court, in all such suits, prosecutions and proceedings, when, in any manner, removed to such Supreme Court.

When in behalf of Officers of Corporation.

SEC. 5. He shall also, whenever directed by the Common Council, appear as attorney and counsel in behalf of any officer of the Corporation, in any suit, prosecution, or other judicial proceeding, brought by or against such officer, in his official character, and, as the case may require, shall prosecute and defend them, to the termination thereof.

Not to commence actions unless directed.

SEC. 6. He shall not commence actions, or other judicial proceedings, in behalf of the Corporation, or any Board thereof, except when so directed to do by the Common Council, or by such Board.

To act as member of Committees when requested.

SEC. 7. He shall also act as a member of any Committee of the Common Council, and discharge the duties of a member thereof, whenever directed by said Council.

To prepare drafts of bills when requested.

SEC. 8. He shall also prepare and report to the Common Council, upon their request, the draft of any bill to amend the Charter of the Corporation, or other bill, to be presented to the Legislature, together with a proper memorial to the Legislature, praying for its passage.

To examine and approve leases, deeds and contracts.

SEC. 9. He also shall examine and approve all leases, deeds and contracts, prepared by the City Attorney, to be entered into by the Corporation, or any Board thereof, or by any agent or officers, in behalf of such Corporation, or Board, and shall certify to the legal correctness, sufficiency and execution of the same.

To make report of moneys received or collected, and of disbursements.

SEC. 10. On the expiration of every quarter of his official term, he shall make a report in writing to the Controller, duly verified by his oath, of all sums of money received or collected by him during such quarter for and in behalf of the Corporation, and from whom and on what account or suit they were received or collected, and shall at the same time pay over the same to the Treasurer, who shall give duplicate vouchers thereof, one of which the Counselor shall file with the Controller. At the same time he shall also make a report in writing to the Controller, duly verified by his oath, of all disbursements which he may have made in conducting the law business of the Corporation, and upon what account or suit and how they were disbursed, and the Controller shall draw his warrant upon the Treasurer for the amount thereof.

Id. of suits, etc.

SEC. 11. He shall, on the first Tuesday in January of each year, make report in writing to the Common Council, duly verified by his oath. of all suits, prosecutions or actions prosecuted or defended by him during the preceding year; of the names of the parties thereto; of the titles of the Courts in which they were commenced; of their progress or final disposition; and when finally disposed of, the mode of their disposition, and all other information concerning the legal interests of the city which he may deem necessary or proper.

Appointment, term of office, etc.

SEC. 12. The Counselor shall be appointed by the Common Council, and shall hold his office for the term of three years; he shall be a practising attorney of the Supreme Court of this State, and of good standing as such; he shall keep an office in some public and convenient place in the city of Detroit, and shall, before entering on the duties of his office, give an official bond, duly conditioned, pursuant to the Charter, for the performance of his duties, in the penal sum of two thousand dollars.

To keep register, and deliver papers, etc., to his successor.

SEC. 13. He shall keep, in proper books, to be provided by the Corporation for the purpose, a register of all actions, prosecutions and proceedings, prosecuted or defended by him, and of the various doings therein; and on the expiration of his official term, he shall forthwith, on demand, deliver to his successor in office such register, together with all deeds, cases, contracts or other papers and writings in his possession, delivered to him by or belonging to the Corporation, any officer or Board thereof, or any Committee of the Common Council, and shall also deliver a written consent of substitution of his successor in all such actions, prosecutions or proceedings then pending and undetermined.

SEC. 14. This Ordinance shall take immediate effect.

CHAPTER III.

OF THE CITY MARSHAL AND HIS ASSISTANTS.

[Ordinance approved July 10, 1861.]

Powers and duties.

SECTION 1. The Marshal, Assistant Marshals, and Constables, as conservators of the peace, shall possess and exercise the powers and duties of township constables, under the general laws of the State of Michigan.

To serve process.

SEC. 2. The Marshal and his assistants shall serve all writs and process in the Recorder's Court, in cases arising under the Ordinances, and in proceedings under the Charter, for opening and extending streets, alleys, etc.

To obey and execute precepts.

SEC. 3. The Marshal and his assistants shall obey and execute all lawful precepts and commands of the Mayor, the Recorder's Court, the Common Council, and the Board of Health.

To attend Recorder's Court.

SEC. 4. The Marshal and his assistants shall attend the sessions of the Recorder's Court when engaged in trials and proceedings under the Charter and Ordinances, and also the sessions of the Common Council, and the Board of Health.

To serve papers and notices.

SEC. 5. The Marshal and his assistants shall serve all papers and notices relating to the business of the City which may be delivered to them by the Mayor, an Alderman, a Member of the Board of Health, the Controller, City Attorney, Treasurer, or City Clerk.

Office, and office hours.

SEC. 6. The Marshal and his assistants shall keep their office in the place provided by the Common Council, and one of them shall be found in their office each day, between the hours of 9 A. M. and 12 noon, and between the hours of 2 and 4 P. M., unless engaged elsewhere on public business.

SEC. 7. Until a Police Department is established, the Marshal shall be the Chief of the Police of the City; and all Constables, Watchmen, and Policemen, whether general or special, shall be subordinate to him, and under his direction; subject, nevertheless, to the orders of the Mayor. To act as Chief of Police.

SEC. 8. The Marshal shall have power to make rules and regulations for the government of his assistants, and for the Constables, Watchmen, and Policemen, when acting under his command, who are hereby required to obey the same. He may direct any Assistant Marshal to perform any duty which he himself might perform. To make rules and regulations.

SEC. 9. The Marshal, Assistant Marshals, Constables, Watchmen, and Policemen, shall aid in the suppression of crimes and misdemeanors; and it is hereby made their duty to arrest all persons guilty of any violation of law or ordinance, and make complaint for the same. To suppress crimes and make arrests.

SEC. 10. The Marshal, Assistant Marshals, Watchmen, and Policemen shall, when on duty, wear a blue coat, with brass buttons, blue pantaloons, and a hat, all to be of uniform style and fashion, and shall carry his police baton fastened in a belt or sash, to be worn about the waist. Uniform.

SEC. 11. The neglect or refusal of the Marshal, Assistant Marshals, Constables, Watchmen or Policemen, or either of them, to perform any of the duties prescribed by the laws of this State, or by the Charter or any Ordinance of the City, or to make complaint for any violation of law or ordinance which may come to his or their knowledge, shall be considered a wilful neglect of the duties of his or their office, and be deemed a sufficient cause for his or their removal from office by the Mayor or Common Council. May be removed from office.

SEC. 12. No Marshal, Assistant Marshal, Watchman, or Policeman, shall be interested, either directly or indirectly, in the keeping of any tavern, saloon, bar-room, coffee or eating house, or beer hall. Shall not be interested in any tavern, etc.

SEC. 13. No person shall be appointed Marshal, Assistant Marshal, Watchman, or Policeman, unless he has arrived at the age of twenty-one years, and is of good moral character, and temperate habits. And any officer named in this section, and any constable who shall be guilty of any drunkenness or lewd conduct, shall be removed from office by the Mayor or Common Council. Qualifications.

To give bond. SEC. 14. The officers named in this ordinance shall, each, before entering upon the duties of their respective offices, execute a bond to the City of Detroit, in the penal sum of two thousand dollars, with two or more sureties, conditioned as provided in Sections twenty-eight and twenty-nine, of Chapter two of the Revised Charter of 1861; and also subscribe the oath of office prescribed by Section fifteen of the same chapter. The bond and oath shall be filed in the office of the City Clerk.

To attend fires. SEC. 15. The Marshal, Assistant Marshals, and Constables, shall attend all fires, and assist in extinguishing the same, and in preserving, removing and securing property. On such occasions they shall be under the direction of the Fire Marshal, whom they are hereby required to obey.

Penalty. SEC. 16. Any violation of the provisions of this Ordinance, in addition to any other penalty therein provided, shall be punished by a fine not to exceed three hundred dollars, and costs of prosecution; and in the imposition of any fine and costs, the Court may make a further sentence, that the offender be imprisoned until the payment thereof: *Provided, however,* That such imprisonment shall not exceed the period of six months.

SEC. 17. Chapter seventy-eight of the Revised Ordinances of 1859, and all Ordinances amendatory thereof, or supplementary thereto, are hereby repealed.

SEC. 18. This Ordinance shall take effect from and after its passage.

CHAPTER IV.

OF THE CITY ASSESSOR AND HIS ASSISTANTS.

[Ordinance approved December 30, 1861.]

Appointment, term of office, etc. SECTION 1. The City Assessor shall be appointed by the Common Council, upon the recommendation of the Mayor, and shall hold his office for the term of three years, and shall devote his whole time to the service of the city in connection with the duties of his office.

SEC. 2. Before entering upon the duties of his office, the Assessor shall take and subscribe the oath provided in section fifteen of Chapter two of the City Charter, and shall execute a bond to the Corporation with one or more sufficient sureties in the sum of ten thousand dollars, conditioned that he will faithfully perform the duties of his office, and on demand, deliver over to his successor or other proper officer, or agent of the Corporation, all books, papers, moneys, effects and property belonging to the Corporation, or appertaining to his office. Oath and bond.

SEC. 3. On the first day of January in each year, the Assessor shall appoint two competent persons to act as Assistant Assessors, who shall hold their offices for the period of three months, take and subscribe the oath herein provided for the Assessor, and receive for their services the sum of two dollars and fifty cents per day each; and in making assessments the Assessor and his assistants shall, as far as practicable, act conjointly. Assistant assessors.

SEC. 4. The Assessor and his assistants shall, between the first days of January and April in each year, in the manner provided in the City Charter, assess all the real and personal property, subject to assessment or taxation within the several wards of the city, and within the same period shall make out and complete the assessment rolls for each ward, in proper books to be provided for that purpose. To assess property and make assessment rolls.

SEC. 5. The Assessor shall keep in his office complete sets of assessment rolls made by him and confirmed by the Common Council, and all books, rolls and records in his office, shall be open to public inspection at all convenient hours of the day. To keep assessment rolls, etc.

SEC. 6. The Assessor may require the services of the City Surveyor in ascertaining the divisions and boundaries of any real estate within the City; and it is hereby made the duty of said Surveyor to render such services whenever applied to by the Assessor. May require assistance of City Surveyor.

SEC. 7. The Assessor is hereby authorized to employ such clerical assistance as the business of his office may render necessary; and such clerical assistants shall receive a compensation of not exceeding the sum of one dollar and fifty cents per day, for the time they are actually employed. May employ clerks. Their compensation.

May procure stationery.

SEC. 8. The Assessor shall have power to procure of the contractor for supplying stationery, books or printing for the city, such books. stationery and printing as he may, from time to time, require for his office, and the same shall be paid for by the City of Detroit.

To prepare tax rolls.

SEC. 9. When required by the City Controller, the Assessor shall prepare the tax rolls for highway, sewer, school and city taxes of each ward in the City, and deliver the same, when completed, to the Controller; he shall also prepare the tax rolls for State and County taxes for each ward in the City, and deliver the same, when completed, to the County Treasurer. [*As amended by Ordinance approved September* 28, 1863.]

To preserve books, etc.

SEC. 10. The Assessor shall carefully preserve and keep all books, papers and records, appertaining to or filed in his office.

To make and file monthly roll.

SEC. 11. The Assessor shall, on the first Monday in each month, make out and file with the City Controller, a monthly roll, with his certificate attached thereto, giving the names of the Assistant Assessors and clerical assistants permanently employed in his office, and the time they were actually employed in their official duties. Upon the receipt of such roll with the certificate of the Assessor, the Controller shall pay such persons for their services the compensation hereinbefore provided. in the same manner as other officers of the city are paid. Temporary clerical assistants shall be paid for their services, upon presenting to the Controller the certificate of the Assessor setting forth the actual time such assistants have been employed.

SEC. 12. Chapter seventy-five of the Revised Ordinances of 1859, and all ordinances amendatory thereto, are hereby repealed.

SEC. 13. This Ordinance shall take immediate effect.

CHAPTER V.

OF THE CITY COLLECTOR.

[Ordinance approved April 10, 1863.]

City Collector to give bond.

SECTION 1. Before entering upon the duties of his office, the City Collector shall execute a bond to the City of Detroit, in the penal sum of five thousand dollars, with two sufficient sureties, conditioned that he will faithfully perform the duties of his office, and will, on demand, or at the expiration of his term of office, deliver over to his successor in office, or other proper officer or agent of the Corporation, all books, papers, moneys, effects and property, belonging to the Corporation, or appertaining to his office, which may be in his custody, as an officer, and that he will pay over to the Corporation, or its legally authorized agent, all money received by him, at the time and in the manner prescribed by the Charter and Ordinances of the City.

To collect special assessments.

SEC. 2. It shall be the duty of the City Collector to collect all special assessments imposed and levied by the Common Council, except such as shall be paid by the person assessed to the Receiver of Taxes, prior to the issue of the warrant for the collection of the same, as is, or may be provided by the Ordinances of the City.

To collect license and other moneys.

SEC. 3. The City Collector shall, in addition to the assessments mentioned in section two, collect all licenses or other moneys due the City, as shall be placed in his hands for collection. by resolution of the Common Council, or direction of the Controller.

To pay over moneys to Receiver of Taxes and file statement.

SEC. 4. It shall be the duty of the City Collector, during the time he has any tax or assessment roll in his hands for collection of special assessment, in the City of Detroit, at least once in seven days, to deposit with the Receiver of Taxes, all sums of money collected by him during said seven days, and since his last deposit, for which sums he shall take the Receiver's receipt, which he shall, within twenty-four hours after receiving the same, show to the Controller of the City, and shall, at the time, file with the Controller a statement, in writing, that the amount so deposited by him with said Receiver of Taxes, was all the money belonging to the Corporation of said city, collected by him, and in his possession at the time of making said deposit, which statement shall be signed by the Collector making the same, and sworn to by him, before the Controller, who shall report said statement to the Common Council, with his allowance or disallowance indorsed thereon, in the same manner as other accounts are audited and indorsed by him. But in case the City Collector shall not have collected any money during seven days, then he shall report the fact to the Receiver of Taxes, and shall make a sworn statement of the same to the Controller.

May levy upon and sell property.

SEC 5. It shall be the duty of the City Collector to collect from the persons named in the respective assessment rolls placed in his hands, the assessment or tax therein specified and set forth as due from such persons, and for such purpose he may levy upon and sell the personal property, of any kind or description, of any person liable to pay, and refusing or neglecting to do so. The Collector may levy upon the property of such person, wherever the same may be found in the City of Detroit.

Salary.

SEC. 6. The City Collector shall receive an annual salary of $500, and one-half of the five per cent. hereby authorized to be collected, in all not exceeding $800.

Proceedings in case of levy and sale.

SEC. 7. Upon receiving the assessment roll, or a copy thereof, and warrant, it shall be the duty of the City Collector to proceed to demand and collect the several sums mentioned therein, and if any person shall neglect or refuse to pay the same, then, if he can find any goods or chattels of the person liable therefor, he shall levy thereon; but before he shall proceed to sell such goods and chattels, he shall give ten days' previous notice of the time and place of sale, by causing the same to be posted up in three of the most conspicuous places in said City, and the property levied upon shall be sold at public auction to the highest bidder; and the City Collector shall render the overplus, if any, after deducting the costs and charges of such distress and sale, to the person entitled thereto The City Collector shall, in all cases, be entitled to demand five cents on the dollar on the amount of the assessment, which the person so assessed shall pay, and which shall be deposited as other moneys received by said City Collector.

To make return

SEC. 8. The City Collector shall make return of his doings within the time mentioned in said warrant to the Common Council, if in session; but if not, then at their next ensuing meeting, and in such return describe the goods and chattels sold, and the amount which each article sold for. But if goods and chattels cannot be found, or if such person or persons mentioned in said roll are non-residents of said city, the City Collector shall state such fact, verified by an affidavit taken before the City Controller, and annex the same to a list of such lands on which the assessments have not been paid.

SEC. 9. Said warrant may be renewed from time to time, if the Common Council shall so direct.

Warrant may be renewed.

SEC. 10. Upon making such return, the Receiver of Taxes shall proceed and sell such lots in the same manner as is prescribed for city taxes.

Receiver of Taxes to sell.

SEC. 11. The following or other sufficient forms may be used in proceedings under this Ordinance:

FORM OF WARRANT.

Form of warrant.

STATE OF MICHIGAN, } ss.
CITY OF DETROIT,

To the City Collector of the City of Detroit, greeting:

In the name of the people of the State of Michigan, you are hereby commanded that you collect from each person or set of persons named in the foregoing tax roll, or of any person liable to pay the amount of money set opposite his, her or their names, respectively, and on the refusal or neglect of such person to pay said tax, costs and charges thereon, including five per cent. for expenses of collection, that you then levy the same by distress and sale of the goods and chattels of such person, according to law, and that you have said roll and this warrant, and the receipt of the Receiver of Taxes of said City, for the amount by you collected, before the Common Council of said City, within thirty days from the date hereof, and fail not at your peril.

In testimony whereof, I have hereunto set my hand and caused the seal of said City to be affixed at the City of Detroit aforesaid, this——day of——, A. D. 18—.

[L. S.]

——— *Controller.*

NOTICE OF SALE OF PROPERTY.

Form of notice of sale.

STATE OF MICHIGAN, } ss.
CITY OF DETROIT,

Notice is hereby given, that pursuant to law in such case made and provided, there will be sold at public auction, to the highest bidder, at——, in the City of Detroit, at—o'clock, in the——noon of—— day of——A. D. 18—, the following goods and chattels, viz: [here description,] or so much thereof as may be necessary to satisfy the amount of a certain assessment made by the Common Council of the City of Detroit, against———for defraying the expenses of———, together with the legal costs and charges which have accrued in the premises.

By order of the Common Council.

——,

City Collector of said City.

Dated at the City of Detroit, this——day of——, A. D. 18—.

Form of return on warrant.

RETURN ON CITY COLLECTOR'S WARRANT.

STATE OF MICHIGAN, }
CITY OF DETROIT, } SS.

To the Honorable the Common Council of said City:

The undersigned begs leave to submit the following list of lands of residents, [or non-residents] which were taxed for [here set forth the object for which the tax was laid,] on the——day of——, A. D. 18—, according to the assessment roll to me heretofore delivered, but which I have not been able to collect.

[Here copy the assessment roll so far as it relates to unpaid assessment.]

Given at the City of Detroit, this——day of——, A. D. 18—.

[Let an affidavit of the following form be added:]

STATE OF MICHIGAN, }
CITY OF DETROIT, } SS.

City Controller of said city, being duly sworn, saith that the foregoing return contains the description of all lands, and the names of all persons taxed on the assessment roll of the——day of——, A. D. 18—, and that the several sums mentioned in the foregoing list, remain due and unpaid, and that he has not, upon diligent inquiry, been able to find or discover any goods or chattels belonging to, or in the possession of the person charged with, or liable to pay the said assessment, whereon to levy the same; and this deponent further says, that the persons mentioned in said list as non-residents, are, as he believes, non-residents.

——, *City Collector.*

Subscribed to and sworn before me.

——, *City Controller, etc.*

Sec. 12. Chapter seven of the Compiled Ordinances of 1859, is hereby repealed, as also all other Ordinances inconsistent herewith.

Sec. 13. This Ordinance shall take immediate effect.

CHAPTER VI.

OF WARD COLLECTORS.

[Ordinance approved September 18, 1862.]

SECTION 1. The Collector of each Ward shall collect all State and County Taxes assessed and imposed upon the real and personal property of such Ward, and all such City, Highway, Sewer and School Taxes as shall be placed in his hands for collection by the Receiver of Taxes.

Ward Collector to collect State and County taxes, etc.

SEC. 2. The penalty of the bond of each Ward Collector given to said City for the faithful performance of his duties shall be in a sum at least double the amount of the taxes placed in his hands for collection on personal property in the Ward for which he is elected, and in such further sum as the Common Council may, by resolution, direct.

Bond.

SEC. 3. It shall be the duty of each Collector, during the time he has any tax roll in his hands for collection of City Taxes, at least once in seven days, to deposit with the Receiver of Taxes, all sums of money collected by him during said seven days, and since his last deposit, for which sums he shall take the Receiver's receipt; which he shall, within twenty-four hours after receiving the same, show to the Controller of the City, and shall at the time file with the Controller a statement, in writing, that the amount so deposited by him with said Receiver of Taxes was all the money belonging to Corporation of said City, collected by him, and in his possession at the time of making said deposit, which statement shall be signed by the Collector making the same, and sworn to by him before the Controller, who shall report said statement to the Common Council, with his allowance or disallowance indorsed thereon in the same manner as other accounts audited and indorsed by him. But in case any Collector shall not have collected any money during seven days, then he shall report the fact to the Receiver of Taxes, and shall make a sworn statement of the same to the Controller.

To pay over moneys to Receiver of Taxes and file statement.

SEC. 4. It shall be the duty of the Collectors to collect from the persons named in their respective assessment rolls, the assessment or tax therein specified and set forth as due from such persons; and for such purposes, they may levy upon and sell the personal property

May levy upon and sell property.

of any kind or description of any person liable to pay and refusing or neglecting to do so. And any Collector may levy upon the property of such person, wherever the same may be found in the City of Detroit.

SEC. 5. Chapter two of the Revised Ordinances of 1859, is hereby repealed.

CHAPTER VII.

TO PUNISH PERSONS RESISTING COLLECTORS.

[Chapter Three of Compiled Ordinances of 1859.]

Penalty for resisting levy or seizure.

SECTION 1. Any person or persons who shall resist, obstruct or hinder any City Collector or Ward Collector of said City in levying upon or taking into possession any goods and chattels under and by virtue of a warrant, legally issued and directed to said City Collector or Ward Collector, for the collection of any tax or assessment of said City—said goods and chattels being legally liable to be so levied on and taken into possession by said City Collector or Ward Collector—shall be punished by a fine not to exceed five hundred dollars, or by imprisonment not to exceed one year, or by both such fine and imprisonment, in the discretion of the Court.

Penalty for resisting entry of collector.

SEC. 2. Any person who shall prevent any City Collector or Ward Collector from entering upon any house or premises occupied by him or her, for the purpose of searching for or levying on goods and chattels, under any warrant legally issued for the collection of tax or assessment, which the person so occupying said house or premises is liable to pay, shall be punished by the same fine or imprisonment, or by both, in the discretion of the Court, as is provided in the preceding section.

SEC. 3. This Ordinance shall take effect on and after its passage

CHAPTER VIII.

OF THE RECEIVER OF TAXES.

[Ordinance approved January 2, 1862.]

Appointment, term of office, and salary.

SECTION 1. There shall be an officer in and for the City of Detroit to be denominated the Receiver of Taxes, with the powers and duties, in addition to those prescribed in the Charter, hereinafter prescribed, to be appointed by the Common Council, on the nomination of the Mayor, and to hold his office for two years, and receive a salary of one thousand dollars per annum.

SEC. 2. Before entering upon the duties of his office, the Receiver of Taxes shall execute a bond to the City of Detroit in the penal sum of twenty-five thousand dollars, with two sureties, conditioned that he will faithfully perform the duties of his office, and will, on demand, or at the expiration of his term of office, deliver over to his successor in office, or other proper officer or agent of the Corporation, all books, papers, moneys, effects, and property belonging to the Corporation, or appertaining to his office, which may be in his custody as an officer, and that he will pay over to the Corporation, or its legally authorized agent, all money received by him. To give bond.

SEC. 3. The Receiver of Taxes shall keep, in books to be provided for the purpose, just and accurate accounts of all moneys received by him, showing the amount of all moneys received and credited to the several funds of the City, and the amount paid over to the City Treasurer; and where money is received by him in payment of any special assessment, for the construction of lateral sewers, or for building of side and crosswalks, or for the paving, grading, graveling, or macadamizing any street, lane or alley, or for repairing or otherwise improving the same, he shall, at the time of receiving such money, note in the proper book the lot or lots upon which such assessments were paid, and also the block or blocks in which such lot or lots are situated. He shall, on Monday in each week, report, under oath, in writing, to the City Controller, the amount of money received by him, the particular funds to which the same has been credited, and if any special assessments, as above provided, have been paid, the lot or lots upon which such assessments have been paid, and the block or the blocks in which such lots are situated, and the name of contractor for doing the work, to pay which such assessment was made, and the amount paid over to the City Treasurer, as hereinafter provided, since the date of his last report. To keep accounts, and make report under oath.

SEC. 4. The Receiver of Taxes shall, on Monday and Thursday, in each week, pay over to the City Treasurer all money received by him, and shall, on Monday of each week, render to the Treasurer in triplicate, a statement, in writing, of the amount of money received To pay over moneys, and render statement.

by him since his last deposit, the funds to which the same was credited, and where special assessments have been received by him, he shall give the number of the lot upon which the same were paid, and the block in which such lot is situated, and take the Treasurer's receipt upon two of such statements, one of which shall be filed with the City Controller, with the report provided for in section three, who shall report the same to the Common Council, at its next session.

Office.

SEC. 5. The Receiver of Taxes shall keep his office in such place as may be provided by the Common Council, where he shall be found at all reasonable hours of the day ; as shall be prescribed by the Common Council.

Books to be open to inspection.

SEC. 6. The books in the office of the Receiver of Taxes shall, at all times, be open for the inspection of the Mayor, Controller, and any member or Committee of the Common Council.

To have assistant when necessary.

SEC. 7. When assistance is necessary for the proper dispatch of the business of his office, he shall apply to the Common Council for the same, and such assistant, when appointed, shall receive not more than two dollars a day, such amount to be determined by resolution of the Common Council, subject to the provisions of this section. [*As amended by Ordinance approved September* 28, 1863.]

SEC. 8. An Ordinance approved April 11, 1861, entitled "An Ordinance relative to the Receiver of Taxes," and all Ordinances and parts of Ordinances amendatory thereof, are hereby repealed.

SEC. 9. This Ordinance shall take effect from and after its passage.

CHAPTER IX.

OF THE CITY SURVEYOR.

[Chapter Five of Compiled Ordinances of 1859.]

City Surveyor to establish the grade of streets, etc.

SECTION 1. It shall be the duty of the City Surveyor, when so directed by the Common Council, to ascertain and establish the proper grade to any avenue, street, lane, alley or sidewalk within the limits of said City, and when required, to run out and stake off the same.

To survey and superintend the construction or alteration of drains, and make report.

SEC. 2. It shall also be his duty to make all necessary surveys, and superintend the construction, enlargement, or alteration of all drains connecting with the main or lateral sewers of said city, and shall record the same in a book to be provided by said Common Council, and deposit the same with the City Clerk at the termination of his said office.

SEC. 3. He shall also make all necessary surveys, and give such information as may be needed by any Committee, or by the Superintendent of the Water Works, in laying down, extending or connecting the water logs or pipes of said Water Works in said City, and shall, at all times, when required, consult and act with any Standing or Special Committee, who may desire any information or assistance in any matter or thing, connected with the duties of his office where the City of Detroit is concerned.

To make surveys and give information to the Superintendent of Hydraulics, and to consult and act with committees requiring official information from him.

SEC. 4. He shall also deliver over to the City Clerk all papers, plans and drafts relating to any survey made by order of the Common Council, and shall also make a written report of his doings and proceedings in all cases, when required so to do by the Common Council.

To deliver books and papers to City Clerk, and, when required, report to the Council.

SEC. 5. The salary allowed by said Council to the City Surveyor shall be in full for all services rendered, and shall also be in full for all incidental, as well as other labor performed by him as said Surveyor, or by any of his assistants.

Salary.

CHAPTER X.

OF STREET COMMISSIONERS.

[Ordinance approved September 28, 1863.]

SECTION 1. Before entering upon the duties of their respective offices, the Street Commissioners shall take and subscribe the oath of office provided in section fifteen of chapter two of the City Charter, and shall execute a bond to the Corporation, with two or more sureties, in the sum of two thousand dollars, conditioned that they will faithfully perform the duties of their respective offices, and, on demand, deliver to their successors in office or other proper officer or agent of the Corporation, all books, papers, property and effects in their hands belonging to the City of Detroit.

Oath and bond

SEC. 2. The Street Commissioners shall keep their office in such places as shall be provided by the Common Council.

Office.

Street Commissioners' Districts.

SEC. 3. The City of Detroit is hereby divided into two Street Commissioners' Districts, as follows: The third, fourth, sixth, seventh and tenth wards shall constitute one district, to be called the "Eastern District," and the first, second, fifth, eighth and ninth wards shall constitute a district, to be called the "Western District."

To superintend construction of pavements, etc., and working and cleaning of highways, etc.

SEC. 4. The Street Commissioners, within their respective districts, under the direction of the Common Council, shall superintend the construction, repairs, and cleaning of pavements, sidewalks, crosswalks. culverts and bridges, and direct the working, cleaning and improving of the highways, streets, alleys and public places, in the City of Detroit.

To keep record of workmen, horses, etc.

SEC 5. It shall be the duty of the Street Commissioners to keep an accurate record of the names of all persons employed by them in the several wards of their respective districts, together with the number of horses, carts, wagons or other vehicles employed by them, and the amount of compensation to be paid for the same.

To make weekly reports.

SEC. 6. The Street Commissioners shall, on Monday of each week, during their terms of office, report, in writing, under oath, to the City Controller, the cost of all repairs upon streets, side and crosswalks, bridges and culverts in their respective districts, and also the number of persons, horses or other animals, carts, wagons and other vehicles employed by them in the several wards of their respective districts, since the date of their last reports, and the length of time each was employed, and also the amount to be paid for the same.

Materials to be purchased and contracts made by City Controller.

SEC. 7. All materials or goods of any kind, to be used by the Street Commissioners, shall be purchased by the City Controller, and all contracts for constructing bridges or culverts, or for repairing streets, crosswalks, bridges or culverts, shall be made by him, under the direction of the Common Council: *Provided, however,* That when the expenses of such supplies shall exceed the sum of two hundred dollars, the same shall be let to the lowest responsible bidder, as provided in section twelve of chapter eight of the City Charter.

To make occasional reports.

SEC. 8. The Commissioners shall, from time to time, report to the Common Council the condition of the side and crosswalks, streets, lanes, alleys and public spaces within their respective districts, and make such recommendations for the improvement of the same as they shall think for the best interest of the City.

SEC. 9. The Street Commissioners shall promptly report to the Controller any negligence or dereliction of duty on the part of the Overseers of Highways in the discharge of their official duties. They shall also make complaint to the City Attorney for all violations of the Ordinances of the City which may come under their observation, whose duty it shall be to file complaints for the same in the Recorder's Court.

To report negligence, and make complaints.

SEC. 10. Chapter four of the Compiled Ordinances of the City of Detroit of the year 1859, is hereby repealed.

SEC. 11. This Ordinance shall take immediate effect.

CHAPTER XI.

OF CITY PHYSICIANS.

[Ordinance approved May 14, 1863.]

SECTION 1. There shall be appointed by the Common Council, on the second Tuesday of January of each year, four Physicians, to be called "City Physicians," and who shall be of good standing in their profession, and shall possess and exercise the powers and duties hereafter prescribed.

Appointment, powers and duties.

SEC. 2. Before entering upon the duties of their respective offices, the City Physicians shall each take and subscribe the oath of office provided for in section fifteen of chapter two of the City Charter.

Oath.

SEC. 3. The City of Detroit is hereby subdivided into four districts, to be called "City Physician Districts," as follows: All that portion of the city of Detroit lying east of the centre of Woodward avenue, and south of Monroe avenue, and south of the centre of Clinton street, shall constitute and be known as City Physician District No. 1.

City Physician Districts.

All that portion of the City of Detroit east of the centre of Woodward avenue, and north of and including Monroe avenue, and north of the centre of Clinton street, shall constitute and be known as City Physician District No. 2.

All that portion of the city of Detroit lying west of the centre of Woodward avenue, and south of Michigan avenue, shall constitute and be known as City Physician District No. 3.

All that portion of the city of Detroit lying west of the centre of Woodward avenue and north of Michigan avenue, and including Michigan avenue, shall constitute and be known as City Physician District No. 4. [*As amended by Ordinance approved October* 16, 1863.

To make sanitary examinations and recommendations.

SEC. 4. The City Physicians, when required by the Common Council, or Board of Health, shall examine in their several districts into all sources of danger to the public health, and shall, from time to time, make such recommendation to the Common Council concerning the sanitary condition of the City as to them shall seem necessary and proper.

To attend sick, etc.

SEC. 5. It shall be the duty of the City Physicians, in their several districts, when directed by the Mayor, an Alderman, or Director of the Poor, to attend any sick, disabled or infirm person who may be a charge upon the City, and render such medical assistance as may be necessary—also, when any person is taken to the pest house, the physician of the district from which the patient is taken, shall attend on the person so taken to the pest house.

To vaccinate without charge.

SEC. 6. It shall be the duty of the City Physicians, in their several districts, to vaccinate, without charge, any inhabitant of the city of Detroit, not previously vaccinated, who may apply to them for that purpose; they shall also give certificates of vaccination to such children as may have been vaccinated by them.

To furnish medicines.

SEC. 7. The City Physicians shall furnish, at their own expense, all medicines which may be necessary in the skillful and proper treatment of such sick or disabled persons as may be a charge upon the City, and also such vaccine matter as may be required to carry into force the provisions of section six of this Ordinance. But each City Physician shall be entitled, at the end of each quarter during his term of office, upon his affidavit, that he has vaccinated, free of charge, all inhabitants of the City of Detroit who have called upon him for that purpose, to receive from the City Treasury the sum of twelve dollars and fifty cents, in addition to the salary of his office.

Names and residences to be published.

SEC. 8. It shall be the duty of the City Clerk to procure, at the expense of the City, suitable cards, upon which shall be printed a copy of section six of this ordinance, and also the names and residences of the City Physicians; such cards shall be placed and kept in conspicuous positions in the office of each City Physician, and in the offices of the Receiver of Taxes, the City Clerk, City Marshal, and Director of the Poor.

SEC. 9. No person shall be eligible to the office of City Physician who has not received a diploma from a respectable Medical College. Must have received diplomas from a Medical College.

SEC. 10. All complaints against the City Physicians shall be made to the Mayor, who shall investigate the same, and, if necessary, report the case to the Common Council, with his opinion thereon. Complaints against.

SEC. 11. In case of the absence or inability, from any cause, of a City Physician to attend to the duties of the office, he shall, with the consent of the Mayor, provide a competent physician to fill his place. Substitute in case of absence.

SEC. 12. An Ordinance entitled "An Ordinance to Define the Duties of Physicians," approved February 6, 1860; and an ordinance entitled "An Ordinance to amend section one of an Ordinance to define the duties of Physicians," and all Ordinances or parts of Ordinances inconsistent with this Ordinance, are hereby repealed.

CHAPTER XII.

OF THE CITY HISTORIOGRAPHER.

[Chapter Six of Compiled Ordinances of 1859.]

SECTION 1. There shall be appointed by the Common Council an officer to be called the Historiographer, who shall hold his office during the pleasure of the Council. Appointment and term of office.

SEC. 2. It shall be the duty of the Historiographer to collect together, receive and safely keep all such books, papers, documents, and other matters, connected with, and illustrating the history of the City of Detroit, as he may be able to procure without expense to the City. To collect and keep all books, papers, etc., connected with the history of the City of Detroit.

SEC. 3. It shall be the duty of the Historiographer to report, annually, (and at such other time as he shall be required to do,) to the Common Council, the state and condition of his department. To make a report annually of the state of his department to the Common Council.

To deliver up all books, papers, etc., and penalty for default.

SEC. 4. The Historiographer shall, at any time when required by the Council, deliver over to such persons as the Council may direct, all books, papers and documents, and other things that may at any time come into his possession as such officer, and in default thereof he shall be liable to a penalty of one hundred dollars.

Office honorary.

SEC. 5. The office of Historiographer being honorary, no compensation shall be allowed to said officer.

CHAPTER XIII.

OF THE DIRECTOR OF THE POOR.

[Ordinance approved January 14, 1862.]

Bond.

SECTION 1. Before entering upon the duties of his office, the Director of the Poor shall execute a bond to the City of Detroit in the penal sum of two thousand dollars, with one or more sufficient sureties, conditioned as prescribed in section twenty-eight of chapter two of the charter of the City of Detroit, and shall also subscribe the oath of office prescribed by section fifteen of the same chapter.

Office and office hours.

SEC. 2. The Director of the Poor shall keep his office in such place as shall be provided by the Common Council, and shall keep the same open from 8 until 11 o'clock, A. M., and from 2 until 5 o'clock, P. M. each day, Sundays excepted, during the months of November, December, January, February, March and April, and from 7½ until 11 o'clock, A. M., and from 3 until 6 o'clock, P. M., during the months of May, June, July, August, September and October.

Duties and powers.

SEC. 3. It shall be the the duty of the Director of the Poor, when any person, being a city pauper, shall, by himself or another, apply to him for relief, to make immediate personal inquiry into the state and circumstances of the applicant, and if it shall appear that he or she is in such indigent circumstances as to require permanent support, and is not so sick, diseased, lame or otherwise disabled as that he or she cannot safely or conveniently be removed, to remove such person to the County Poor House, to be relieved and cared for as their necessities may require; but if such person cannot be safely or conveniently removed for any of the reasons hereinbefore specified, the Director of the Poor may afford such persons relief under the provisions of this Ordinance, until such time as he or she can be safely removed to the County Poor House. And if it shall appear that any person applying for relief as aforesaid, requires only temporary or partial support, he shall afford him or her such relief as the circumstances of the case may require. Whenever, from sickness or other disability, the Director of the Poor shall deem it necessary and proper to place any city pauper in a hospital, he shall do so by removing such pauper to any proper hospital belonging to the City of Detroit, or to any hospital with which the City has a contract, as prescribed in section eight of this Ordinance, and the board and care of such pauper shall be paid for in the same manner as other claims and demands against the Corporation.

SEC. 4. The Director of the Poor shall, on or before the first Monday of July, in each and every year, report to the Controller the quantity of wood, flour, groceries, meats, articles of clothing, and such other articles as in his judgment may be necessary for the support of the Poor for the ensuing year, such estimate to be based upon the quantity of such articles used for that purpose during the preceding year; within twenty days after the receipt of such report, the City Controller shall advertise for at least ten days in two or more of the daily newspapers published in this city, for sealed proposals to furnish and supply so many and such quantity of the articles enumerated in the report of the Director of the Poor as the City may require; such articles to be delivered at convenient places in the city of Detroit, and in such quantities as the City may, from time to time, require: *Provided*, *however*, That immediately after the approval of this Ordinance, the City Controller shall advertise in the three daily newspapers published in this City, for a period of ten days, for sealed proposals to supply and furnish the city so much wood, groceries, flour, meat, and such other articles as he may deem necessary and proper, as the City may require between the day of making such contract and the first day of November next, for the purposes hereinbefore enumerated, such articles to be furnished at the place and in the manner provided in this section. Supplies for support of poor.

SEC. 5 It shall be the duty of the Director of the Poor, when any person, being a city pauper, shall apply to him for relief, and whose state and circumstances are such as to render relief neces- When to give orders for supplies and money.

sary and proper, to give such person an order on the contractor or contractors, furnishing the article or articles needed by such person. In any case where the Director of the Poor shall deem it for the best interest of the City to furnish pecuniary aid to any pauper, he shall give such pauper a certificate for the amount which he may deem necessary, and the Controller, upon presentation to him of such certificate, shall draw his warrant for the amount thereof on the City Treasurer, payable out of any money which shall have been previously appropriated for such purposes by the Common Council.

Common Council shall appropriate funds.

SEC. 6. The Common Council shall, from time to time, upon the report of the Controller that an appropriation is necessary for that purpose, appropriate out of the poor fund, limited sums to be subject to the warrant of the Controller, to meet the cases provided for in the last clause of the preceding section.

Contractors for supplies, how paid.

SEC. 7. It shall be the duty of all contractors furnishing supplies to the Corporation for the purposes hereinbefore specified, to present to the Controller on the first Monday in each month, a monthly account of supplies furnished by him, together with all orders which shall have been drawn upon him by the Director of the Poor, which account shall be accompanied by an affidavit as required by section twenty-five of chapter four of the City Charter, and shall be audited and allowed like other claims and demands against the Corporation. and paid out of the poor fund.

Controller to contract for boarding poor.

SEC. 8. It shall be the duty of the City Controller, on or before the first day of July in each and every year, to make a contract or agreement with some public hospital in the City of Detroit, for the boarding and taking care of such indigent persons as may be a charge on the City, and may be sent to such hospital by the Director of the Poor.

Medical aid to poor.

SEC. 9. It shall be the duty of the Director of the Poor to give to paupers needing medical aid, an order therefor on the City Physician in whose district such pauper resides.

Railroad tickets for paupers leaving State.

SEC. 10. It shall be the duty of the Controller to procure railroad tickets for paupers who may wish permanently to leave the State, when recommended so to do by the Director of the Poor.

CHAPTER XIV.

OF THE CLERK OF THE MARKET.

[Ordinance approved January 2, 1862.]

SECTION 1. The Clerk of the Market shall be appointed by the Common Council on the second Tuesday in January of each year, and shall possess and exercise the powers and duties hereinafter prescribed. Appointment.

SEC. 2. He shall have charge of the City Hall Market, take care of the buildings thereof; attend therein daily during market hours; keep the same in a clean and orderly condition; collect all rents of stalls and stands, and such fees from wagons, carts and other vehicles as may be fixed by the Controller and Committee on Markets; see that market wagons and other vehicles occupy such positions so as not to interfere with public travel, as may be prescribed by the Controller and Committee on Markets; carefully observe that the rules and regulations of the market are properly observed and respected, and make complaint for any infractions of such rules and regulations or of any Ordinances of the City. Powers and duties.

SEC. 3. He shall examine all articles offered and provisions exposed for sale in the market, and see that the same is of good and wholesome quality. To examine articles offered for sale.

SEC. 4. Under the direction of the Committee on Markets and the Controller, he shall let any of the stands in the vegetable market. To let stands in Vegetable Market.

SEC. 5. He shall promptly report to the Controller the names of all persons renting stalls and stands in the market who are in arrears for rent; and immediately after their collection he shall pay into the City Treasury all money received for the rent of stalls and stands, or for fees received from wagons and other vehicles; he shall, on Saturday of each week, make a report under oath, in writing, to the Controller, in which he shall give the amount of money received by him for rent of stalls and stands, or for fees, of whom received, and when paid into the City Treasury. On the first Monday in each month he shall report, in writing, under oath, to the Controller, the names of all persons renting and occupy- To make reports and pay over moneys.

ing stalls or stands in the market, the time for which such stalls or stands are leased or rented, and the amount for which each of such stalls is rented.

To visit meat markets.

SEC. 6. It shall be the duty of the Clerk of the Market to visit, from time to time, the several meat markets in the City, and see that the same are licensed as provided by law, and that all the provisions of the Ordinance relative to private meat markets are properly enforced. He shall make complaint for any infractions of the provisions of that Ordinance.

May be removed.

SEC. 7. Any neglect or refusal of the Clerk of the Market to comply with any duty imposed upon him by law, shall be cause for his removal from the office by the Mayor or Common Council.

SEC. 8. This Ordinance shall take effect from and after its passage.

CHAPTER XV.

OF WEIGHMASTERS.

[Ordinance approved January 2, 1862.]

Appointment and term of office.

SECTION 1. There shall be two or more officers in and for the City of Detroit, to be denominated Weighmasters, to be appointed by the Common Council on the second Tuesday in January of each year, and shall hold their offices for one year, or until their successors are appointed, and possess and exercise the powers and duties hereinafter provided.

Bond.

SEC. 2. The Weighmasters before entering upon the duties of their respective offices, shall each execute a bond to the City of Detroit in the penal sum of $500, with one or more sureties, conditioned as prescribed in section twenty-eight of chapter two of the city charter, and shall also subscribe the oath of office prescribed by section fifteen of the same chapter.

To weigh hay, coal, etc. Fees.

SEC. 3. It shall be the duty of the Weighmasters to weigh any load of hay, coal or straw which may be brought to the public scales under their charge, and after deducting the weight of the cart, wagon or sled, they shall deliver to the owner a certificate specifying the weight. They shall receive for their services one cent and a half per hundred weight upon each and every load they shall weigh, not including, however, the deduction made as above provided. [*As amended by Ordinance approved March* 13, 1863.]

Where carts and other vehicles to stand. Hay not to be sold unless weighed.

SEC. 4. Persons owning or having in charge carts, wagons or sleds, loaded with hay, or straw, shall not permit the same to stand in any street, avenue, alley or public space; but all such carts, wagons or sleds, shall stand at, or adjoining the public hay scales, in such order as shall be prescribed by the Weighmaster. No person or persons shall sell or offer for sale any hay in said city by the cart, wagon or sled load, unless the same has been weighed by one of the Weighmasters of said City, as provided by this Ordinance. [*As amended by Ordinance approved September* 6, 1862.]

Ordinance not to apply to straw in bundles.

SEC. 5. This Ordinance shall not apply to straw made up into and sold by the bundle.

Cattle, etc., not to be kept for sale in streets.

SEC. 6. No person shall keep for public sale, in any of the streets, lanes, alleys or public spaces, in this city, any horse or neat cattle, sheep or hogs.

Weighmasters to designate places where cattle may be exposed for sale.

SEC. 7. The Weighmasters shall designate the places in the public wood yards where animals may be exposed for sale, and all persons owning, or having animals in charge, shall strictly comply with the rules and regulations prescribed by the Weighmasters, for the good order and government of their respective yards.

Fees for weighing cattle, etc.

SEC. 8. The Weighmaster shall be entitled to demand and receive from the owner, or person having in charge any horse or neat cattle, the sum of ten cents per head; and for any sheep or hogs the sum of five cents per head.

Weighmasters to pay $150 per annum into city treasury.

SEC. 9. The Weighmaster of the Eastern District shall pay into the City Treasury for the use of the hay scales in said District, one hundred and fifty dollars per annum. The Weighmaster of the Western District shall pay into the City Treasury for the use of the hay scales in said District, one hundred and fifty dollars per annum; the said sums to be paid quarterly. [*As amended by Ordinance approved March* 13, 1863.]

Calves not to be muzzled.

SEC. 10. No person offering or exhibiting for sale a cow having a sucking calf, shall muzzle, or in any way prevent the calf from taking its natural nutriment from its mother.

Removal for fraud or peculation.

SEC. 11. Any Weighmaster who shall be guilty of taking or demanding more compensation for his services than is prescribed by this Ordinance, or who shall be guilty of any fraud or peculation in his office, shall, in addition to the punishment hereinafter prescribed, be removed from office by the Mayor or Common Council.

Penalty.

SEC. 12. Any violation of, or failure to comply with the provisions of this Ordinance, shall be punished by a fine not to exceed one hundred dollars and costs; and in the imposition of any such fine and costs, the Court may make a further sentence, that the offender shall be committed to the County Jail, or Detroit House of Correction, until the same be paid, for any period of time not exceeding six months.

SEC. 13. Chapters thirty and eighty-six of the Revised Ordinances of 1859 are hereby repealed.

To have powers of assistant marshal.

SEC. 14. Weighmasters shall possess and exercise the powers and duties of an Assistant Marshal for the enforcement of the provisions of this Ordinance, and the preservation of the public peace in and about the hay scales.

SEC. 15. This Ordinance shall take effect from and after its passage.

CHAPTER XVI.

OF THE SEALER OF WEIGHTS AND MEASURES.

[Ordinance approved April 25, 1862.]

Appointment.

SECTION 1. There shall be in and for the City of Detroit, an officer to be denominated the Sealer of Weights and Measures, who shall be appointed by the Common Council, on the second Tuesday in January in each year, and possess and exercise the powers and duties hereinafter prescribed.

Oath and Bond.

SEC. 2. Before entering upon the duties of his office, the Sealer of Weights and Measures shall take and subscribe the oath of office, provided for in section fifteen, of chapter two, of the City Charter, and shall execute a bond to the Corporation, with one or more sufficient sureties, in the sum of one thousand dollars, conditioned that he will faithfully perform the duties of his office, and, on demand, deliver over to his successor, or other proper officer or agent of the Corporation, all books, papers, property and effects in his hands, belonging to the City of Detroit.

SEC. 3. The Sealer of Weights and Measures shall keep his office in a suitable and convenient place in the City of Detroit, in which shall be kept correct and approved standard weights and measures, scales, beams, and other instruments used for weighing and measuring, to be provided by the City of Detroit, which shall conform to the standard weights and measures established by the laws of the United States. **Office.**

SEC. 4. Once in each year, from the first day of January, 1862, the Sealer of Weights and Measures, for the time being, shall cause all standards in his office to be tried, proved, and sealed by the standards of the State of Michigan, in the office of the Clerk of the county of Wayne. **To test standards.**

SEC. 5. The Sealer of Weights and Measures shall, once in each year, and oftener, if he deems it necessary, inspect and prove all weights and measures, scales, beams, and other instruments used for weighing and measuring, by any merchant, retailer, trader or dealer, for the purpose of buying or selling merchandise, groceries, provisions, or property of any description whatsoever, sold by weight or measure; and such as shall be found conformable to the standards kept in his office, he shall stamp with the word "approved," or the letter "M," and the year in which such inspection is made; and such as shall be found not to be conformable to the standard in his office, he shall stamp with the word "condemned," and the year in which inspection is made: *Provided, however,* That when any weights, measures, scales, beams, or other instruments, are inspected more than once in any one year, and found to be correct, the Sealer of Weights and Measures shall not be entitled to any fees for such re-inspection. **To test and stamp weights, measures, etc.**

SEC. 6. The Sealer of Weights and Measures shall be provided by the City of Detroit with a book, to be kept in his office, in which he shall register, in alphabetical order, the name of each person whose weights, measures, scales, beams, or other instruments he has inspected; the number and size of the same, and what number of each was approved and condemned, with the time of inspection; **To keep records.**

and such book shall at all reasonable times be open to the inspection and examination of the public.

May require exhibition of weights, etc.

SEC. 7. No person shall neglect or refuse to exhibit any weights, measures, scales, beams, or other instruments used by him or her, in weighing or measuring, to the Sealer of Weights and Measures, when demanded by him, for the purpose of having the same inspected.

Weights, etc., not to be used unless inspected and stamped.

SEC. 8. No person shall use, for buying or selling, any weights, measures, scales, beams, or other instruments, unless the same have been inspected and stamped "approved," or with the letter "M," by the Sealer of Weights and Measures.

Fees.

SEC. 9. The Sealer of Weights and Measures shall, for inspecting and proving, as hereinbefore provided, be entitled to demand and receive the following fees:

For a hay, coal, cattle or depot scales, weighing two tons or more, $2.00.

For a platform scale weighing from 1,000 to 2,500 pounds, $1.00.

For a platform scale weighing less than 1,000 pounds, 50 cents.

For a beam weighing 1,000 pounds or more, 40 cents.

For a beam weighing less than 1,000 pounds, 25 cents.

For a counter, union counter and grocer's scales, 25 cents.

For a union counter platform scales, weighing from 160 to 240 pounds, 40 cents.

For spring balances or butcher's scales, 25 cents.

For weights of seven pounds or more, 3 cents each

For a nest of weights of four pounds, 12 cents.

For a nest of weights of eight pounds or more, 15 cents.

For comparing a bushel measure, 15 cents.

For comparing a half bushel measure, 10 cents.

For comparing any dry measure less than a half bushel, 5 cents.

For comparing wine, ale and beer measures, containing three gallons or more, 10 cents.

For any measure containing less than three gallons, 5 cents each.

For each yard measure and each subdivision, 6 cents each. [*As amended by Ordinance approved March* 13, 1863.]

SEC. 10. The Sealer shall receive 25 cents an hour for drilling out weights. [*As amended by Ordinance approved March* 13, 1863.] Id.

SEC. 11. Any person who shall neglect or refuse to exhibit his weights, measures, scales, beams, or other instruments used for the purpose of weighing or measuring, to the Sealer of Weights and Measures, for the purpose of having the same inspected, as hereinbefore provided, or who shall use, in buying or selling, any weights, measures, scales, beams, or other instruments used for weighing or measuring, which shall have been inspected and condemned by the Sealer of Weights and Measures, or which, not having been inspected and approved, shall not be conformable to the standards provided by law, shall be punished by a fine not to exceed one hundred dollars, and costs of prosecution; and the Court may make a further sentence, that the offender be imprisoned in the Detroit House of Correction till the payment of such fine and costs: *Provided,* That such imprisonment shall not exceed the period of six months. Penalty for refusing to exhibit weights, etc.

SEC. 12. Chapter seventy-nine, of the Revised Ordinances of 1859; an Ordinance entitled "An Ordinance relative to Assistant Sealer of Weights and Measures," approved January 26, 1860; an Ordinance entitled "An Ordinance to repeal section two of an Ordinance relative to Assistant Sealer of Weights aed Measures," approved May 29, 1860; "An Ordinance supplementary to an Ordinance relative to Weights and Measures," approved April 20, 1861, and all other Ordinances and parts of Ordinances supplementary to, or amendatory of chapter seventy-nine of the Revised Ordinances of 1859, are hereby repealed.

SEC. 13. This Ordinance shall take effect from and after its passage.

CHAPTER XVII.

OF THE INSPECTOR OF GAS METERS.

[Ordinance approved December 2, 1861.]

SECTION 1. There shall be an officer in the city of Detroit, to be denominated "The Inspector of Gas Meters," with the powers and duties hereinafter prescribed, to be appointed by the Common Appointment and term of office.

Council, and to hold his office for one year, or until his successor is appointed.

Salary. SEC. 2. The Inspector of Gas Meters shall receive a salary of $600 per annum, to be paid by the Detroit Gas Company, in equal monthly payments.

Bond. SEC. 3. Before entering upon the duties of his office, the Inspector of Gas Meters shall execute a bond to the city of Detroit, in the penal sum of one thousand dollars, with two sureties, conditioned as provided in section twenty-eight, of chapter two, of the revised Charter of 1861, and shall also subscribe the oath prescribed in section fifteen of the same chapter. The bond and oath shall be filed in the office of the City Clerk.

Office. SEC. 4. He shall keep his office in a room to be provided by the Common Council, where he shall be found at all convenient hours of the day.

To keep Photometer, etc. SEC. 5. He shall keep in his office a good and accurate standard photometer, meter and prover, to be furnished by the City of Detroit.

To test meters. SEC. 6. Whenever requested, he shall examine and test, without charge, any meter furnished by the Gas Company, which may be brought to his office, and shall give notice to the consumer and the Gas Company of the time when any meter is to be examined and tested; and after testing and proving any meter, he shall duly stamp the same.

Inspection to be conclusive. SEC. 7. His inspection shall be conclusive upon both the Gas Company and the consumer, as to the accuracy of any meter; and whenever any meter shall be found to be imperfect or inaccurate, it shall be replaced by the Gas Company with a good and sufficient one.

To supervise public lamps and meters. SEC. 8. It is hereby made the duty of the Inspector of Gas Meters to keep a supervision over the public lamps of the City, and see that they are kept clean, and at all times provided with good and sufficient burners, of equal size. He shall, at the end of each month, examine the public meters, and make a record of the number of feet of gas indicated by such meters, and shall compare the same with the bill of gas presented to the City by the Gas Company.

To make and report tests. SEC. 9. The Inspector of Gas Meters shall, from time to time, make photometrical tests of the gas furnished by the Gas Company, and shall communicate to the Common Council the result of such tests.

SEC. 10. He shall, from time to time, give the Council information of the condition of the public lamps of the city, and of the quality of the gas furnished by the Gas Company. To make report.

SEC. 11. He shall keep a book in his office, in which he shall record the number of each meter, and the time when it was tested and proved by him, and such record shall be open at all times for public inspection. To keep books.

SEC. 12. He may be suspended at any time by the Mayor, without charges, who shall report the same to the Common Council. May be suspended.

SEC. 13. This Ordinance shall take effect from and after its passage.

CHAPTER XVIII.

OF INSPECTORS OF FIREWOOD.

[Ordinance approved January 2, 1862.]

SECTION 1. There shall be four officers in and for the City of Detroit, to be denominated "Inspectors of Firewood," to be appointed by the Common Council, and to hold office for one year, or until their successors are appointed, and who shall possess and exercise the powers and duties hereinafter provided. Appointment and term of office.

SEC. 2. The City of Detroit is hereby divided by Woodward avenue and Fort street, into four wood inspection districts, to be known as the Eastern, Western, Northern and Southern Districts. To each of said districts there shall be appointed one of the aforesaid Inspectors. Inspection Districts.

SEC. 3. The Inspectors, before entering upon the duties of their respective offices, shall execute a bond to the City of Detroit, in the penal sum of $500, with one or more sureties, and conditioned as prescribed in section twenty-eight, of chapter two, of the Charter of the City of Detroit, and shall also subscribe the oath prescribed by section fifteen of the same chapter. Bond and oath.

Offices and office hours of Inspectors for Northern and Southern districts. To have charge of wood yards.

SEC. 4. The Inspectors for the Northern and Southern Districts shall keep their respective offices at or near the public woodyards, and shall keep the same open each day, Sunday excepted, between the hours of 7 o'clock A. M. and 6 o'clock P. M. They shall have charge of the wood yards in their respective districts, and all persons using such yards shall conform to the rules and regulations prescribed by the Inspector.

Offices and office hours of Inspectors for Eastern and Western districts.

SEC. 5. The Inspector for the Eastern and Western Districts shall keep their respective offices in some convenient place near the dock, and the same shall be open each day, Sunday excepted, between the hours of 7 o'clock A. M. and 6 o'clock P. M.

Inspectors for Northern and Southern districts to measure wood in public wood yards. Fees.

SEC. 6. The Inspectors of the Northern and Southern Districts shall measure all wood which may be sold, or offered for sale, in the public wood yards, and they shall receive for their services the following compensation, and no more: For measuring a load drawn by one horse, or other animal, three cents; for measuring a load drawn by two or more horses, or other animals, five cents.

Wood in wagons, etc., not to be sold until measured.

SEC. 7. No person shall sell, or offer to sell, wood by the wagon, cart or sled load, unless the same has been measured by the Wood Inspector, at one of the wood yards, nor shall such wood be kept for sale in any place in said city, except at one of the public wood yards.

Wood carts, etc., not to stand in streets.

SEC. 8. No person owning or having in charge any wagon, cart or sled containing wood for sale, shall permit the same to stand in any street, alley, or public space.

Inspectors for Eastern and Western districts to measure wood in boats. Fees.

SEC. 9. The Inspectors for the Eastern and Western Districts shall measure all wood which may be brought to the city in boats, or other water craft, for the purpose of being sold. They shall receive for their services the following compensation, and no more: For measuring ten cords, or under, five cents per cord, and three cents for each additional cord.

Wood in boats, etc., not to be sold until measured.

SEC. 10. Persons bringing wood to this city in boats or other craft, for the purpose of selling the same, shall, before selling the same, cause it to be measured by the Wood Inspector of the district; and if necessary to the more accurate measurement of the same, they shall cause it to be piled in a convenient place on the wharf or dock.

SEC. 11. On the receipt of their legal compensation, the several Wood Inspectors shall deliver to the person employing them a certificate, stating the number of feet contained in the wagon, cart, or sled load measured by them; or the number of cords, or parts of a cord, contained in any boat, or water craft, or pile, measured by them; and in making their measurements, they shall examine carefully the manner in which the wood is piled in the vehicle, boat, craft or pile, and make a reasonable and fair deduction for improper or unfair piling, or for the crookedness or unevenness of the wood. Certificate of measurement.

SEC. 12. Any Inspector who shall be guilty of taking or demanding more compensation for his services than is prescribed by this Ordinance, or who shall be guilty of any fraud or peculation in his office, shall, in addition to the punishment hereinafter prescribed, be removed from office by the Mayor or Common Council. Inspectors may be removed for fraud or peculation.

SEC. 13. Any violation of, or failure to comply with, the provisions of this Ordinance, shall be punished by a fine not to exceed one hundred dollars, and costs; and in the imposition of any such fine and costs, the Court may make a further sentence, that the offender be committed to the County Jail, or Detroit House of Correction, until the payment thereof, for any period of time not exceeding six months.

SEC. 14. Chapter thirty-five of the Revised Ordinances of 1859, is hereby repealed.

SEC. 15. This Ordinance shall take effect from and after its passage.

CHAPTER XIX.

OF CHIMNEY SWEEPS.

[Chapter Eight of Compiled Ordinances of 1859.]

SECTION 1. There shall be nominated by the Mayor of the City of Detroit, subject to the approval of the Common Council, one Chimney Sweeper for the City, who shall have full power to appoint others under him, according to the subsequent provisions of this chapter. Appointment.

To give bonds and register their names with Clerk, and Clerk to give them certificates.

SEC. 2. No person shall hereafter follow the business or occupation of a Chimney Sweeper, either by himself, or others, within the City of Detroit, unless he shall have been approved in the manner prescribed in section one, and shall give bonds to the City of Detroit, in the penal sum of fifty dollars, conditioned for the faithful performance of his duties, according to the provisions hereinafter contained, and shall have registered his name, and the names of all persons employed by him as assistants, with a number affixed to every such name, in a book to be kept by the City Clerk, and shall have obtained from said Clerk a certificate of such registry, containing the name of the person and the number affixed in said registry, under a penalty of five dollars for every day he shall follow, by himself or others, the said business; and the said Clerk is hereby required to make out and deliver to the person so appointed such certificates, for each of which he shall be entitled to demand and receive one dollar.

To wear a badge and penalty for default.

SEC. 3. Every person following the aforesaid business within said City, shall wear, and cause to be worn by the persons employed by him, on the front of their caps or hats, in full view, the same figures and numbers, respectively, as shall be so, as aforesaid, entered in the said book, and contained in his or their respective certificates, in large figures, not less than two inches in length, to be made of durable tin or copper, with the word "Sweep" legibly painted on said badge. Every person who shall violate the provisions of this section, shall forfeit one dollar.

Duty of.

SEC. 4. Every such Chimney Sweep, so appointed, who shall not, within forty-eight hours after application to him, made by any inhabitant of the district to which he belongs, sweep, or cause to be swept, such chimney, or chimneys, as he shall be required to sweep, shall, for every such offence, forfeit and pay the sum of three dollars.

Fees of.

SEC. 5. Each Chimney Sweeper so appointed, shall be entitled to demand and receive, for each chimney so swept, the following sums, and no more, to wit: For each chimney with a single flue, the sum of one shilling for every story through which said flue shall pass, and six cents for each additional flue, the same to be paid by the persons respectively owning the same.

Penalty on persons whose chimneys being unswept, take fire.

SEC. 6. If any chimney in this City shall take fire, and blaze out at the top, (the same not having been swept within three months next before the time of taking fire,) the occupant of such premises shall forfeit and pay the sum of one dollar and costs. But if the same shall have been swept within three months, then the person having swept the same shall forfeit and pay one dollar and costs.

CHAPTER XX.

OF SCAVENGERS.

[Ordinance approved July 24, 1861.]

SECTION 1. No person shall follow the business or occupation of a Scavenger without a license from the Mayor. Scavengers must be licensed.

SEC. 2. The Mayor is hereby authorized to license proper persons to act as Scavengers, upon their paying into the City Treasury the sum of one dollar, and executing a bond to the Corporation in the sum of fifty dollars, with one or more sufficient sureties, conditioned for the faithful observance of the Charter and Ordinances. License fee and bond.

SEC. 3. Such Scavengers, under the direction of the Mayor, City Marshal, an Alderman, or a member of the Board of Health, shall have the power to enter upon any premises, between sunrise and sunset, and examine any vault, sink, privy, or private drain. Power to enter on premises and examine sinks, etc.

SEC. 4. Whenever, in the opinion of the Mayor, Marshal, an Alderman, or a member of the Board of Health, any sink, privy, or private drain shall need cleaning, altering, relaying, or repairing, in order to protect the public health, he shall notify, in writing, the owner or occupant thereof to cause the same to be cleansed, altered, re-laid or repaired, within six days from the date of the service of such notice, and in case of the neglect or refusal to comply with the requirement of such notice, the Common Council may direct the proper officer to cleanse, alter, re-lay or repair such sink, private drain or privy, and assess the expenses thereof on the lot or premises attached thereto, which assessment shall be a lien on such lot or premises, and be collected in the same manner as other assessments imposed by authority of the Common Council. How sinks, etc. to be cleansed, altered, or repaired. Assessment of expense thereof.

SEC. 5. Scavengers shall not empty or remove the contents of any tub, vault, sink, privy or private drain, otherwise than in boxes or casks made tight and closely covered. Sinks, etc., to be emptied in tight and covered boxes.

Scavengers to clean sinks, etc., and remove nuisances when requested.

SEC. 6. When requested, the Scavenger shall cleanse or empty any vault, sink, private drain or privy, and remove any and all nuisances. They may demand and receive their fees for such services in advance.

Fees of Scavengers.

SEC. 7. The Scavengers shall receive eight cents for each cubic foot of the contents of any sink, private drain, vault or privy, by them cleaned out or removed; and for removing any dead dog, cat, hog or other animal, or other nuisance, they shall receive such fees as may be, from time to time, fixed by resolution of the Common Council.

Penalty.

SEC. 8. Any violation of, or neglect or refusal to comply with, the provisions of this Ordinance, shall be punished by a fine not to exceed fifty dollars and costs of prosecution; and in the imposition of any fine and costs, the court may make a further sentence that the offender be imprisoned until the payment thereof: *Provided*, That the term of such imprisonment shall not exceed the period of six months.

SEC. 9. This Ordinance shall take effect from and after its passage.

CHAPTER XXI.

OF THE DUTIES OF STANDING COMMITTEES.

[Chapter Eighty-one of Compiled Ordinances of 1859.]

SECTION 1. The following shall be the duties of Standing Committees of the Common Council, to wit:

Committee on Claims to examine all accounts.

1. The Committee on Claims shall examine into and report upon all matters of account or claim, either in favor of or against the City.

Committee on Ways and Means to report and examine into all matters of finance.

2 The Committee on Ways and Means shall examine into and report upon all such matters relative to the revenue of the City, as shall be referred to them; they shall inquire into the state of the City debt, the revenue, and the expenditures of the City; and whether any or what retrenchment can be made with advantage; and shall report, from time to time, such provisions and arrangements as may be promotive of order, economy and accountability in the conduct

of the fiscal concerns of the City. They shall examine into and report upon the sufficiency of all official bonds, and all such matters not constituting a claim against the City, as shall be referred to them, and shall, with the City Controller, make and report the estimates for the yearly expenditures.

3. The Committee on Streets shall examine into and report upon all such matters as may be referred to them relative to streets, alleys and sidewalks within the City, and shall, at the end of each year, report to the Common Council what improvements of any nature will be needed upon the streets, alleys and sidewalks of the City, during the ensuing year, and an estimate of the expense of the same.

Committee on Streets, all matters relative to streets, etc.

4. The Committee on Health shall examine into and report upon all matters relating to, or in any way affecting the public health, which shall be referred to them; and it shall be their duty to report, from time to time, to the Common Council, such plans and suggestions relative to the cleanliness and health of the City, as they may deem proper.

Committee on Health, all matters relative to public health.

5. The Committee on Fire Department shall examine into and report upon all matters connected with the Fire Department of the City, and the suppression of fires, which may be referred to them; and shall, at the end of each year, report to the Common Council an estimate of all the expenses which will be necessary for the operation of the Fire Department of the City during the ensuing year.

Committee on Fire Department, all matters relative thereto.

6. The Committee on Hydraulics shall examine into and report upon the condition of the Hydraulics of the City, whenever so directed by the Common Council; and to them shall be referred all reports and communications from the Board of Commissioners of the Water Works.

Committee on Hydraulics, all matters relative to water works.

7. The Committee on Markets shall examine into and report upon all matters connected with the Public Markets, which may be referred to them.

Committee on Markets, all matters relative to public markets.

8. The Committee on Taxes shall examine into and report upon all questions brought before the Common Council concerning Taxes, which may be referred to them.

Committee on Taxes, all matters relative to taxation.

9. The Committee on Printing shall examine into and report upon all matters connected with the City Printing, which may be

Committee on Printing, matters relative thereto.

referred to them. They shall also, at the end of the year, report to the Common Council an estimate of the expense necessary for the City Printing in the ensuing year.

Committee on Gas Lights, all things relative to street lamps, etc.

10. The Committee on Gas Lights shall report upon all matters connected with the lighting of the City, which may be referred to them. To them shall be referred all reports of the Gas Company; and they shall, at the end of each year, report to the Common Council, the number, location and cost of lights which will be necessary in the ensuing year.

Committee on Public Buildings, relative to all buildings owned by city.

11. The Committee on Public Buildings shall examine into and report upon the condition of all buildings belonging to the City; all questions and plans for repairs, erection and construction of public buildings, shall be referred to them; and they shall, at the end of each year, report to the Common Council the estimated expenses of their department for the ensuing year.

Committee on Parks, relative to same.

12. The Committee on Parks shall examine into and report upon the condition of all public parks; upon the improvements, adornment and protection thereof; and shall, at the end of each year, report the estimated expenses of their department during the ensuing year.

Committee on Sewers, to examine all matters relative to same.

13. The Committee on Sewers shall examine into and report upon all questions connected with the construction of sewers, which may be referred to them.

Committee on Licenses, all matters relative to licenses.

14. The Committee on Licenses shall examine into and report upon all questions connected with licenses, which may be referred to them.

Committees may require the services of any officer.

SEC. 2. Every Committee, in the discharge of their duty, may require the services of any officer of the City, whose duties are in any manner connected with the subject under investigation by the Committee.

Committees not to make contracts.

SEC. 3. No Committee shall exercise any executive functions, nor perform any duty save that usual to legislative bodies; nor shall they in any case order the doing of any work, or the cessation thereof, enter into any contract, or change or vary one already made; and any act performed by them, which is unauthorized by this Ordinance, shall be null and void.

Matters to be referred to the appropriate committees.

SEC. 4. The Common Council shall always refer matters to the appropriate Committee; nor shall any matter be referred to a committee which does not directly relate to the department which that Committee has been appointed to.

CHAPTER XXII.

OF TAKING TESTIMONY BEFORE COMMITTEES.

[Chapter Eighty-two of Compiled Ordinances of 1859.]

SECTION 1. The presiding officer of any Board, or the Chairman of any Committee of the Common Council, who are engaged in the consideration, or to whom have been referred the investigation, of any claim for damages, money or recompense against said Board, or against the City, may issue subpœnas under their hands, and sealed with the corporate seal of said City, directed to any person whom said Board or Committee deem necessary as a witness in any matter pending before them, and ordering said person to appear before said Committee or Board at such time and place, and to testify concerning such matter or thing, as in said subpœna shall be designated.

Chairman of any Committee may issue subpœnas and compel the attendance of witnesses.

SEC. 2. If the person so subpœnaed shall fail to appear at said time and place, an attachment shall be issued to compel his appearance, which attachment shall be signed and sealed, as is provided for subpœnas in the preceding section

May issue attachment.

SEC. 3. The person or party making such claim shall be entitled to a hearing before said Board or Committee, and to process to compel the appearance of witnesses in his behalf.

Party making claim to be heard.

SEC. 4. The Marshal or Assistant Marshals of said City shall serve all process issuing under this Ordinance. Said process shall be served in the manner like processes are served in courts of Justices of the Peace, and shall be returned to the Presiding Officer or Chairman issuing them: *Provided, always,* That in case of the absence of the Chairman of any Committee, the person whose name appears next to his in the order of appointment of said Committee, shall act as Chairman, and may issue all processes herein provided for.

Marshal or deputy to serve process.

Statement of parties to be under oath.

SEC. 5. The statements of all persons concerning any such claim, made before any Board or Committee, as herein provided, shall, in all cases, be taken under oath, and reduced to writing by the Chairman of said Committee, or the presiding officer of said Board, and signed by the person making the same, which statement, so signed. shall be returned by the Chairman of said Committee to the City Attorney, who shall file and preserve the same in his office, subject to the order of the Common Council.

TITLE II.

OF TAXES AND ASSESSMENTS.

CHAPTER XXIII.

OF THE ASSESSMENT AND COLLECTION OF CITY TAXES.

[Chapter Ten of Compiled Ordinances of 1859, as amended.]

SECTION 1. It shall be the duty of the City Attorney to meet with the Assessors, and give them all necessary advice relative to the manner of making the general assessment, and if any property belonging to the Corporation should be assessed, to request that the same should be stricken from the roll.

Duty of Attorney relative to general assessment.

SEC. 2. That whenever it shall be necessary to call a meeting of the freemen of said city, for the purpose of authorizing the said Common Council to assess or lay a tax on the real and personal property, within the limits of said City, the notice or proclamation for convening such meeting, shall be left or filed with the City Clerk, who shall cause a copy thereof to be duly published in said City, in one of the City papers, and handbills.

Proclamation for public meeting to authorize tax to be published by the City Clerk.

SEC. 3. If such meeting shall authorize the Common Council to assess and levy any such tax, the chairman, or other officer of the meeting shall certify the same to the Common Council, as soon as may be, and such authority so certified shall be recorded in the Journal, and filed by the City Clerk.

Proceedings of meeting to be filed and recorded.

SEC. 4. Whenever any tax roll for city, highway, sewer and school taxes shall be placed in the hands of any Ward Collector, or the City Collector, by the Receiver of Taxes, in accordance with

Collectors to collect city taxes and make returns.

7

section twelve, of chapter nine, of the City Charter, said Collector shall proceed to collect the amounts appearing unpaid thereon, and shall make returns to the Receiver of Taxes, as commanded in the warrant annexed to said tax roll. The following shall be a sufficient form of warrant:

Form of warrant.

FORM OF WARRANT.

STATE OF MICHIGAN, CITY OF DETROIT, } ss.

To—— Collector of the —— Ward of the City of Detroit, Greeting:

In the name of the people of the State of Michigan, You are hereby commanded, that you collect from the several persons named in the foregoing Tax Roll, or of any person liable to pay the same, the amount of highway, sewer, school and city taxes opposite to their names respectively, together with —— per cent. for your services for collecting the same; and on the neglect or refusal of any such person to pay such taxes, that you then levy the same by distress and sale of goods and chattels of such person, occupant, or lessee refusing or neglecting to pay the same, according to law; and that you have said roll, and the money so collected by you, and this warrant, before the Receiver of Taxes of said City, on the —— day of —— 18—.

In testimony whereof, I have hereunto set my hand and caused the seal of said City to be affixed, at the City of Detroit [L. S.] aforesaid, this —— day of —— A. D. 18—.

—————— *Controller.*

Levy and sale.

Sec. 5. In case of levy and sale, in accordance with section thirteen, of chapter nine, of the City Charter, the following shall be a sufficient form of notice of sale of property levied upon. Any such sale may be adjourned from time to time by the Collector making the same.

Form of notice of sale.

NOTICE OF SALE OF PROPERTY.

STATE OF MICHIGAN, CITY OF DETROIT, } ss.

Notice is hereby given, that, pursuant to law in such case made and provided, there will be sold at public auction, to the highest bidder, at —— ——, in the City of Detroit, at —— o'clock, in the

—— noon of —— day of —— A. D. 18—, the following goods and chattels, viz.: [here description,] or so much thereof as may be necessary to satisfy the amount of —— taxes imposed upon —— —— for the year 18—, and which are to be levied by said sale.

Dated at Detroit, this —— day of —— A. D. 18—.

——— *Collector for* —— *City of Detroit.*

SEC. 6. The following shall be a sufficient form of return: Form of return.

COLLECTOR'S RETURN.

STATE OF MICHIGAN, } ss.
CITY OF DETROIT, }

To the Receiver of Taxes of said City of Detroit:

The undersigned begs leave to submit the following list of persons named in the annexed assessment roll, who were taxed for the year 18—, upon personal property, according to the assessment roll of said City, and the taxes imposed upon such persons, which I have been unable to collect:

NAMES.	TAX.		
	DOLLS.	CENTS.	

Given at the City of Detroit, this —— day of —— A. D. 18—.

——— *Collector for* —— *City of Detroit.*

STATE OF MICHIGAN, } ss.
CITY OF DETROIT, }

——— ———, Collector of the —— Ward of said City, being duly sworn, deposes and says that the several sums mentioned in the foregoing returns of the city, school, highway and sewer taxes for the year 18—, remain due and unpaid, and that he has not, upon diligent inquiry, been able to discover any goods and chattels belonging to the persons charged with or liable to pay said sums of money whereon he could levy the same.

——— *Collector for* —— *City of Detroit.*

Subscribed and sworn before me this —— day of —— A. D. 18—.

——— *Clerk of said City.*

CHAPTER XXIV.

OF THE SALE OF LANDS FOR UNPAID GENERAL TAXES AND ASSESSMENTS.

[Ordinance approved July 10, 1862.]

Receiver of Taxes to sell real estate when tax or assessment is unpaid.

SECTION 1. Whenever any general tax or assessment on any lands, tenements, hereditaments or premises in said City, shall remain due and unpaid, after publication of notice by the Receiver of Taxes, as required by the provisions of section twelve, chapter nine, of the Charter, and after the expiration of the time therein mentioned, it shall be the duty of the Receiver of Taxes, on behalf of the Common Council, to proceed and sell such lands, tenements, hereditaments and premises, in the manner herein prescribed.

To publish notice of sale.

SEC. 2. The Receiver of Taxes shall, on or before the first day of May in each year, make out a list of all such lands, tenements hereditaments, or premises, the names, if known, of the owners or occupants of, or parties in interest, and the amount of the unpaid tax or assessment due thereon, and shall, on behalf of the Common Council, cause to be published in the daily newspaper published by the Printer for the City, once a week, for four successive weeks, such list with a notice thereto attached, requiring the owners, or occupants of, or parties in interest in such lands, tenements, hereditaments, or premises, to pay any such assessment or tax ; and further notifying them that if default be made in making any such payment, any such real estate will be sold, at public auction, at a day and a place therein to be specified, for the lowest term of years, at which any person will offer to take the same in consideration of advancing and paying the sum assessed or taxed on the same, with the costs and charges in the premises, and shall, at the same time cause said list, with said notice thereto attached, to be posted in three or more public places in each ward in said City : *Provided, however,* That for any unpaid general tax, assessed or levied during the year 1861, on any lands, tenements, hereditaments or premises, in said City, the Receiver of Taxes shall make out said list, and cause the same to be published, with the notice thereto attached, as above specified, on or before the first Monday in November, 1862. [*As amended by Ordinance approved September* 18, 1862.]

SEC. 3. If the owner or owners, occupant or occupants, party or parties, in interest, in any such real estate, do not pay any such assessment or tax, with the costs and charges thereon, within the period above prescribed for the publication of said notice, then the Receiver of Taxes, on behalf of the Common Council, at the place, and on the day mentioned in such notice, shall commence the sale of such lands, tenements, hereditaments and premises, at public auction, and shall continue the same from day to day, (Sundays excepted,) until the same is sold for the lowest term of years at which any person shall offer to take the same, for the purpose, and in the manner already above expressed, but each lot, or parcel of lot, owned by any one person, or set of persons, against whom any such tax or assessment has been made, shall be sold by itself.

To sell according to notice if tax or assessment remains unpaid.

SEC. 4. The Receiver of Taxes shall report to the Common Council, within ten days after the close of such sale, the terms for which each lot was sold, the amount bid therefor, and the name of the purchaser; and if there be no sufficient objection, the several purchasers shall, on payment of the amount of their respective bids, as hereinafter provided, be entitled to the necessary conveyances of said premises, when the time for the redemption fixed by law shall have fully expired, upon paying for the expense of such conveyance the further sum of fifty cents, unless said lot shall have been sooner redeemed, in which case the purchaser shall be entitled to recover his money and interest, at the rates hereinafter established.

To make report of sales.

SEC. 5. The purchasers at such sale shall pay the amount of their respective bids to the Receiver of Taxes, within forty-eight hours after the sale has been finally closed, and, on payment of the same, it shall be the duty of the Receiver of Taxes, on behalf of the Common Council, to execute to the purchaser of each lot a proper certificate of such sale, describing the lands purchased, and the amount paid therefor, and the term of years for which the same was bid off; and such certificate shall be regularly numbered, and a copy of each shall be filed in the office of the Controller.

Payment of bids and certificates of sale.

SEC. 6. The Receiver of Taxes may, in his discretion, require immediate payment of any person to whom any such real estate shall be struck off, and in case of his neglect or refusal to pay any bid made by him, he may declare the bid cancelled, and, at his discretion, sell the lands again, and any person so neglecting or refusing

Immediate payment may be required or sale cancelled.

to pay any bid made by him, shall not be entitled, after such neglect and refusal, to have any bid made by him received during such sale.

Names of persons failing to pay bids to be reported to Common Council.

SEC. 7. If any purchaser shall neglect or refuse to pay the amount of their respective bids to the Receiver of Taxes, within forty-eight hours after the sale, the Receiver of Taxes shall report the names of such persons to the Common Council, who may elect to take the lots bid off by such purchaser.

Deed.

SEC. 8. On presentation of certificate of sale, heretofore referred to, to the Controller, after the expiration of the time provided by law for the redemption of real estate, sold as aforesaid, unless such real estate has been previously redeemed, the Controller shall, in the name of, and for the City of Detroit, execute and deliver to such purchaser, or his assignee, a proper deed for the conveyance of such real estate, for the term for which the same was sold, which said deed shall be under the corporate seal of the City, and attested by the Clerk.

Record of sales.

SEC. 9. The Receiver of Taxes, within forty days after such sale, shall make a correct record of all land sales, showing the time when the tax or assessment was levied, and the amount thereof, the cost and charges, the time when the lands were sold, the name of the purchaser, or his assignee, the term for which the same was bid off, with such other entries as may be necessary in the premises, and shall deposit said record in the office of the Treasurer.

Redemption of lands sold.

SEC. 10. Any person entitled to redeem any such real estate, may, within one year from the time of sale, deposit with the Treasurer, for the use of the purchaser, the full amount of the assessment, or tax, for which such real estate was sold, and interest, as hereinafter mentioned, and the Treasurer shall give proper receipt for the same, and shall enter a note of such redemption in said record. Interest on unpaid taxes shall be at the rate of twelve per cent per annum, up to, and until the date of the sale of such real estate, and at the rate of twenty-five per cent. per annum from and after such sale, and no person shall be entitled, after sale, to redeem any real estate sold without payment of the said interest and principal, in the manner prescribed by law.

Treasurer to conduct sales in the absence of Receiver of Taxes.

SEC. 11. If, on the day mentioned in such notice of sale, the Receiver of Taxes shall neglect, or be unable, from any cause, to be present at, and conduct said sale, then it shall be the duty of the

Treasurer, in behalf of the Common Council, to proceed with said sale, in the same manner, and with the like effect, as if the same had been conducted by the Receiver of Taxes, and he shall receive payments of bids, make the like returns, issue certificates of purchase, and make out the same record, and perform all other acts, as are required of the Receiver of Taxes, under like circumstances.

SEC. 12. The following, or other sufficient forms, may be used in proceedings under this chapter: Form of notice of sale.

NOTICE OF SALE.

STATE OF MICHIGAN, } ss.
CITY OF DETROIT, }

Notice is hereby given, that, pursuant to law, there will be sold at the Common Council Hall, in the City of Detroit, and State of Michigan, between the hours of —— and ——, of the ——— day of ———, A. D. 18—, at public auction, the several lands, tenements, hereditaments, and premises, hereinafter described, each parcel separately, for the lowest term of years, at which any person will offer to take the same, in consideration of advancing the sum or sums which were assessed or taxed by the Common Council of said City, for the year 18—, unless the said sum, or sums, with the costs and charges thereon, shall, before that time, be paid and satisfied, which the owners, or occupants of, or parties in interest in said lands, tenements, hereditaments and premises, against whom said sum or sums have been assessed, are hereby required to do. [Here insert an accurate description of the several premises, and add to the description of each the amount assessed, the name of the individual or individuals against whom the amount is assessed, and also the amount of the costs and charges, if any, up to that time.]

NAMES.	DESCRIPTION OF LOTS.	AMOUNT OF TAX.	COSTS AND CHARGES.

Dated at the City of Detroit, this —— day of ——, A. D. 18—.
By order of the Common Council.

—— ——, *Receiver of Taxes.*

CHAPTER XXV.

OF THE SALE OF LANDS FOR UNPAID SPECIAL ASSESSMENTS.

[Ordinance approved July 10, 1862.]

Receiver of Taxes to sell real estate when special tax or assessment is not paid.

SECTION 1. Whenever the City Collector or other officer of said City, authorized to collect any assessment to defray the expense of constructing lateral sewers, side and crosswalks, paving, grading, macadamizing, graveling, or otherwise improving streets, lanes or alleys, or for defraying the expense of any local improvements properly payable from the proceeds of special assessment, shall make due return that such tax or assessment remains due and uncollected, it shall be the duty of the Receiver of Taxes to proceed and sell any real estate on which any such assessment shall be a lien, in the manner hereinafter prescribed.

To publish notice of sale.

SEC. 2. The Receiver of Taxes shall, within ten days after such return, make out a list of all such real estate on which any such assessment remains due and unpaid, the names of the owners, and the amount of the unpaid assessment due thereon, and shall, on behalf of the Common Council, cause to be published in the daily newspaper published by the Printer for the City, once a week for four successive weeks, such list, with a notice thereto attached, requiring the owner or occupants, or parties in interest in any such lands, tenements, hereditaments or premises, to pay any such tax, and further notifying them that if default be made in making any such payment, any such real estate will be sold at public auction, at a day and place therein to be specified, for the lowest term of years at which any person will offer to take the same, in consideration of advancing and paying the sum assessed on the same, with the costs and charges in the premises; and shall at the same time cause a printed copy of said list, with said notice thereto attached, to be posted in three or more public places in each Ward in said City.

To sell according to notice if tax or assessment remain unpaid.

SEC. 3. If the owner or owners, occupant or occupants, party or parties in interest, in any such real estate, do not pay any such assessment or tax, with the costs and charges thereon, within the period above prescribed, then the Receiver of Taxes, on behalf of the Common Council, at the place and on the day mentioned in said notice, shall commence the sale of such lands, tenements, hereditaments and premises, at public auction, and shall continue the same from day to day (Sundays excepted) until the same are sold for the lowest term of years at which any person shall offer to take the same, for the purpose and in the manner already above expressed, but each lot or parcel of lot, owned by any one person or set of persons, against whom any such tax or assessment has been made, shall be sold by itself.

To make report of sales.

SEC. 4. The Receiver of Taxes shall report to the Common Council, within ten days after the close of such sale, the terms for which each lot was sold, the amount bid therefor, and the name of the purchaser; and if there be no sufficient objection, the several purchasers shall, on payment of the amount of their respective bids, as hereinafter provided, be entitled to the necessary conveyances of said premises, when the time for the redemption fixed by law shall have fully expired, upon paying for the expense of such conveyance the further sum of fifty cents, unless said lot shall have been sooner redeemed, in which case the purchaser shall be entitled to recover his money and interest at the rate hereinafter established.

Payment of bids and certificates of sale.

SEC. 5. The purchasers at such sale shall pay the amount of their respective bids to the Receiver of Taxes within forty-eight hours after the sale has been finally closed, and on payment of the same it shall be the duty of the Receiver of Taxes, on behalf of the Common Council, to execute to the purchaser of each lot a proper certificate of such sale, describing the lands purchased and the amount paid therefor, and the term of years for which the same was bid off, and such certificate shall be regularly numbered, and a copy of each shall be filed in the office of the Controller.

Immediate payment may be required or sale cancelled.

SEC. 6. The Receiver of Taxes may, in his discretion, require immediate payment of any person to whom any such real estate shall be struck off, and in case of his neglect or refusal to pay any bid made by him, he may declare the bid cancelled, and at his discretion sell the lands again, and any person so neglecting or refusing to pay any bid made by him, shall not be entitled, after such neglect and refusal, to have any bid made by him received during such sale.

Names of persons failing to pay bids to be reported to Common Council.

SEC. 7. If any purchaser or purchasers shall neglect or refuse to pay the amount of their respective bids to the Receiver of Taxes within forty-eight hours after the sale, the Receiver of Taxes shall report the names of such persons to the Common Council, who may elect to take the lots bid off by such purchaser.

Deed.

SEC. 8. On presentation of certificate of sale heretofore referred to, to the Controller, after the expiration of the time provided by law for the redemption of real estate sold as aforesaid, unless such real estate has been previously redeemed, the Controller shall, in the name of and for the City of Detroit, execute and deliver to such purchaser or his assignee, a proper deed for the conveyance of such real estate, for the term for which the same was sold, which said deed shall be under the Corporate seal of the City and attested by the Clerk.

Record of sales.

SEC. 9. The Receiver of Taxes, within thirty days after such sale, shall make a correct record of all land sales, showing the time when the tax or assessment was levied, and the amount thereof, the cost and charges, the time when the lands were sold, the name of the purchaser or his assignee, the term for which the same was bid off, with such other entries as may be necessary in the premises, and shall deposit said record in the office of the Treasurer.

Redemption of lands sold.

SEC. 10. Any person entitled to redeem any such real estate, may, within one year from the time of sale, deposit with the Treasurer, for the use of the purchaser, the full amount of the assessment or tax, for which such real estate was sold, and interest as hereinafter mentioned, and the Treasurer shall give proper receipt for the same, and shall enter a note of such redemption in said record. Interest on unpaid taxes shall be at the rate of twenty-five per cent. per annum from and after such sale, and no person shall be entitled after sale to redeem any real estate sold without payment of the said interest and principal in the manner prescribed by law.

Treasurer to conduct sale in the absence of Receiver of Taxes.

SEC. 11. If, on the day mentioned in such notice of sale, the Receiver of Taxes shall neglect, or be unable from any cause to be present at and conduct said sale, then it shall be the duty of the Treasurer, in behalf of the Common Council, to proceed with said sale, in the same manner, and with the like effect as if the same had been conducted by the Receiver of Taxes, and he shall receive payments of bids, make the like returns, issue certificates of purchase, and make out the same record and perform all other acts as are required of the Receiver of Taxes under like circumstances.

SEC. 12. The following or other sufficient forms, may be used in proceedings under this chapter: Form of notice of sale.

NOTICE OF SALE.

STATE OF MICHIGAN, }
CITY OF DETROIT, } ss.

Notice is hereby given, that pursuant to law, there will be sold at the Common Council Hall, in the City of Detroit and State of Michigan, between the hours of —— and —— of the —— day of ———, A. D. 18—, at public auction, the several lands, tenements, hereditaments and premises hereinafter described, [each parcel or description separately,] for the lowest term of years at which any person will offer to take the same, in consideration of advancing the sum or sums which were assessed by the Common Council of said City, on the —— day of —— 18—, [here describe the improvement for which the assessment was levied,] together with the costs and charges thereon, unless the said sum or sums, with the costs and charges thereon, shall before that time be paid and satisfied, which the owners or occupants of, or parties in interest in said lands, tenements, hereditaments and premises, against whom said sum or sums have been assessed, are hereby required to do. [Here insert an accurate description of the several premises, and add to the description of each the amount assessed, the name of the individual or individuals against whom the amount is assessed, and also the amount of the costs and charges, if any, up to that time:]

NAMES.	DESCRIPTION OF LOTS.	AMOUNT OF TAX.	COSTS AND CHARGES.

Dated at the City of Detroit, this —— day of ——, A. D. 18—.
By order of the Common Council.

——— ———, *Receiver of Taxes.*

SEC. 13. All Ordinances conflicting with this are hereby repealed.

SEC. 14. This Ordinance shall take immediate effect.

CHAPTER XXVI.

OF THE MANNER OF OBTAINING POSSESSION OF LOTS SOLD FOR TAXES.

[Chapter Thirteen of Compiled Ordinances of 1859.]

Possession of lots under tax title, how obtained.

SECTION 1. Whenever the title of any person shall become absolute by virtue of the sale or lease of any lot or parcel of land in said City, in pursuance of the second section of an act, entitled "An Act to amend the several acts relative to the City of Detroit," approved April 22, 1833, such person, his legal representative or attorney, shall make demand, in writing, of the person in possession, and notify him that he claims possession of such lot, by virtue of a sale or lease under said section.

Persons refusing to deliver possession may be cited before Recorder's Court.

SEC. 2. If the person in possession shall neglect or refuse for the space of six days, after such demand, to give up possession of such lot, then the person claiming the same may present a petition to the Recorder's Court of said City, verified by his own oath, or by some person for him, setting forth his right to such possession, and praying that a citation may issue, directed to the person in possession; upon filing such petition, the Court may order that a citation issue accordingly, which shall be issued, and be returnable in the same manner as a summons: *Provided,* The petitioner enter into a bond to the Corporation of the City of Detroit, with such sureties as the Court shall direct, conditioned to pay all costs that may accrue in such proceedings.

Proceedings to obtain possession of lots leased by the city.

SEC. 3. If the defendant appears, he may plead the general issue, and give notice of any special matter which he intends to give in evidence.

Whenever, according to the laws of the State, relative to forcible entry and detainer, the Corporation of said City are entitled to the possession of any lands and tenements, the same proceedings shall be had in such case in the Recorder's Court of said City, so far as the same apply, as are authorized before Justices of the Peace: *Provided,* That in all cases the Marshal of said City shall give notice, in writing, to the persons in possession to quit the same, and in default thereof for the space of six days thereafter, the Marshal shall make report thereof to the City Attorney.

CHAPTER XXVII.

OF THE DISPOSITION OF LANDS BID IN BY THE CITY FOR TAXES OR ASSESSMENTS.

[Chapter Seventy-six of Compiled Ordinances of 1859.]

Treasurer may dispose of lands bid in by City in certain cases.

SECTION 1. Whenever any lands, bid in for the City under the provisions of section twenty-one of chapter nine of the Revised Charter of said City of the year 1857, shall not be redeemed by the owner or other persons interested in said lands, within one year from the day on which said lands are so bid in, it shall be lawful for the City Treasurer, and he is hereby authorized to sell, assign and transfer to any person or persons who shall pay the tax or assessment, together with the costs and charges for which said land was sold, all the interest which the City has acquired in said land by reason of said bid. And he shall give to the person or persons who shall so pay said tax or assessment, together with said costs and charges, a certificate of the fact of such payment, in which certificate the land or lands for which such payment is made shall be particularly described.

Treasurer to give certificate of such sale.

Controller to make transfer on presentation of such certificate.

SEC. 2. Upon presentation to him of the certificate provided for in the foregoing section, the City Controller shall, under the seal of the City, execute to the person named in the certificate a full and absolute assignment and transfer of the conveyance or certificate of sale of the land or lands for which the person or persons named in said certificate of the Treasurer shall have made said payment.

Treasurer to report the fact of purchasers failing to make good their bids, to the Council.

SEC. 3. It shall be the duty of the City Treasurer, whenever persons bidding for lands at any sale for delinquent taxes or assessments, shall fail to pay the amount of their said bid, to report the fact to the Common Council.

TITLE III.

OF STREETS, SIDEWALKS, AND PUBLIC PLACES.

CHAPTER XXVIII.

OF PAVING AVENUES AND STREETS, AND CONSTRUCTING AND REPAIRING SIDEWALKS AND CROSSWALKS.

[Ordinance approved March 26, 1860.]

Sidewalks, crosswalks and streets to be paved or planked.

SECTION 1. The side and crosswalks of all streets and avenues, which are or shall be graded, and all streets and avenues, shall be paved or planked with such materials as the Common Council may direct.

Owners of lots may pave or plank, etc.

SEC. 2. The owners of all lots on streets which have been graded and prepared for the laying down of sidewalks, under the direction of the Common Council, are hereby authorized to pave or plank in front of their lots, under the direction of such officer or committee as the Common Council may direct.

How money raised for sidewalks or crosswalks.

SEC. 3. Whenever the Common Council of said City shall deem it necessary to provide funds for defraying the expenses of paving or planking any sidewalks within the limits of said City, they shall do so by assessment on the owners or occupants of the lots or premises in front of, or adjacent to, the sidewalks paved or planked, or directed so to be; and whenever it may be necessary to provide for the expense of constructing any crosswalks in said City, the assessments for the same shall be made in accordance with the provisions of this chapter particularly relating thereto.

When sidewalks are directed by Common Council to be paved or planked, Street Commissioner shall notify owners of lots, who may construct same within ten days.

SEC. 4. Whenever the Common Council shall direct any sidewalks to be paved or planked, it shall be the duty of the Street Commissioner of the proper district to ascertain the proper description and the names of the owners of the premises, within the limits embraced in the order of the Common Council, in front of which sidewalks are not already paved or planked, and he shall forthwith serve, or cause to be served, upon all persons therein interested, a written or partly written and partly printed notice, by delivering the same to them personally, or leaving it at the party's usual place of abode or business, or when the persons therein interested are not residents, or cannot be found, by posting such notice in some conspicuous place on said premises, which said notice shall fully set forth the place where said sidewalk, paving or planking is ordered, and that said party is allowed ten days within which to construct the same; and if completed within that time, to the satisfaction of the Street Commissioner of the proper district, that no expense of proceedings to collect the same shall be incurred by them; and upon the expiration of said ten days, the Street Commissioner of the proper district shall make a full return to the City Surveyor of his doings, under this section, and state fully whether such notices have or have not been complied with by said parties.

If not so constructed, Street Commissioner shall make return to City Surveyor.

City Surveyor shall make report to Common Council.

SEC. 5. If from such return it appears that said sidewalks, paving or planking have not been constructed by the parties notified within the ten days prescribed, the said City Surveyor shall, with all due diligence, ascertain from the best evidence in his power, all the necessary facts, and shall then make out a written report or assessment roll, stating therein the names of the owners or occupants of the lots or premises in front of, or adjacent to which such sidewalks may be paved or planked, or directed so to be; describing by itself, with sufficient accuracy, each lot or portion of a lot owned by any one person or company of persons, and also the names of such owner or several owners; and when he cannot ascertain the names of any such owners or occupants, or either of them, he shall state such fact in his report; and said City Surveyor shall also, in as accurate a manner as possible, ascertain, and in said report set forth the space or number of square yards or feet paved or planked, and the quantity of curbing placed, or to be placed in front of or adjacent to the lots or premises owned or occupied by any one person or set of persons, the sum of money which such person or set of persons shall be assessed at and pay for such paving or planking, and also thirty cents for each description, to defray the expense of making such assessment, which report the said City Surveyor shall present to said Common Council. [*As amended by Ordinance approved September* 7, 1863.]

City Clerk shall notify persons assessed.

SEC. 6. The City Clerk shall then make out a notice, directed to the several persons in said report named and proposed to be assessed, notifying them that they are about to be assessed, to defray the expenses of paving or planking the sidewalks adjacent to certain premises owned or occupied by them in said City, and that a report or assessment roll made out in the premises is on file in the office of said Clerk, for inspection, and further notifying them of the time and place when the Common Council will meet and review said report or assessment, on the request of any person conceiving himself aggrieved; which said notice shall be published in some daily newspaper printed in said City, for four successive days.

Common Council to examine and approve assessment.

SEC. 7. The said Common Council shall, at the time and place in said notice specified, or at some session thereafter, take said assessment into consideration, and if no person appears to object to said report or roll, and no good cause to the contrary appears, and an affidavit of publication of the requisite notice having been made by some one acquainted with the facts, they shall, by a written resolution to be entered on their journal, declare that they approve of said report or assessment roll, that they receive as correct the description of the premises and the names of the individuals therein contained, and that the sum which said report states to be the correct one, which each individual or set of individuals should be assessed at and pay, be the assessment, and be collected from the respective persons liable, according to law; but if any sufficient cause appears, or is shown to said Common Council, they shall review said report or roll, and make such assessment as may be just and right in the premises; and said Common Council may, if necessary, adjourn from one time to any reasonable time, for the purpose of finishing said review of said assessment.

Contractor to construct sidewalks. How assessments collected.

SEC. 8. Upon the confirmation of the assessment roll by the Common Council, it shall be the duty of the Street Commissioner of the proper district to notify the contractor to construct said sidewalks, and when the same shall have been constructed, the amount of such assessment, together with all costs and charges incident to the collection thereof, shall be collected by warrant issued for that purpose by the Common Council, according to the provisions of chapter five of these Ordinances, relative to City Collector and special assessments.

SEC. 9. The Common Council may, from time to time, authorize that good and substantial plank sidewalks shall be laid down and constructed in any street or part of a street, whether graded or not, as hereinbefore described, and under the direction of the Street Commissioner of the proper district. Common Council may authorize plank sidewalks.

SEC. 10. Such sidewalks shall be constructed of good pine or oak plank, which shall not be less than two inches in thickness, nor more than twelve inches wide, on pine, oak, cedar or hemlock sleepers, not less than four inches square, to be placed not more than three feet apart; the plank shall not exceed eight inches in width, shall be laid in a line at right angles to the line of the sidewalk, and shall be nailed with nails not less than forty-penny, with at least three in each end of each plank and not less than two at any other bearing; and said sidewalks shall be of the following width: On Jefferson and Woodward avenues, not less than twelve feet, and on all other streets not less than six feet: *Provided, however,* That the Common Council may, at any time, direct that such sidewalk, on any street, or part thereof, be of more or less width than is hereinbefore described, and all crosswalks shall be constructed of oak plank, not less than two and one-half inches thick, and twelve inches wide, to be laid and fastened as in this section above prescribed for sidewalks; such crosswalks to be of such width as shall be ordered by the Common Council. How constructed.

SEC. 11. When the Common Council shall direct the construction of any such plank sidewalk, such proceedings shall be had as are required by sections four, five, six, seven and eight of this chapter, in the case of paving or planking sidewalks. Proceedings as required in case of paving or planking sidewalks.

SEC. 12. Any parties interested shall have the privilege of constructing a plank sidewalk in front of their respective premises after the same shall have been ordered by the Council, within the time and after the same manner as is hereinbefore provided in sec- Persons may construct their own sidewalks.

tion four, and shall be entitled to all the rights and privileges secured by said section.

Property of persons failing to pay assessments liable for expenses of construction.

SEC. 13. Whenever an assessment has been duly levied, according to the provisions of this chapter, and a return of the warrant issued for the collection of the same by the City Collector, under the provisions of section eight, has been made, the Common Council shall proceed to the construction of the sidewalk as ordered, and the property of all persons whose assessments have not been paid shall be held liable for all costs, charges, and interest incurred on their behalf in the construction of said sidewalks, and may be sold for the same, as in the case of delinquent taxes.

Certain mistakes not to vitiate assessment.

SEC. 14. Whenever, by mistake or otherwise, any person may be improperly designated as the owner or occupant of any lot or premises in proceedings under this chapter, or any other Ordinance of said City relative to taxes or assessments, the tax or assessment shall not for such cause be vitiated, but the same shall be a lien on such lot or premises, and collected as in other cases.

Persons may pave or grade streets.

SEC. 15. Any person or number of persons shall be allowed to grade and pave the street opposite to his or their property, where the same shall extend from the intersection of one cross street to the intersection of another: *Provided,* The same shall be done in conformity with the regulations of the Common Council. [*As amended by Ordinance approved August* 16, 1860.]

How money raised for paving, etc.

SEC. 16. Whenever the Common Council of said City shall order any highway, street, avenue, lane, alley, cross-walk, or interior public space, created by the intersection of streets in said City, or any portions thereof, to be graded, paved or planked, the funds necessary for defraying the expenses thereof, shall be provided by causing an assessment to be made by the City Surveyor on the owner or owners of the lot or premises in front of or adjacent to which such highway, street, avenue, lane, alley, crosswalk or interior public space, may be directed to be graded, paved or planked. [*As amended by Ordinance approved August* 16, 1860.]

City Surveyor to make report.

SEC. 17. The City Surveyor shall, with all due diligence, ascertain from the best evidence in his power all the necessary facts, and shall then make out an assessment roll, stating therein the names of the owners of the lots or premises in front of or adjacent to which such highway, street, avenue, lane, alley, crosswalk or interior public space, may be graded, paved or planked, or directed so to be, describing by itself with sufficient accuracy, each lot or portion of a lot owned by any one person or company of persons, and also the names of such owner or several owners, and when he cannot ascertain the name of such owner or owners, or either of them, he shall state such facts in said roll, and said City Surveyor shall also, in as accurate a manner as possible, ascertain and in said roll set forth, in separate columns, the space or number of yards or feet graded or to be graded, the space or number of square yards or feet paved or to be paved, the quantity of curbing placed or to be placed, and the quantity of tile drains placed or to be placed, in front of, or adjacent to, the lots or premises owned by any one person or set of persons, the sum of money which such person or set of persons shall be assessed for said work, and also five cents for each description to defray the expense of making such assessment. For defraying the expense of grading, paving, or otherwise improving crosswalks, and the interior spaces created by the intersection of streets, the City Surveyor shall make a separate assessment upon the real property of one-quarter of each of the blocks to be connected by such crosswalks, and being the two quarters which respectively lie nearest to such crosswalk; which said assessment shall be made *pro rata* according to the superficial area of each lot or parcel, to be separately described and assessed: *Provided*, Each block shall only be assessed to the centre of such cross street or interior space each way, which said assessment rolls said City Surveyor shall present to said Common Council. [*As amended by Ordinance approved August* 16, 1860.]

City Clerk shall notify persons assessed.

SEC. 18. The City Clerk shall then make out a notice, directed to the persons named in said assessment rolls, and proposed to be assessed, notifying them that they are about to be assessed, to defray the expenses of grading, paving, or planking the street or streets, or alley or alleys, in front of and adjacent to certain premises owned by them, in said City, and that a report, or assessment roll, made out in the premises, is on file in the office of said Clerk, for inspection, and further notifying them of the time and place when the Common Council will meet and review said report or assessment, on the request of any person conceiving himself aggrieved; which said notice shall be published in some daily newspaper printed in said City,

Common Council shall examine and approve of assessment roll.

for four successive days. The said Common Council shall, at the time and place in said notice specified, or at some session thereafter, take said assessment into consideration, and if no person appears to object to said report or roll, and no good cause to the contrary appears, and an affidavit of publication of the requisite notice having been made by some one acquainted with the facts, they shall, by a written resolution, to be entered on their journal, declare that they approve of said report, or assessment roll; that they receive, as correct, the description of the premises, and the names of the individuals therein contained, and that the sum which said report states to be the correct one, which each individual, or set of individuals, should be assessed at and pay, be the assessment, and be collected from the respective persons liable, according to law; but if any sufficient cause appears, or is shown to said Common Council, they shall review said report, or roll, and make such assessment as may be just and right in the premises; and said Common Council may, if necessary, adjourn from one time to any reasonable time, for the purpose of finishing said review of said assessment. After the assessment rolls shall have been fully and finally confirmed, as provided in the preceding section, the proper officer shall proceed in the collection of said assessment, as directed and provided by the Charter, and the Ordinances relative to City Collector and special assessments. [*As amended by Ordinance approved August* 16, 1860.]

How streets, etc., planked.

SEC. 19. Such avenues or streets, or such portions thereof, as the Common Council may direct to be planked, shall be done with good sound pine, oak, or hemlock plank, not less than four inches in thickness, nor more than ten inches in width; said planks to be spiked or pinned down solid, on timbers not less than four inches in thickness, nor eight inches in width, of the same material, and firmly imbedded in the earth, so that the lower surface of the plank shall rest on the earth as well as the bed timbers, which shall be put down not more than four feet apart; said planks to be laid crosswise, in the said avenues or streets, and the ends placed firmly against the curb-stones of the sidewalks, so as to leave the upper surface of the planks five inches below the top of the curb-stones, and the corner to be filled with one-half of a stick of timber five inches square, sawed through the extreme corners, the back well fitted to the curb, and spiked down solid to the plank, so as to prevent the water from washing the sand from between the curb-stones and pavement. All planks to be laid according to the established grade of the avenue or street. The work to be done to the satisfaction of the Common Council, or such committee as they shall appoint to inspect the same.

"Block" defined.

SEC. 20. The term "block," whenever used in this Ordinance, shall be held to mean either the interior space enclosed by streets most contiguous to each other, or the interior space enclosed on one side by the line of an undivided farm, and on all other sides by streets the most contiguous to each other, or that part of an unsubdivided farm, or tract, which would be included between streets already opened, the most contiguous to each other, and running in an easterly or westerly direction, if said streets were extended across said unsubdivided farm, or tract: *Provided,* That in determining in what block any premises lie, the said several definitions or limitations shall be applied, and take precedence in the order in which they are herein stated.

How expense of constructing crosswalks over streets defrayed.

SEC. 21. The expense of construction of all crosswalks over the streets of the City, hereafter to be made, and not already provided for, shall be defrayed by a rateable assessment upon the real property of one-quarter of each of the blocks so to be connected, and being the two quarters which respectively lie in the line of direction of the crosswalk; and said assessment shall be made *pro rata,* according to the superficial area of each lot, or parcel, to be separately described and assessed.

Id. over alleys.

SEC. 22. The expense of constructing all crosswalks hereafter to be made over each of the alleys of the City, shall be defrayed by an assessment upon the real property of, as near as may be, one-half of the block through which such alley runs, being that half most contiguous to the point where such crosswalk is directed to be laid: *Provided, however,* That the line dividing said block, for the purposes of said assessment, shall be parallel to the line of the crosswalk to be constructed, and at right angles to the line of the alley across which said crosswalk is to be made Said assessment shall be made *pro rata* according to the superficial area of each lot, or parcel, to be separately described and assessed.

When Council to direct construction of crosswalks.

SEC. 23. Whenever a majority of the taxable inhabitants of each of any two blocks to be connected, shall petition the Common

Council to have a crosswalk constructed to connect said blocks, the Common Council will order the construction of such crosswalk, at such point or points of connection as the petitioners may designate, and of the width prayed for; and whenever a less number than such majority shall so petition, or the Common Council shall direct without petition, the construction of such walk shall not be ordered, except upon a report thereon by the Committee on the Streets of said City, or the Street Commissioner of the proper District.

Street Commissioner to construct crosswalks, and warrant to issue for collection of assessment for same.

SEC. 24. As soon as a crosswalk shall be ordered, in pursuance of the foregoing provisions, the Street Commissioner shall proceed, without delay, to cause the same to be constructed by the contractor for building walks in the respective Districts, and the City Surveyor shall report the assessment for constructing the same at the next succeeding meeting of the Common Council, for confirmation, and upon such confirmation, a warrant shall issue for the amount of said assessment, and the City Collector shall proceed at once to collect the same, in the same manner as other special assessments.

How expense of repairing crosswalks defrayed.

SEC. 25. The expense of repairing all crosswalks over the streets and alleys of the City, shall be defrayed out of the district road funds of the respective districts, in which the crosswalks are situated.

When Street Commissioner to notify persons to repair.

SEC. 26. All sidewalks in the City of Detroit shall be kept in good repair by the owner or occupant of the house, lot, or premises adjoining or fronting on such, and whenever any sidewalk within the limits of said City shall require repairing, it shall be the duty of the Street Commissioner of the district in which the same is situated, to notify, by a written or printed, or a partly written or partly printed notice, the owner or occupant of such house, lot, or other premises, adjacent to, or fronting on, such parts of said sidewalk needing such repairs, to repair the same within forty-eight hours; and if the person thus notified shall refuse or neglect to comply with the exigency of said notice, then the said Street Commissioner shall have said repairs made, and shall report the making of the same, together with a detailed statement of the cost of making said repairs, to the City Surveyor, who shall prepare and transmit to the Common Council a proper assessment roll, assessing the expense of said repairs upon said lot or premises, which roll shall be confirmed by the Common Council, in the same manner as other special assess-

City Surveyor to make assessment roll.

ments, and said Common Council may thereupon issue their warrant for the collection of said assessment, and all costs and charges relating to such assessments, and on failure of the proper officer to collect the same, the said lots or premises shall be sold, agreeably to the provisions of the Charter and Ordinances relative to such cases: *Provided, however,* That where the said Commissioner shall estimate that the expense of any repair herein provided for will exceed the sum of two hundred dollars, he shall report the fact of notice, and the estimate of expense, to the said Common Council, who shall then provide for the making of said repair by contract, as is prescribed by law. It shall be the duty of said Street Commissioners to keep, in a book, a copy of all notices served under this section, on which shall be made a memorandum, signed by the Commissioner serving the notice, of the time when, the person on whom, and the manner in which said notice was served. If any lot, or premises, in front of, or adjacent to which said repairs shall be required, shall be unoccupied, and the owner or owners, or lessee thereof, cannot be found in the City of Detroit, said Street Commissioner may serve said notice to repair by posting the same in some conspicuous position upon said lot or premises. If any person shall neglect or refuse to repair any sidewalk, after notice, as aforesaid, shall, on conviction thereof, in the Recorder's Court, be subject to a penalty of two dollars for each offence. He shall be liable for all damages which the City may incur, by reason thereof, to be recovered by the City in an action of assumpsit.

Proviso.

Expense of making assessment to be paid by person assessed.

SEC. 27. All expenses for making assessments under this chapter, or any other Ordinance of the City, incurred after the confirmation, by the Common Council, of the assessment roll, including the expense of printing notices, shall be justly apportioned by the City Treasurer to the persons liable to pay said assessments, and shall be collected at the same time. The said Treasurer shall endorse upon each roll which comes into his hands a detailed statement of the expenses apportioned by him to the persons named in said rolls, under the provisions of this section.

Common Council may authorize any other person to do duty of Street Commissioner.

SEC. 28. The Common Council may, at any time, by resolution, to be entered on their journal, authorize or require any person, or officer of the Corporation of said City, to perform the same duties which are hereinbefore required to be performed by the Street Commissioner, or other officer.

Penalty for injuring streets, etc.

SEC. 29. Any person, or persons, who shall, in any manner, be guilty of a wanton injury to any side or crosswalk, paving or planking, within the limits of the City, by impairing, destroying, or removing the same, or any part thereof, shall, on conviction thereof, in the Recorder's Court, be subject to a fine not exceeding fifty dollars.

Forms of proceeding under this chapter.

SEC. 30. The following, or other sufficient forms, shall be used in proceedings under the provisions of this chapter:

No. 1.

RESOLUTION.

Resolved, That a ("plank," "brick," or "stone," as the case may be,) sidewalk be constructed on —— street, between —— street and —— street, except where such walk is already built within said limits, and that the several officers named in chapter twenty-eight, of the Ordinances of the City, perform the duties imposed upon them by the provisions of said chapter.

No. 2.

Resolved, That the sidewalks on the —— side of —— street, between —— street and —— street, be repaired forthwith, except where the walks within said limits are in good repair, to the satisfaction of the Street Commissioner of the —— District, and that the several officers named in chapter twenty-eight, of the Ordinances of the City, perform the duties imposed upon them by the provisions of said chapter.

No. 3.

NOTICE TO PERSONS TO BE ASSESSED.

STATE OF MICHIGAN, }
CITY OF DETROIT, } ss.

To (here insert the names of those to whom directed, and add,) *or to any other person interested in the premises, within the limits hereinafter mentioned:*

You are hereby notified that assessments are about to be made upon you to defray the expenses of constructing plank sidewalks, (or paving the sidewalks or streets, as the case may be,) in front of, or adjacent to, certain premises, or lots of land, owned or occupied by you, respectively, on —— street, in the City of Detroit, State of Michigan; and, also, that a report, or assessment roll, has been made in the premises, which is on file in the office of the Clerk of said City, where it will remain open for your inspection until the —— day of ——, A. D. 18—, when and where you may appear and show cause, before the Common Council, in the Common Council house, in said City, why the said assessment should not be made and collected, according to law.

By order of the Common Council.

—— ——, *City Clerk.*

Dated at the City of Detroit, this —— day of ——, A. D. 18—.

[After the time mentioned in the notice, and on filing affidavit thereof, let a resolution of the following form be entered on the journal:]

Whereas, It appears, by affidavit on file, that due notice has been given to the owners and occupants of premises fronting on —— street, in the City of Detroit, that the Common Council would, on the —— day of ——, A. D. 18—, meet and review the report or assessment roll filed by the City Clerk, on the —— day of ——, A. D. 18—, for the expense of constructing —— in front of said premises: *And whereas,* No person has appeared before the Common Council, to object to said assessment, or the confirmation thereof; (if there be any objection, say after the word "whereas"—all objections thereto have been duly considered,) therefore

Resolved, That said assessment roll is hereby approved and confirmed; that the description of premises, and the names of persons contained therein, are received as correct; and that the sums which the said assessment roll states to be the correct ones, which each individual, or set of individuals, should be assessed at and pay, be the assessment, and be collected from the several persons liable to pay the same, according to law.

[Then let the Clerk endorse on the roll the words: "Approved and confirmed by the Common Council, this —— day of ——, A. D. 18—."]

SEC. 31. All by-laws and ordinances, or parts of by-laws and ordinances, repugnant to, or in any manner inconsistent with the provisions of this Ordinance, are hereby repealed, and this Ordinance is hereby designated as chapter twelve, of title two, of the Ordinances and By-laws of the City of Detroit: *Provided, however,* That the provisions of this Ordinance shall not be so construed as to alter or repeal any part or portion of chapter eighty-four of the Revised Ordinances.

SEC. 32. This Ordinance shall take effect, and be in force, from and after its passage.

CHAPTER XXIX.

OF THE USE OF STREETS AND ALLEYS.

[Ordinance approved December 30, 1861.]

Snow and ice to be removed from sidewalks.

SECTION 1. No person shall permit any snow or ice to remain on the sidewalk in front of any house, building or lot occupied by him or her, or on the sidewalk in front of any unoccupied house, building or lot owned by him or her, longer than twenty-four hours after the same has fallen or formed; and where ice is formed on any sidewalk, such owner or occupant as above provided, shall, within four hours after the same has formed, cause salt, sand or ashes to be strewn thereon.

Buildings not to be removed in streets without permission.

SEC. 2. No person shall remove, or cause to be removed, or aid or assist in removing any building into, along or across any street, alley or other public space, without permission first obtained from the Mayor, Common Council, or Street Commissioner.

Animals not to be driven on sidewalks.

SEC. 3. No person shall drive, lead or back any horse, mule, ox, cow, or other animal, or team, cart or wheel carriage, on any sidewalk.

Building materials not to remain on sidewalks.

SEC. 4. No person owning, building, or repairing any house or other building, shall permit any lumber, brick, plaster, mortar, earth, clay, sand, stone, or other material, to remain on the sidewalk after sunset of the day upon which it was placed there, without the permission of the Mayor, Common Council, or Street Commissioner.

Streets, wharves, etc., not to be obstructed.

SEC. 5. No person shall obstruct or encumber any public wharf, street, alley, or other public space, with any article or thing whatsoever. This section shall not be construed to prohibit merchants and other business persons from using and occupying the side of the sidewalks next to their places of business, for a distance of three feet, for the purpose of displaying their goods and wares, or merchandise; nor shall it be construed to prevent the moving of goods, wares or merchandises across any sidewalk in the way of trade, or for the use of families.

SEC. 6. No person shall leave any wagon, cart, carriage, sleigh, or other vehicle, standing in any street, alley, or public space, without the same is actually in use at the time.

Vehicles not to stand in streets.

SEC. 7. No person shall place, by himself or another, any stone, timber, lumber, planks, boards, bricks or other materials, in or upon any street, alley or other public space, except for the purpose of building, and not for that purpose, except under permission first obtained from the Mayor, Common Council or the Street Commissioner; and such material shall not be allowed to remain in such street, alley, or other public space, after the completion of such building, or for a longer period than four months, and the same shall not be allowed to occupy and obstruct more than the one-half of any street or alley; and after such building has been completed, all building material, dirt and rubbish arising therefrom, shall be removed.

Building materials not to be placed in streets without permission.

SEC. 8. No person shall leave any horse, mule, oxen, or team, in any street, alley or public space, without being sufficiently tied; and no person shall halt any wagon, cart, carriage, sleigh, or other vehicle, on any crosswalk or footway.

Animals to be tied, etc.

SEC. 9. No person shall make or construct any drain or sewer, in any street or other public space, within four feet of the curb-stone of the sidewalk, unless it be the drain or sewer leading to or from the building or lot for which the same is designed.

Construction of drains and sewers.

SEC. 10. No person shall dig or tear up any pavement, side or crosswalk, or dig any hole, ditch, drain or sewer in any street, alley or other public space, without permission first obtained from the Mayor, Common Council or Street Commissioner; and it shall be the duty of any person digging or tearing up any pavement, side or crosswalk, or digging any hole, ditch, drain, or sewer, in any street, alley or other public space, as speedily as practicable to repair and put the same in as good order and condition as before; and in order to do this, such person shall pound down the earth so as to make it firm and solid, and if the earth shall settle, such person shall fill the same, from time to time, as may be necessary; and any person digging in any street, alley, or other public space, for any of

Digging up and replacing pavements.

the purposes hereinbefore mentioned, or for any purpose whatever, shall erect and maintain a good and sufficient fence, railing or barrier around such excavation, in such a manner as to prevent accidents, and to place and keep upon such railing, fence or barrier, suitable and sufficient colored lights during the night.

Cattle not to be herded in streets.

SEC. 11. No person shall herd together, or detain in any street, alley, or other public space, any cattle, horses, hogs, sheep or goats.

Cattle troughs.

SEC. 12. No person shall place or put any trough for feeding or watering horses, cattle, or other animals, in any street, alley or other public space.

Stands on sidewalks.

SEC. 13. No person shall keep or maintain on any sidewalk, any wagon or stand for the sale of goods, wares or merchandise, vegetables or fruits, to project more than three feet from the wall of his or her house or store.

Exhibition of stud-horses prohibited.

SEC. 14. No person shall display or detain for exhibition any stud-horse in any street, alley or other public space.

Fast driving through streets prohibited.

SEC. 15. No person shall ride or drive any horse, carriage, sleigh or other vehicle, through any street or avenue in this City, at a faster rate than six miles per hour.

Balustrades and balconies.

SEC. 16. No person shall erect any balustrade or balcony, to extend beyond the line of any sidewalk or street, and less than twelve feet from the ground, without permission first obtained from the Common Council, and iron braces and railings shall be used in the construction of any such balustrades or balconies, and the same shall not project beyond the line of the sidewalk more than three feet.

Games not to be played in streets.

SEC. 17. No person shall play any game of nine or ten pins, ball, wicket or other games, in any street, alley or other public space.

Nor crowds gathered.

SEC. 18. It shall not be lawful to gather in crowds on any sidewalk or in any street, so as to obstruct travel therein, or encumber the same.

Hitching posts.

SEC. 19. No post, except for the purpose of supporting awnings or hitching horses, shall be erected or put up in any street, alley, or public space, without permission first obtained from the Common Council.

SEC. 20. No wooden post for the purpose of supporting any awning, shall be erected or set up in any paved street, avenue or public space, and all iron posts erected in any paved street, avenue or other public space, for the purpose of supporting awnings, shall be not less than eight feet in height, and to be placed next to and alongside the curb-stone; and no rails or strips of boards shall be used to connect such posts with the buildings. Awning posts.

SEC. 21 No awning, or cloth or canvas used as an awning, shall be permitted to hang within eight feet of the sidewalk. Awnings.

SEC. 22. No person shall suspend from any house, shop or store, into or over any street, alley or other public space, any lamp, sign, goods, clothes, wares or other article or substance, so that the same shall extend or project from the wall or front of such building more than three feet. Suspended lamps, signs, goods, etc.

SEC. 23. No person shall make or continue any cellar door, windows or area, so that the same shall extend more than four feet beyond the line of any sidewalk; and all areas shall be protected by sufficient grating or illuminated pavement. Cellar doors, etc.

SEC. 24. Every entrance or flight of steps projecting beyond the line of the sidewalk, and descending into any cellar or basement story, where such entrance or flight of steps shall not be covered, shall be enclosed with a good iron railing on each side, permanently put up, not less than three feet high, with a gate opening inwardly, unless such entrance steps be thoroughly lighted, so as to prevent accidents; and such steps and railing shall not occupy more than one-fifth of the width of the sidewalk. Entrances, etc.

SEC. 25. No person shall construct or continue any porch over a cellar door so that the same shall project beyond the line of any alley or other public space. Porches.

SEC. 26. No person shall dig or construct, or cause to be dug or constructed, any area to or around any cellar or basement story, so that the same shall extend more than four feet beyond the line of any sidewalk; and no vault shall be dug or constructed to extend beyond the curb line of the street. Areas.

SEC. 27. No person shall swim or bathe in any of the waters in or adjoining the City of Detroit, so as to be exposed to the view of spectators. Bathing in sight of spectators prohibited.

Hoisting goods, etc.

SEC. 28. No person shall hoist or raise from any street into any building, loft, store or room, or lower from any building, store, loft or room into any street, any cask, bale, bundle, box, crate, or any goods, wares or merchandise, boards, joists, timber, or article whatever, by means of any rope, pulley, tackle or windlass.

Penalty.

SEC. 29. Any violations of the provisions of this Ordinance shall be punished by a fine not to exceed one hundred dollars and costs of prosecution, and the offender may be imprisoned in the Detroit House of Correction until the payment thereof: *Provided, however,* That the term of such imprisonment shall not exceed six months.

Marshals, etc., to enforce ordinance.

SEC. 30. It is hereby made the duty of the Marshal, Assistant Marshals and Street Commissioners of the City, to see that the provisions of this Ordinance are faithfully observed, and to make complaint for all violations of the same.

SEC. 31. Chapters fourteen, fifteen, seventeen, eighteen and nineteen of the Revised Ordinances of 1859, and an ordinance entitled "An Ordinance to prohibit and punish the obstruction of streets and alleys," approved Dec. 23, 1859; and an ordinance entitled "An Ordinance relative to the use of certain streets and alleys," approved July 11, 1860, and all Ordinances and parts of Ordinances amendatory of the foregoing chapters, or inconsistent with this Ordinance, are hereby repealed.

CHAPTER XXX.

OF SIDEWALKS.

[Chapter Eighty-four of Compiled Ordinances of 1859.]

Sidewalks on Jefferson avenue and other streets to be flagged.

SECTION 1. Hereafter, all sidewalks laid down on Jefferson avenue, between Third street and Beaubien street, in said City; on Woodward avenue, between Grand River street and the Detroit river, in said City; and on Griswold street, from Atwater street to Michigan avenue, in said City, shall be constructed of stone flagging, and of no other material.

SEC. 2 All sidewalks in the City of Detroit shall be raised from the curb-stone in the proportion of eight inches on twenty feet, and in conformity to the established grade.

How sidewalks raised from curb stone.

SEC. 3. All sidewalks laid under this Ordinance shall be constructed in the following manner, that is to say:

How constructed.

1st—The stone flagging shall be laid upon six inches of clean sand, and in water lime.

2d—Said flagging shall not be less than three inches in thickness, and not less than two feet square, and dressed even on the sides, so as to form close and even joints.

3d—Old flagging, when good, may be re-cut and laid next to the curb or the building, but the central portion of the sidewalk, for not less than six feet in width, shall be laid with new flagging.

4th—The curb-stones laid for the purpose of supporting the sidewalk shall not be less than thirty inches in length, four inches thick, and eighteen inches wide throughout; the top of the stone to be beveled so as to correspond with the inclination of the sidewalk; the front to be cut smooth; the ends, from top to bottom, to be truly squared, so as to form close and even joints.

5th—The curb-stones shall be set perpendicular and in conformity to the established grade. At the intersection of streets with other streets, or with alleys, the curb-stones shall be set upon a proper curve, and to the satisfaction of the Street Commissioner of the proper district.

SEC. 4. No sidewalk, or any part of a sidewalk, laid with flagging in any part of the City of Detroit, shall hereafter be taken up, or the flagging removed therefrom, for any purpose whatever, without the written permission of the Street Commissioner for the proper district.

Sidewalks not to be taken up.

SEC. 5. The expense of constructing said sidewalks shall be defrayed in the same manner in which the expense of constructing street pavements is now defrayed; and all ordinances and parts of ordinances relative to the manner of constructing and of making assessments for the construction of street pavements are hereby made parts of this Ordinance, except so far as they relate to the material of which said sidewalk shall be constructed, or are inconsistent with this Ordinance.

How expense of constructing sidewalks defrayed.

Penalty.

SEC. 6. Any person violating any of the provisions of this Ordinance shall pay a fine of not more than twenty dollars, nor less than five dollars, in the discretion of the Court, and costs of prosecution. [*Sections two, three, four, five and six added by Ordinance approved April* 11, 1860.]

CHAPTER XXXI.

OF SIDEWALKS ON WAYNE STREET.

[Chapter Eighty-five of Compiled Ordinances of 1859.]

Width of sidewalks on Wayne street, (portion of.)

SECTION 1. The sidewalks on both sides of Wayne street, in said City of Detroit, shall, and hereby are directed to be made and maintained the width of twelve feet, from Fort street to Michigan avenue.

CHAPTER XXXII.

OF CLEANING STREETS.

[Chapter Sixteen of Compiled Ordinances of 1859.]

Committee on Streets and City Controller authorized to contract with suitable persons to clean streets.

SECTION 1. The Committee on Streets and the City Controller are hereby authorized to contract with the lowest bidder, who shall propose to clean such portions of the paved or planked streets, squares or alleys, as the Corporation are liable to clean.

Such persons to furnish security.

SEC. 2. The said lowest bidder, or person contracting with the Corporation, as aforesaid, shall furnish satisfactory security for the performance of such contract: *Provided,* Notice shall be published for one week, in the City paper, previous to receiving proposals for said work.

CHAPTER XXXIII.

OF NUMBERING BUILDINGS.

[Chapter Twenty of Compiled Ordinances of 1859.]

SECTION 1. Whenever the Common Council shall, by resolution, direct the public streets or avenues, or any part of said streets or avenues, to be numbered, said streets or avenues shall be numbered as hereinafter provided, and the owners or agents of the said buildings or premises so directed to be numbered, lying alongside said streets or avenues, shall pay the costs of numbering the same; and any owner or agent refusing or neglecting to have his premises or buildings so numbered, whenever a public street or avenue is directed to be numbered, as aforesaid, such person or persons shall, for every such offence, on conviction before the Recorder's Court, forfeit a sum of five dollars, and costs of prosecution. *Streets to be numbered when Council shall direct.* *Penalty.*

SEC. 2. The numbering on Jefferson avenue, Woodbridge street, and Atwater street, shall commence at the western termination of each of said streets, and the numbers one, three, five, seven, etc., shall be used on the left hand of each of said streets, and the numbers two, four, six, eight, etc., shall be used on the right hand of each of said streets, and proceed easterly, as far as it may, from time to time, be deemed necessary or expedient. *How numbered.*

SEC. 3. On all streets parallel to Jefferson avenue, the numbering shall commence where such street crosses Woodward avenue, and proceed easterly and westerly, as far as necessary, using the odd numbers, one, three, five, seven, etc., on the left, and even numbers, two, four, six, eight, etc., on the right hand side of each of said streets. *Id.*

SEC. 4. On Woodward avenue, and all streets running parallel to it, the numbering shall commence at the channel of the Detroit river, and proceed northerly, as far as may be required, using the numbers one, three, five, seven, etc., on the left, and the numbers two, four, six, eight, etc., on the right hand side of each of said streets, respectively. *Id.*

Vacant lots how numbered.

SEC. 5. Whenever there are vacant lots along the line of said streets, one number shall be allowed to every twenty feet of such vacant lot.

CHAPTER XXXIV.

OF LAMPS AND LAMP POSTS.

[Ordinance approved December 2, 1861.]

Lamps and lamp posts to be supervised by Inspector of Gas Meters.

SECTION 1. The public lamps and lamp posts in the City shall be under the supervision of the Inspector of Gas Meters.

Lamps and lamp posts not to be injured.

SEC. 2. No person shall willfully, maliciously, or negligently injure, pull down, break, remove, or in any manner deface, or injure any public lamp, lamp post, crotchet, or gas light, within the City of Detroit.

Nor lighted nor extinguished without authority.

SEC. 3. No person shall light, or cause to be lighted, or extinguish, or cause to be extinguished, any public lamp or gas light, without being authorized so to do, either by the Common Council, the Mayor, Controller, Inspector of Gas Meters, or the Detroit Gas Light Company.

Animals not to be hitched to lamp posts.

SEC. 4. No person shall hang or place any article or substance whatever upon, or place any box, or other heavy material, against, or hitch any horse, or other animal, to any public lamp or lamp post, in this City.

Lamps not be be suspended or lamp posts erected without authority.

SEC. 5. No person shall erect, place or suspend any lamp or lamp post, in any public street, lane or alley, in this City, without permission from the Common Council.

Penalty.

SEC. 6. Any violation of the provisions of this Ordinance shall be punished by a fine not to exceed the sum of twenty-five dollars and costs, and in the imposition of any fine and costs, the Court may make a further sentence, that the offender be imprisoned in the Detroit House of Correction until the payment thereof, for any term not exceeding six months.

SEC. 7. Section four, of chapter fifty-one, of the Revised Ordinances of 1859, and all other ordinances, and parts of ordinances, inconsistent herewith, are hereby repealed.

SEC. 8. This Ordinance shall take effect from and after its passage.

CHAPTER XXXV.

OF PUBLIC PARKS AND PLACES.

[Ordinance approved June 12, 1861.]

SECTION 1. No person shall place any building, or obstruction of any kind, on a public park or space. Public parks and spaces not to be obstructed.

SEC. 2. No person shall take down, climb over, interfere with, disturb or displace any rails, posts, boards, chains or fences, enclosing any public park or space. Fences, etc., not to be taken down, etc.

SEC. 3. No person shall play at any game, or sport, in any enclosed public park or space. Games not to be played.

SEC. 4. No person shall climb, peel, cut, deface, remove, injure or destroy any tree, in any public park or space. Trees not to be defaced.

SEC. 5. No person shall stand, walk, or lie upon any part of a public park or space, laid out and appropriated for grass or shrubbery. Grass and shrubbery not to be trodden on.

SEC. 6. No person shall pluck, break, trample upon, or interfere with any flower or shrub, in any public park or space. Flowers not to be plucked.

SEC. 7. No person shall dig, remove, or carry away any sward, gravel, sand, turf or earth, in any public park or space. Earth, etc., not to be removed.

SEC. 8. No person shall place or deposit any dead carcass, ordure, filth, dirt, stones, or other matter or substance, on any public park or space. Nuisances not to be placed.

SEC. 9 No person shall hang, post, place, or put any bill, notice, sign, placard, carpet, or other incumbrance, on any tree, fountain, post, railing, fence, or other erection, in or surrounding any public park or space. Bills, etc., not to be posted.

SEC. 10. No person shall wade into, or throw any wood, sand, stone, or other substance, into any basin, pool or fountain, in any public park or space. Fountains, etc., not to be disturbed.

SEC. 11. No person shall molest, or in any manner disturb or annoy the fish, or other animals, which may be placed in any fountain, pool or basin, in any public park or space. Fish, etc., not to be molested.

SEC. 12. The person or person in charge of the public parks or spaces, shall have and possess the powers of policemen, and it is Persons in charge of public parks, etc., to have powers of policemen.

hereby made the duty of such person or persons, to observe that the provisions of this Ordinance are strictly complied with, and to make complaint to the Recorder's Court, for any violation of its provisions.

Penalty. SEC. 13. Any violation of the provisions of this Ordinance shall be punished by a fine not to exceed one hundred dollars, and costs; and in the imposition of any fine and costs, the Court may make a further sentence, that the offender be imprisoned in the County Jail, or in the Detroit House of Correction, until such fine and costs be paid: *Provided, however*, That the term of such imprisonment shall not exceed the period of six months.

SEC. 14. This Ordinance ordered to take effect immediately.

CHAPTER XXXVI.

OF HOISTWAYS.

[Ordinance approved December 2, 1861.]

Hoistways to be enclosed. SECTION 1. The owner or occupant of any building in which there is a hoistway, shall cause the same, in each story, to be enclosed by a good and sufficient railing, except when in actual use, and provide for the closing of such hoistways by a trap door, to be closed at the conclusion of the business of each day.

Fire Marshal to enforce ordinance. SEC. 2. It shall be the duty of the Fire Marshal to examine into all violations of the preceding section, and make complaints for the same.

Penalty. SEC. 3. Any violation of this Ordinance shall be punished by a fine not to exceed fifty dollars; and in the imposition of any such fine, the Court may make a further sentence, that the offender be imprisoned until such fine be paid: *Provided, however*, That the period of such imprisonment shall not exceed six months.

SEC. 4. This Ordinance shall take effect from and after its passage.

CHAPTER XXXVII.

OF THE PREVENTION OF ACCIDENTS.

[Ordinance approved December 2, 1861.]

Barriers to be erected.

SECTION 1. It shall be the duty of each and every person engaged in paving any avenue, street, lane, or alley, or in digging or building any sewer, drain, trench, or cistern, in or through any avenue, street, lane, or alley, or in the performance of any other work whatever, requiring the digging or excavating of any street, avenue, lane, or alley, under a contract with the City of Detroit, or by virtue of any permission granted by the Common Council, or any department or officer of the City, where, if left exposed, such work would be dangerous to passengers, to erect and maintain a good and sufficient fence, railing, or barrier, around the same, in such a manner as to prevent accidents; and it shall also be the duty of such persons to place upon such railing, fence, or barrier, at twilight, on each day, suitable and sufficient colored lights, and keep them burning during the night.

Contracts for public work must contain provisions for erecting barriers, etc.

SEC. 2. It shall be the duty of the City Attorney, or other legal adviser of the Corporation, to insert in all contracts for paving or grading streets, avenues, lanes, or alleys, or for constructing sewers, drains, or reservoirs, or for doing any work whatever, whereby accidents or injuries may occur in consequence of any neglect or carelessness on the part of the contractor, a covenant requiring the contractor to place and maintain the fences, railing, or barriers, in the manner provided for in the preceding section, for the prevention of accidents, and keep and save the City harmless and indemnified against all loss and damage, which may be occasioned by reason of any negligence or carelessness in the manner of doing such work.

Liability of contractors.

SEC. 3 In all cases where any person or persons shall perform any work, as provided in the preceding section, either under contracts with the Corporation, or by virtue of any permission from the Common Council, or any department or officer of the City, such person shall be liable to the City of Detroit for any and every loss or damage which said Corporation may sustain, and for all sums which it may have to pay to any person, or persons, by reason of any loss or injury sustained in consequence of any carelessness or negligence in doing the work, or by reason of any neglect or failure to comply with the provisions of this Ordinance. [*As amended by Ordinance approved October* 16, 1863.]

Penalty.

SEC. 4. Any person performing work, as provided in this Ordinance, who shall neglect or refuse to comply with its provisions, shall be punished by a fine not to exceed one hundred dollars and costs; and in the imposition of any such fine and costs, the Court may make a further sentence, that the offender may be imprisoned in the Detroit House of Correction until the payment thereof, for any period of time not exceeding six months.

SEC. 5. This Ordinance shall take effect from and after its passage.

CHAPTER XXXVIII.

OF THE DEPARTURE AND ARRIVAL OF BOATS AND CARS.

[Chapter Seventy-one of Compiled Ordinances of 1859.]

Carriages not to be kept within twenty feet of depot on arrival of cars.

SECTION 1. No person shall, on the arrival of any railroad cars in said City, nor for the period of thirty minutes previously to the departure of any railroad cars from said City, have or keep any carriage, wagon, cart, or other vehicle, within twenty feet of the place where such railroad cars shall have ceased running, or are about to depart from said City.

Where carriages to stand on arrival and departure of steamboats.

SEC. 2. No person shall, on the arrival of any steamboat or vessel at any wharf in said City, nor for the period of thirty minutes thereafter, nor for the period of thirty minutes previously to the departure of such steamboats or vessels, have or keep any carriage, wagon, cart, or other vehicle, within sixty feet of the place where such steamboat or vessel has, or is about to be made fast, or depart from said City. Any person violating this, or the preceding section, shall, for every violation, on conviction before the Recorder's Court, forfeit a sum not exceeding one hundred dollars, and costs of prosecution.

SEC. 3. All carriages, wagons, carts, and other vehicles, the keepers whereof are waiting for employment from any railroad cars, steamboats or vessels, shall stand on either side of the street or alley, so as to leave the centre thereof, and access to each house thereon, open and unobstructed, for the free passage of carriages, wagons, carts, and other vehicles, and foot passengers. Any person violating this section, shall, for every violation, on conviction before the Recorder's Court, forfeit a sum not exceeding fifty dollars, and costs of prosecution.

Further regulations.

SEC. 4. If any person shall, on the arrival or departure of any railroad cars, steamboats or vessels, at or from said City, or for the period of thirty minutes after the arrival, or before the departure of such railroad cars, steamboats or vessels, and within sixty feet of the wharf or depot where such railroad cars, steamboats or vessels have, or are about to stop running, or being made fast, or depart from said City, make, aid, countenance, or assist in making any loud or boisterous noise, disturbance, or improper diversion, or shall be guilty of any indecent, immoral, or insulting conduct, language, or behavior, such person shall, for every such offence, on conviction before said Recorder's Court, forfeit a sum not exceeding one hundred dollars, and costs of prosecution.

Disorderly conduct at boats and cars prohibited.

SEC. 5. If any person shall, by any false or deceitful representations to any stranger traveler in said City, induce or prevail on such stranger or traveler to go to, and put up at any hotel, tavern, grocery, or other house of entertainment in said City, such person shall, for every such offence, on conviction before the Recorder's Court, forfeit a sum not exceeding one hundred dollars, and costs of prosecution.

False representation to strangers, punishment.

SEC. 6. It shall be the special duty of the Marshal, and all the Constables of said City, to make complaint of all violations of this Chapter.

Duty of officers.

SEC. 7. Nothing contained in the first and second sections of this Chapter shall be construed to prevent any teamster from hauling freight to any steamboat or vessel about to depart from said City.

Teamsters may haul freight.

SEC. 8. No propeller shall be permitted to approach within fifty feet of any wharf in this City, or lie at any wharf in this City, while fired up, unless her smoke pipe shall be covered with a good and sufficient spark catcher, or other covering, to prevent the emis-

Propellers to be provided with spark catchers

sion of sparks or coals from her said pipe; and in case the captain or officers of any propeller shall permit the same to approach, or lie at any wharf, contrary to the provisions of this section, he or they shall be liable to a fine not exceeding one hundred dollars, to be recovered, with costs, by prosecution in the Recorder's Court.

Penalty.

CHAPTER XXXIX.

OF THE SPEED OF CARS AND ENGINES WITHIN THE LIMITS OF THE CITY.

[Chapter Seventy-four of Compiled Ordinances of 1859.]

Not to exceed six miles per hour.

SECTION 1. The rate of speed of engines and cars on railroads, within the limits of the City, shall not exceed six miles per hour, and any engineer, driver, or conductor, having charge of an engine, car, or train of cars, upon any railroad in said City, who shall suffer or cause said engine, car, or train of cars, to go over said railroad, within said City, at a greater rate of speed than six miles an hour, shall be punished by a fine of not less than twenty-five dollars, nor more than one hundred dollars, or by imprisonment not to exceed six months, or by both said fine and imprisonment, in the discretion of the Court.

SEC. 2. This Ordinance shall take effect and be in force five days after its passage.

CHAPTER XL.

OF THE IMPROVEMENT OF WASHINGTON AVENUE.

[Ordinance approved June 29, 1860.]

Width of wagon way.

SECTION 1. The width of the wagon way on Washington avenue shall be forty feet from curb to curb, running through the central portion of said avenue.

Width of grass plat.

SEC. 2. The width of the grass plat on each side of the wagon way shall be twenty-four feet.

Width of sidewalks.

SEC. 3. The width of the sidewalks on said avenue shall be sixteen feet, running parallel to and adjoining said grass plat.

SEC. 4. The said grass plat of twenty-four feet shall be ornamented with two rows of shade trees; one to be placed two feet from the curb-stone, and the other two feet from the sidewalk on each side of said wagon way. The trees shall not be less than twenty feet apart, and shall be protected by suitable guard boxes of a uniform pattern and size. Trees on grass plat.

SEC. 5. Said wagon way shall be paved or graveled, under the direction of the Street Commissioner for the Western District, according to the adopted plans and specifications for paving for the year 1860. Wagon way to be paved or graveled.

SEC. 6. The remaining portions of said avenue on each side thereof, and between said sidewalks and the line of said avenue, shall be improved and ornamented by turfing and planting ornamental trees and shrubbery. Said ornamental grounds shall be protected by a suitable iron fence or railing. Turfing and planting trees.

SEC. 7. The said grass plat of twenty-four feet shall be subdrained with suitable tile drains, in accordance with the plan hitherto submitted, and the entire of said improvements on said avenue, to wit: the paving or graveling, grading, turfing, subdraining, planting of trees, boxing the same, and the fencing or railing, shall be done by the property owners on said avenue without any expense to the City, and the said improvements shall at all times be kept in good and substantial repair by the said property owners, at their own expense and costs: *Provided, however,* that if said improvements are not made and completed within eighteen months from the passage of this Ordinance, and if there shall, at any time, be any neglect on the part of said property owners, their heirs and assignees, to keep said improvements in good order and repair, or if they in any way neglect to comply with the provisions of this Ordinance, no rights or privileges shall accrue to said property owners on said avenue, but all such rights and privileges under this Ordinance shall cease at the election of the City. Grass Plat to be sub-drained. Improvements to be made by property owners without expense to the city, and by them to be kept in repair.

SEC. 8. The entire ornamental grounds on said avenue shall, at all times, be under the supervision of the Common Council, through their Committee on Parks. Grounds to be under supervision of Common Council.

SEC. 9. Unless the property holders upon Washington Grand Avenue shall, within thirty days from the taking effect of this Ordinance, file their written assent to the same in the office Assent of property owners to be filed within thirty days.

12

of the City Clerk, the said Ordinance and all its provisions shall cease and become inoperative, and of no effect.

SEC. 10. All Ordinances or parts of Ordinances conflicting with this Ordinance are hereby repealed: *Provided,* That nothing in this Ordinance contained, shall be construed in a manner to affect the existing legal rights of the City in and to the enclosed portions of said street.

SEC. 11. This Ordinance shall take effect from and after its passage.

CHAPTER XLI.

TO VACATE CAMPUS MARTIUS.

[Ordinance approved March 14, 1860.]

Campus Martius to be vacated as public ground for the purpose of using it as a site for the City Hall.

SECTION 1. All that portion of the public grounds in said City of Detroit, known and described as the *Campus Martius*, lying west of Woodward avenue and between Michigan avenue and Fort street, in said City, shall be, and the same is hereby discontinued and vacated as public ground, for the following purposes, and no other, to wit: For the purpose of using and occupying the same as a site for the erection and use of a building, and the necessary appurtenances, to be known as the City Hall, and to be used for the purposes of a hall for the sessions of the Common Council, City Courts, and such other Courts as the City authorities may see fit to allow; City offices and such other public offices as the said authorities may see fit to allow to be kept therein; and for any other objects or purposes connected with the interests of said City, the County of Wayne, or the State of Michigan, which said authorities may, from time to time, see fit to countenance and permit.

SEC. 2. This Ordinance shall take effect and be in force from and after its passage.

TITLE IV.

OF THE DETROIT RIVER, FERRIES, AND WHARVES.

CHAPTER XLII.

OF THE NAVIGATION OF DETROIT RIVER, ETC.

[Ordinance approved July 10, 1862.]

SECTION 1. No steam tug or other vessel, while having one or more vessels in tow; and no vessel while made fast to any other vessel by lines or otherwise, shall approach within five hundred feet of any dock in said City, unless compelled to do so by unavoidable accident: *Provided*, This section shall not be so construed as to prevent steam tugs from approaching other vessels to take them in tow. Vessels, etc., not to approach within 500 feet of docks.

SEC. 2. No person shall throw or deposit in said river, within said limits, any substance which may, in any respect, tend to injure the navigation thereof. Navigation not to be impeded.

SEC. 3. All steamboats, ships, brigs or other vessels shall have kept outboard during the night time a conspicuous light, elevated at least six feet above decks. Vessels to maintain lights.

SEC. 4. All steamboats coming to or going from the docks, shall be moved under a low head of steam, and slowly, so as not to endanger the docks, or other crafts in port. To move slowly

Vessels unloading to obtain permission.

SEC. 5. No person shall unload any boat or vessel at or on any of the public wharves or docks in said City, or otherwise place or deposit on any such wharf or dock, any stone, lumber, timber, or firewood, or other material, without permission from the Harbor Master of said City.

Harbor Master. Appointment and term of office.

SEC. 6. The Common Council may annually appoint, on the second Tuesday of January, or at any regular meeting of the Common Council thereafter, on the nomination of the Mayor of the City, a Harbor Master for the port of Detroit, who shall hold his office for one year, subject to removal under the Charter. His term of office to commence on the third Tuesday of January—the person appointed this summer to hold until the third Tuesday of January, 1863. Before entering upon his office he shall give bonds to the said City, with sufficient sureties, conditioned as required by section twenty-eight, chapter two, of the Revised Charter of the City of Detroit, in the penal sum of two thousand dollars. And in case of the sickness or other disability of said Harbor Master, he may appoint a deputy, subject to the approval of the Mayor, to perform his duties during such sickness or disability.

Salary.

SEC. 7. Such Harbor Master, when appointed as herein provided for, shall receive for his services one dollar and fifty cents a day, payable monthly: *Provided,* No salary shall be paid in any one year, for any such services, before the first day of April, and shall cease on the first day of December in each year.

Duties.

SEC. 8. It shall be the duty of said Harbor Master to enforce the execution of the several provisions of this Ordinance, and of all other laws and ordinances passed in pursuance of the Revised Charter for regulating and preserving the navigation of said river within the limits of said City, and to make the necessary complaint for violations thereof.

Powers.

SEC. 9. The Harbor Master authorized to be appointed by this Act, shall have authority to protect the owners and occupants of wharves and docks within the limits of the City, in the free and undisturbed use of the same. And he is authorized to regulate the anchorage of all vessels lying within said City limits, and to give such orders and directions relative to the location and change of station of every steamboat, or other vessel, as shall be for the interests of trade and navigation, having respect at all times to the rights of occupants of wharves and docks ; and to this end he shall have full authority to go on board of and move any steamboat or vessel that shall be, without right or consent, occupying any of said docks or wharves ; and every owner, captain, master, consignee, or other person, having in charge any such steamboat or vessel, shall be liable to the penalties of this Act for refusing to comply with such order or direction.

SEC. 10. Every owner, master, captain, consignee, or any other person having in charge any steamboats or other vessels used in violation of this Act, and any person or persons violating or failing to comply with the provisions thereof, shall be punished by a fine not exceeding one hundred dollars and costs of prosecution ; and in the imposition of any such fine and costs, the Court may make a further sentence that the offenders be imprisoned in the Detroit House of Correction until the payment thereof, for any term not exceeding six months. Penalty.

SEC. 11. The Harbor Master appointed under and by virtue of this Ordinance is hereby invested with all the powers of Special Policeman, appointed under the Revised Charter of the City of Detroit. Harbor Master to have powers of Special Policeman.

SEC. 12. This Ordinance shall take effect from and after its passage.

CHAPTER XLIII.

OF FERRIES.

[Ordinance approved July 24, 1861.]

SECTION 1. No person shall keep a ferry or boat for carrying and transporting persons and property across the Detroit River to the opposite shore, without a license therefor from the Mayor. Persons keeping ferries to be licensed.

SEC. 2. The Mayor is hereby authorized to grant a license as hereinafter provided, to any person, or company, to keep a ferry or boat to carry and transport persons and property across the Detroit River to the opposite shore, on his or their paying into the City Treasury the sum of fifty dollars for each boat which carries and transports passengers, teams and animals, and the sum of twenty- Terms and conditions of license.

five dollars for each boat which transports and carries passengers only, and executing a bond to the City of Detroit in the penal sum of two hundred dollars, with one or more sureties, conditioned as provided in power sixty-three, of chapter five, of the City Charter.

Application for license.

SEC. 3. Any person or company desiring a license for a ferry to carry and transport persons across the Detroit River, shall make application therefor, in writing, to the Mayor; and such application shall state the points or wharves upon each shore between which it is proposed to run the ferry.

Boats and trips

SEC. 4. The person or company licensed, as provided in section two, shall keep at all times during the continuance of his or their license, a good and sufficient boat or boats, manned with a sufficient number of trusty and experienced hands to work and manage the same; and shall make, between sunrise and dark of each day, trips across and back, at least once in each half hour, unless prevented by the ice.

Mayor may issue more than one license.

SEC. 5. The granting of any license by the Mayor for a ferry between any wharves or points on each side of the Detroit River, shall not deprive him of the power to grant other licenses for ferries between the same points.

Ferries not to be run between other points than those designated in license.

SEC. 6. No person or company licensed, as provided in this Ordinance, shall run his or their ferry between any other wharves or points than those designated in his or their application and license.

Disorderly conduct on ferries prohibited.

SEC. 7. No gaming, drunkenness, quarreling, fighting, blasphemy, or any rude, disorderly or immoral conduct, shall be allowed on any ferry.

Rates of ferriage to be printed and posted.

SEC. 8. Persons and companies licensed to keep ferries, shall cause a list of the rates of ferriage to be printed in legible characters, and posted in a conspicuous place on their boat or boats.

Rates of ferriage.

SEC. 9. Ferriage, at any ferry established under this Ordinance, shall not exceed the following rates, to wit: For a foot passenger, except children under ten years of age, ten cents; and for such children, five cents. For a horse and rider, twenty cents. For a horse, fifteen cents. For one horse and vehicle, with two persons, twenty-five cents. For two horses and vehicle, with not more than four persons, fifty cents, and ten cents for each additional horse. For each head of horned cattle, ten cents. For each sheep or hog, five cents. For each one hundred pounds of baggage, or other article, five cents.

SEC. 10. The Mayor is hereby authorized to revoke any ferry license, whenever he shall be satisfied that the person or company keeping such ferry has intentionally violated any of the provisions of this Ordinance; and after such person or company, or its agent, has been notified of such revocation, it shall not be lawful to continue such ferry. Mayor may revoke licenses.

SEC. 11. Any violation of, or failure to comply with, the provisions of this Ordinance, shall be punished by a fine not to exceed two hundred dollars and costs; and in the imposition of any such fine and costs, the Court may make a further sentence, that in default of the payment thereof, such offender be imprisoned in the Detroit House of Correction or County Jail, for any period of time not exceeding six months. Penalty.

SEC. 12. Chapter sixty, of the Revised Ordinances of 1859, being "An Ordinance relative to Ferries," and all Ordinances amendatory thereof, or supplementary thereto, are hereby repealed.

SEC. 13. This Ordinance shall take effect from and after its passage.

CHAPTER XLIV.

OF WHARVES.

[Chapter Twenty-one of Compiled Ordinances of 1859.]

SECTION 1. It shall be the duty of the owner or owners, occupant or occupants, lessee or lessees, of any of the wharves of this City, bordering upon the Detroit River, and which are not fenced in, or otherwise enclosed, so as to prevent the passage of travelers or others over or across them, to keep the same in good order and condition, and whenever any of the plank, boards, timber or other materials composing or forming a part of any of the wharves of said City shall, from any cause, become loose, or be removed, or whenever any of said wharves shall in any manner, and from any cause whatever, be out of repair, it shall be the duty of the City Marshal to Wharves to be kept in repair.

Marshal to notify to repair.

notify either the owner or owners, occupant or occupants, lessee or lessees, of any such wharf or wharves, to immediately replace and securely fasten the plank, board, or other material so removed as aforesaid, or otherwise to repair such wharf or wharves as to the Marshal may seem necessary: *Provided,* That the notice so to be given may be either a verbal or written notice, and may be given by either of the Constables, or by the Mayor, or any of the Aldermen, or other officers of the City; and if a written notice, it may be either served personally upon, or left at the place of business or residence of the person or persons notified.

Penalty for not repairing.

SEC. 2. In case the person or persons so notified, as provided for in the preceding section, shall neglect for twenty-four hours after such notice, to comply with the requisitions thereof, he, she or they shall, on conviction thereof before the Recorder's Court, be liable to a fine of not less than five, nor more than fifty dollars for each and every day he, she or they shall neglect to comply with the requisitions of said notice.

CHAPTER XLV.

OF THE STATIONING, ANCHORING, AND MOORING OF VESSELS IN THE DETROIT RIVER.

[Chapter Twenty-two of Compiled Ordinances of 1859.]

Marshals and assistants, Dock Masters.

SECTION 1. The Marshal of said City shall be, and hereby is, made Dock Master of said City, for the purpose of directing the stationing, anchoring and mooring of vessels, agreeably to the provisions of this Ordinance, within said City; and all Policemen, Assistant Marshals, Constables, or other officers appointed and paid by the City to serve, and stationed on any of the docks of said City, shall, at their respective stations, enforce the provisions of this Ordinance.

Steamboats and vessels how long to remain at public wharves.

SEC. 2. No steamboat or vessel of any kind shall stop at or use any public wharf in said City for a longer space of time than one hour, nor shall any person land from said steamboat or vessel, or place upon any public wharf aforesaid, any article or thing, unless for the purpose of being immediately transported from said wharf to some other place; and if any article or thing so landed or placed upon said wharf shall remain there for the space of fifteen minutes after the same was so landed or placed on said wharf, the person so landing or placing the same on said wharf, and the owner, agent, captain, master, or any officer or employee of said steamboat or vessel, who actually landed, caused or directed to be landed, on said wharf, said article or thing, shall be punished by a fine not to exceed one hundred dollars, or by imprisonment not to exceed ninety days.

Goods landed to be immediately removed.

SEC. 3. No person shall land or place upon any public wharf in said City any firewood, stones, brick, building materials, lime-bed, locomotives, cumbrous or heavy castings, or any material or thing calculated to injure or obstruct said wharf; and any person violating the provisions of this section shall be punished by a fine not to exceed one hundred dollars, or by imprisonment not to exceed ninety days.

Certain articles not to be landed on public wharves.

SEC. 4. No steamboat or other vessel shall load or unload cargo, or lay out or receive ballast, or careen or be careened for repairs at any public wharf; and any person violating the provisions of this section shall be punished by a fine not to exceed one hundred dollars, or by imprisonment not to exceed ninety days.

Vessels, etc., not to repair at public wharves.

SEC. 5. The officers mentioned in the first section of this Ordinance are authorized, whenever any article or thing is landed on any public wharf of said City, contrary to the provisions of this Ordinance, to remove such article or thing to a place to be designated by the Common Council, which said article or thing shall remain in said place, in charge of the Street Commissioner of the District in which said article or thing was found, who shall receipt for the same to the officer bringing the same to him, and said article or thing shall be sold, and the proceeds of said sale disposed of and accounted for in the same manner, and the same costs and charges collected thereon, as is provided in regard to the sale of certain articles by section five of an Ordinance relative to the use of streets and alleys.*

Goods landed on public wharves to be removed and placed in charge of Street Commissioner.

SEC. 6. No steamboat or any other vessel shall anchor within one hundred feet of any wharf in said City; and if any person, hav-

Where steamboats and vessels to anchor.

* Section five, of chapter fifteen, of the Compiled Ordinances of 1859, is here referred to, but that chapter is repealed by chapter twenty-nine, of this compilation.

ing charge of a steamboat or vessel, shall anchor the same nearer to any wharf than one hundred feet, the said person shall be punished by a fine not to exceed one hundred dollars, or by imprisonment not to exceed ninety days: *Provided, always,* That nothing herein contained shall be construed to prevent any vessel from laying alongside of any dock with the consent of the owner of said dock.

Proviso.

Marshal and officers may board vessels to enforce this Ordinance.

SEC. 7. The officers mentioned in the first section of this Ordinance are hereby authorized to board any vessel or steamboat in the waters of the Detroit river, and within the limits of said City, which may be violating the provisions of this Ordinance, and to order any person on board of, and having charge of said steamboat or vessel, either officer or seaman, to remove said steamboat or vessel, or otherwise to comply with this Ordinance; and any person who shall neglect or refuse to obey said order, who shall obstruct, hinder or resist said officer in going aboard of said steamboat or vessel, or who shall take off, or attempt to take off, said officer in saia steamboat or vessel, when he has boarded the same in conformity to the powers herein vested in him, shall, upon conviction thereof, be punished by a fine of not less than fifty dollars, nor more than two hundred and fifty dollars, or by imprisonment not to exceed one year.

Marshal or other officer to visit the place on information of any violation of Ordinance.

SEC. 8. Whenever the Marshal or any officer mentioned in this Ordinance, shall receive a written or verbal complaint or information, or in any manner know of a violation of this Ordinance, it shall be the duty of said Marshal or other officer forthwith to repair to the place where such violation has occurred or is occuring, and to exercise any and every power vested in him to enforce this Ordinance, and to complain of the person or persons guilty of said violation; and if said Marshal or other officer shall refuse or neglect to comply with the provisions of this section, he shall be punished by a fine of twenty-five dollars, cr by twenty days' imprisonment.

Construction of Ordinance as to vessels loading, etc.

SEC. 9. This Ordinance shall not be so construed as to prohibit vessels projecting in front of the foot of streets or public docks while discharging or receiving freight or passengers from or on an adjoining dock or wharf.

TITLE V.

OF DRAINS AND SEWERS.

CHAPTER XLVI.

OF THE BOARD OF SEWER COMMISSIONERS.

[Chapter Twenty-five of Compiled Ordinances of 1859.]

SECTION 1. The Board of Sewer Commissioners shall, annually, dating from the time of their organization, elect one of their number President. Board to elect President annually.

SEC. 2. The Engineer of Sewers shall act as Secretary of said Board, and shall, under the direction of said Board, superintend the construction and repairs of all public sewers or drains, and pools, and sewers and drains built by special assessments. His salary shall be fixed by resolution of the Common Council. Engineer to act as Secretary; his duties and salary.

SEC. 3. Said Board, when specially authorized by resolution of the Common Council, may appoint such inspectors of work, and other agents, as may be required for carrying out the work committed to their charge, by the Charter and by this Ordinance, which inspectors and agents shall receive such compensation for their services as the Common Council may allow or prescribe. Board may appoint inspectors.

SEC. 4. Said Board shall have the supervision of the construction of all sewers hereafter to be built, whether they be built at the expense of the City, or by special assessment upon the individuals to General supervision of sewers.

be benefited thereby, and of all repairs of sewers and pools hereafter to be performed, and are hereby fully authorized and empowered to enforce, or otherwise carry out all contracts for the building or repairing of sewers, drains and pools within said City.

Board to submit plans to Council and report.

SEC. 5. Said Board shall, as soon as may be, submit to the Common Council "a plan for constructing sewers and drains for the whole City, having reference, however, to the sewers and drains already constructed, or in process of construction," and shall, at the first meeting of the Common Council, in February of each year, report to said Common Council what public sewers and drains they deem necessary to build in that year, and shall accompany the report with an estimate of the cost of each and all of said sewers, and of all the probable expenses of the construction of public sewers during the year then next ensuing.

Council to decide on sewers to be built, etc.

SEC. 6. The Common Council shall decide what public sewers and drains shall be built in said year, and shall, through the City Clerk, notify said Board of their decision; and said Board shall, without delay, report to said Common Council an estimate of the cost of any sewer or drain which the Common Council shall thus order to be built, and which was not embraced in the estimate provided for in the foregoing section, and shall proceed to advertise for proposals to build all the sewers and drains ordered to be built by the Common Council, under such specifications and forms as the said Board may deem necessary; which advertisement shall be published at least ten days in the newspaper published by the contractor to do the City printing, and shall state the time when, and place where said proposals shall be received and opened, and shall require each party making a proposal, to accompany the same with a statement, in writing, signed by at least two persons, who agree thereby to become sureties in an amount at least double the estimated cost of the work proposed to be performed, for the faithful performance of said work.

Board to advertise for proposals for building sewers.

Proposals where opened.

SEC. 7. Said proposals shall be received and opened by said Board publicly, in the office of the City Controller, and in his presence, and a copy of each proposal shall be recorded by the said City Controller, and also by the Secretary of said Board.

Board to examine proposals.

SEC. 8. When said proposals shall have been received and opened, as aforesaid, said Board, together with the City Controller, shall proceed to examine the same, and determine who are the lowest responsible bidders, possessing the qualifications required by the Charter of said City, whereupon the Controller shall communicate their determination, together with all said proposals, to the Common Council, who shall consider said proposals and communication, and award the contract proposed to be performed to the lowest responsible qualified bidder, and shall return said proposals, and communicate their decision to said Board. The said Board shall transmit the proper specifications of the work to be performed to the City Attorney, who shall draw a contract for the performance of said work, in accordance with said specifications, and of the Charter and Ordinances of said City, which said contract shall be signed, on the part of the City, by said Board, and attested under the corporate seal by the City Clerk, and shall, when executed, be placed in the keeping of said Board, whose duty it shall be to see that the contractor, or contractors, shall comply therewith.

Controller to make statement to Council.

Attorney to draw contract.

To be attested by Clerk.

SEC. 9. Said Board shall certify to the amount due upon all contracts, and for all materials furnished, and labor performed, in building or repairing sewers and pools; and all bills and accounts thus certified, for amounts so due, shall be audited by the Controller, and presented by him to the Council, in the same manner as other bills and accounts against said City.

Board to certify to all accounts for work, etc.

SEC. 10. Said Board shall keep, or cause to be kept, an accurate record of all their proceedings, which shall, at all times, be subject to the examination and inspection of any citizen of said City, and shall, once in each year, or oftener, if required, submit to said Common Council a report of all their proceedings, with the names of their employees, and the total expenses of the construction and repairs of sewers and pools, since the last report, and such other information as they may deem necessary, or as said Council may require.

To keep record of proceedings and submit the same yearly to Council.

SEC. 11. Said Board shall not lay down or construct any sewer or pool in said City, or purchase any materials, or enter into any contract, except as provided in this Ordinance, and except in case of any unexpected casualty or damage to the sewers or pools of said City, in which case said Board may cause the same to be repaired, to the amount of not exceeding two hundred dollars, and

In certain cases may order work to the amount of $200.

shall report their proceedings therein, and the necessity therefor, to the next regular meeting of the Common Council.

Board to give permit for connecting with sewers.

SEC. 12. No connection shall be made with any public sewer or drain, except with the permission of said Board, and under the direction of the Engineer, who shall, at least once in each month, notify the City Assessor of all such connections, made since the last notice; and any person connecting with any public sewer, without such permission, shall be fined not to exceed one hundred dollars, or imprisoned three months, or both, in the discretion of the Court.

City Clerk to supply stationery.

SEC. 13. The City Clerk shall supply the said Board with all necessary stationery.

SEC. 14. This Ordinance shall take effect, and be in force from and after its passage.

CHAPTER XLVII.

OF PUBLIC AND PRIVATE DRAINS AND SEWERS.

[Chapter Twenty-three of Compiled Ordinances of 1859.]

No lot to be drained without application to the Common Council and payment of assessment.

SECTION 1. No person or persons shall be permitted to connect any drain from his, her, or their premises, with any public drain or sewer now made or constructed, or hereafter to be made or constructed, in said City, nor with any private drain, whereby his, her, or their premises will be drained into any public drain or sewer, except on previous application, in writing, to, and permission by the Common Council, or Board of Sewer Commissioners, and the payment of the assessment hereinafter mentioned.

Council to determine the size of drains and to be entered under supervision of Engineer of Sewer Commissioners.

SEC. 2. All private drains to be hereafter made by individuals in any public street, lane or alley, in said City, and connecting with any public drain or sewer, shall be of such size, dimensions and materials, and constructed and laid as directed by the Board of Sewer Commissioners, and shall enter such public drain or sewer under and according to the personal supervision and direction of their Engineer, nor shall any person or persons enter any public drain or sewer at any other places than those designated and fixed for that purpose in the construction thereof.

SEC. 3. The amount which individuals using, or being benefited by any public drain or sewer, shall pay for such use, is hereby fixed as follows, to wit: the sum of one dollar and fifty cents annually, for each cellar drained by box, directly or indirectly, into any public drain or sewer, which assessment shall be taken to include all other drainage of the premises to which said cellar especially belongs; and the sum of fifty cents annually for each lot, or subdivision of lot, being without a cellar, drained by box, as aforesaid, into any public drain or sewer; and such sums as may be fixed by the Common Council for all establishments requiring an unusual or extraordinary amount of drainage, drained as aforesaid, upon actual inspection of, and report thereon, by the assessors.

Assessment for draining cellars.

SEC. 4. Said assessment shall, in all instances, be paid when the City and School taxes are collected.

When to be paid.

SEC. 5. Any person whose premises are drained, directly or indirectly, into any public drain or sewer, or any person using said premises thus drained, or for whose benefit or family the same is used, shall be liable to the payment therefor, and, in addition, said assessment shall become, and be a charge and lien on the premises thus drained, and be recovered, and the same proceedings had in every respect for the recovery thereof, as are provided for the recovery of other special assessments; and the Corporation may also, at their option, stop such private drain, and prevent any person from draining his premises into any public drain or sewer, where such assessment shall not be paid in advance, on the second application, and said privilege shall not be restored, unless on the payment of the tax, and a forfeiture of double the amount of the assessment.

Persons using drain or sewer liable to assessment.

Assessment lien on lots. How collected.

Drain may be cut off.

SEC. 6. Any person who shall remove any grate from the pool over which it is placed, or in any way, directly or indirectly, injure any public drain or sewer, or any part thereof, shall, on conviction thereof, before the Recorder's Court, be liable to a penalty for each offence, not exceeding one hundred dollars, and costs.

Penalty for injuring drain.

SEC. 7. Any person who shall connect any drain from his premises with any public drain or sewer, or who shall drain his premises into any private drain which enters into any public drain or sewer, without first making the application, procuring the permission, and paying the assessment, provided for in the first section of this Chapter, shall, on conviction of each offence, before the Re-

Penalty for connecting drains without permission.

corder's Court, be liable to a penalty not exceeding one hundred dollars, and costs; and any person who shall construct and lay any private drain, connecting with any public drain or sewer, or who shall enter any public drain or sewer, in any other manner except as is provided for in the second section of this Chapter, shall be liable, for each offence, on like conviction, to a penalty not exceeding one hundred dollars, and costs; and any person who shall enter any public drain or sewer at any other place than is designated and fixed for that purpose in the construction thereof, shall be also liable to pay for each offence, on like conviction, a penalty not exceeding one hundred dollars and costs; and if any person shall drain his premises along the side of any public drain or sewer, he shall also be liable to pay a penalty not exceeding one hundred dollars, and costs, on like conviction: *Provided,* That this section shall not be construed to extend to any case where a private drain has heretofore been laid down along the side of any public drain or sewer; but such private drain shall not be repaired by any person without having received from the Common Council, or some authorized officer of said City, a certificate that such repair will not endanger the safety and preservation of any public drain or sewer along the side thereof.

How to enter drains.

Drain not to be placed by public drain.

When sewers may be entered.

SEC. 8. No person shall be permitted to connect any drain from his premises with the grand sewer, nor enter the same between the first day of December and the first day of April, in each year, and any person offending against this section, shall, on conviction of such offence, before the Recorder's Court, be liable to pay a fine of one hundred dollars, and costs.

What drains are public.

SEC. 9. All drains now made and constructed, or which shall hereafter be made and constructed by the Corporation, shall be deemed to be public drains or sewers, within the purview of this Chapter; and all sums of money received under the provisions of this Chapter, shall be stated and kept in a separate account, and are hereby specifically pledged and appropriated to the following uses and objects, and no other, to wit: *First,* To defray the expense of indispensable repairs of existing sewers; *Second,* To defray the cost of additional public sewers, and their repairs; *Third,* To apply on the interest of the City debt accruing on account of the cost of construction and maintenance of such sewers.

How sewer assessments to be appropriated.

SEC. 10. The assessment provided for in this chapter shall be collected in the manner prescribed by the chapter relating to the collection of special assessments, the provisions of which are made applicable hereto, except that the time of the warrants, and provision of per centage, shall be made to correspond with the terms of the warrants, and the provisions for per centage, in the collection of the City and School taxes.

How sewer assessments may be collected.

SEC. 11. No person shall be permitted to connect any drain from his, her, or their premises, with any drain or sewer made by one or more individuals, in any street, lane or alley, as aforesaid, unless on payment to the proprietors of such drain or sewer of a rateable proportion of the expense of making the same, the amount to be ascertained and determined by the Marshal or Surveyor, with the right of appeal to the Common Council; nor shall any person make or construct a sink, drain or sewer, leading into any other drain or sewer, without putting a sufficient strainer at the head of it, under a penalty not exceeding ten dollars, and costs, for each offence.

Certain portion of expense to be paid before connection with drains.

SEC. 12. Every person having any drain from his, her, or their premises, that shall be connected with any drain or sewer now made, or that shall hereafter be made, as aforesaid, shall pay a rateable proportion of all expenses necessary for maintaining and keeping such drains or sewers in repair, such proportion to be ascertained and determined in the manner provided for in the foregoing section; and if any person shall neglect to pay the same, when so ascertained, such person shall forfeit and pay the sum of two dollars, and costs, for every week during which the same shall remain unpaid.

How expense of repairs ascertained.

Penalty.

SEC. 13. In all cases where drains or sewers shall be obstructed so as to become, in the opinion of the Marshal, a nuisance, it shall be his duty to give notice to the persons using the same, to repair such drains or sewers, and if the same be not forthwith repaired, it shall be the duty of the Marshal to cause the necessary repairs to be made, and to charge the said persons with a rateable proportion of the expense incurred, including a reasonable allowance to the Marshal for his own services, subject to an appeal to the Common Council, as is provided in the tenth section; and all such appeals shall be made within the time in which such person is required to pay the sums above required; and if any person shall refuse or

Marshal to notify persons to repair.

Proceedings in case of neglect.

neglect to pay their proportion of the charges, for the space of ten days after notice, he or they shall be liable, upon conviction, before the Recorder's Court, to pay a fine not exceeding fifty dollars, and costs of suit.

No connection to be made until Surveyor shall have ascertained the grade.

SEC. 14. No connection with public or private sewers, or drains, shall be made under the provisions of this Chapter, until the Surveyor shall have designated the grade therefor, under the penalty of twenty dollars.

CHAPTER XLVIII.

OF LATERAL SEWERS OR DRAINS.

[Chapter Twenty-four of Compiled Ordinances of 1859.]

Common Council may order lateral sewers to be built, etc.

SECTION 1. The Common Council may, by resolution, direct the construction, cleansing, or repair of lateral sewers or drains, through, or in any streets or alleys, or the construction, cleansing, or repairs of drains from any house, yard or lot, when, in their opinion, the same shall be necessary. Such drains or sewers to be built of such materials as the said Common Council shall direct, and be laid or constructed in such direction, of such size and width, such descent, and with such strainers or grates, as said Common Council shall direct.

City Surveyor to assess the expense of building, repairing, etc.

SEC. 2. Whenever the Common Council shall direct, as aforesaid, the construction, cleansing, or repair of any lateral sewer or drain, as provided for in section one, it shall be the duty of the City Surveyor to assess the expense of constructing, cleansing or repairing the same, in a rateable proportion to the owners or occupants of all land or lots adjoining said street or alley, or to the owner or occupant of the land or lot through which such drain shall run; and it shall be the duty of the Street Commissioners of their respective districts, whenever such resolution shall be passed, to cause notice of the intended improvement to be served on the owners of all lots or premises intended to be assessed; such notice shall be served personally on such owner, or his agent, or by leaving the same at the residence of such owner or agent, or in case they or their residence cannot be found, the same shall be served on any occupant of the premises, and if the same be unoccupied, by posting the same in some conspicuous place upon the premises. The said Street Commissioner shall file with the City Clerk a due certificate of his doings, and all persons served with notice in either of the modes herein provided, who do not make and file objections before its confirmation by the Common Council, shall be precluded from thereafter questioning or making any objections to the assessment roll for such improvement. [*As amended by Ordinance approved Sept.* 7, 1863.]

City Treasurer to retain rolls five days in his office, and receive pay.

SEC. 3. The City Clerk shall cause the assessment rolls to be delivered to the City Treasurer, who shall retain them in his office for the space of five days, from and after the date of such delivery; and during said period, any person assessed therein may pay the amount of his or her assessment to the City Treasurer. Upon the expiration of the said period of five days, it shall be the duty of the City Treasurer to deliver the said assessment rolls, or a certified copy thereof, adding thereto all costs incurred in the premises, to the Controller, who shall issue a warrant under his hand and the seal of the City, directed to the City Collector of said City, with a command to levy and collect all sums or assessments then remaining unpaid, with the costs and charges thereon, and five cents on the dollar for his services, by distress and sale of the goods and chattels of the person against whom said assessment has been made, or those who may be liable to pay the same; and, further, commanding the City Collector to make returns to the Common Council within five days thereafter.

Controller to issue warrant for collection.

Collector to make return within five days.

Collector in case of neglect and refusal, to make a levy and sale at public auction.

SEC. 4. Upon receiving the assessment roll, or a copy thereof, and warrant, it shall be the duty of the City Collector to proceed to demand and collect the several sums mentioned therein, and if any person shall neglect or refuse to pay the same, then, if he can find any goods or chattels of the person liable therefor, he shall levy thereon, and shall proceed to sell such goods and chattels at public auction, to the highest bidder, and shall render the surplus, (if any,) after deducting costs and charges, of such distress and sale, to the person entitled thereto.

Only persons named in roll to make connections except by permission of Common Council.

SEC. 5. No parties, except those embraced in the said assessment roll, shall connect with any such lateral sewer or drain, without permission of the Common Council, and without payment to the City Treasurer of such sum or sums as the City Surveyor shall decide it to be right and proper for them to pay; and any person or persons who shall violate this section, shall be prosecuted before the Recorder's Court, and fined not to exceed ten dollars, and costs of prosecution, and the amount so decided upon by the Surveyor, shall also be recovered before said Court.

Penalty.

Lots sufficiently drained to be exempt.

SEC. 6. Whenever any lot or premises subject to assessment, under and by virtue of this Ordinance, shall, in the opinion of the Common Council, be already sufficiently drained by a private drain or sewer, said lot or premises shall not be assessed for any of the purposes for which an assessment is provided by this Ordinance: *Provided, always,* That it shall be the duty of the owner or occupant of said lot or premises to inform the Common Council of the fact that said lot or premises are so drained, in the manner hereinafter provided.

Proviso.

City Clerk to publish notice of assessment five days.

SEC. 7. Whenever an assessment shall be ordered to be made under this Ordinance, it shall be the duty of the City Clerk of said City to publish a notice for five days in the daily newspaper published by the contractor to do the printing of the City, which said notice shall state the fact that said assessment has been ordered by the Common Council, the purposes for which it has been ordered, and that said Common Council will, at their next regular meeting, after the expiration of said five days, permit any person whose lot or premises are liable to be included in said assessment, to show to said Council that said lot or premises are drained in the manner set forth in the preceding section.

City Surveyor to omit lots in certain cases.

SEC. 8. If the Common Council resolve that said lot or premises are sufficiently drained by a private drain or sewer, the City Surveyor shall omit said lot or premises from said assessment.

SEC. 9. All Ordinances, or parts of Ordinances, of the Revised Ordinances of 1855, in contravention of this Ordinance, are hereby repealed.

SEC. 10. This Ordinance shall take effect and be in force from and after its passage.

CHAPTER XLIX.

OF THE OPENING AND CLEANING OF SEWER POOLS.

[Chapter Forty-three of Compiled Ordinances of 1859.]

Overseers of Highways to clean and keep open grates, etc.

SECTION 1. It shall be and hereby is made the duty of Overseers of Highways to clean and keep open and unobstructed the grates or other openings of pools within their respective Wards, connecting with any of the public sewers of said City, so that, at all times, said grates or other openings shall be unobstructed, and in condition to perform the office of carrying off the water from the public streets of said City.

SEC. 2. This Ordinance shall take effect, and be in force, from and after its passage.

CHAPTER L.

OF SLUICES AND LOW GROUNDS.

[Chaper Forty-one of Compiled Ordinances of 1859.]

Assessment for low grounds, sluices, etc.

SECTION 1. Whenever it may be deemed necessary or expedient to make and open any sluice, and make any wharf or embankment on the margin of the Detroit river, or fill up any low grounds or lots covered, or partially covered, with water, adjacent to said river, or when it shall be necessary, for the abatement of any nuisance, to fill up or level any lots or low grounds not adjacent to said river, but within the limits of said City, the Common Council shall, by a written resolution, to be entered on their journal, authorize some competent person to make an assessment for making such sluice, wharf, embankment, or filling up such low ground, or abating such nuisances; and upon approving and filing such assessment, the Common Council shall order that the owner, occupant or proprietor of such wharf, low grounds or lots, (describing them,) shall make such sluice, wharf or embankment, or fill up such low grounds or lots, or abate such nuisance, within a certain time, and in such manner as may be in such order specified.

Marshal to give notice of order to fill low grounds.

SEC. 2. It shall be the duty of the Marshal to give notice, in writing, to such owner, occupant, or proprietor personally, or by leaving the same at his place of residence in said City, requiring him to comply with such order, a copy of which shall be annexed to such notice, and also that, within ten days after the service of such notice, he shall enter into a bond to the City of Detroit, with approved security, conditioned for the performance and execution of such order, and the Marshal shall make due return or report to the Common Council of his doings in the premises: *Provided,* That if any such person cannot be found, or has no place of residence in said City, the Marshal shall cause such notice to be published four weeks in some paper in said City, unless the Common Council shall otherwise order, and an affidavit thereof shall be filed with the Clerk.

When Council may order a lot to be filled.

SEC. 3. Whenever it shall appear to the Common Council that the notice required by the preceding section has been given, and that such bond has not been executed, within the time limited therefor, then the Common Council may cause such sluice, wharf, or embankment to be finished and completed, or such low ground or lots to be filled up, or such nuisance abated, in such manner as they may deem expedient and necessary; and the expense thereof shall be deemed a valid assessment, from the time of filing the same, as aforesaid.

Clerk to deliver the assessment to collector to be collected.

SEC. 4. The Clerk shall record, in the assessment register, all assessments made by virtue of this Chapter, and the date of the same; and immediately after said work mentioned in said order shall have been finished and completed, the Clerk shall make out and deliver to the Collector a copy of such assessment, to be collected as other special assessments.

CHAPTER LI.

OF THE MANNER OF DRAWING JURORS IN THE MATTER OF DRAINING WET AND LOW LANDS.

[Chapter Forty-two of Compiled Ordinances of 1859.]

Common Council may declare whose lands they deem should be drained.

SECTION 1. Whenever the said Common Council shall deem it necessary to drain any swamp, marsh, wet or low lands, in accordance with the power conferred upon said Council by subdivision twenty-fifth, of section twenty-second, of chapter fifth, of the Revised Charter of said City, they shall so declare by resolution, which resolution shall describe the size and location of the ditch proposed to be opened for draining said lands, and shall also describe what private lands, if any, it will be necessary to take to make said ditch. A copy of said resolution, certified to by the City Clerk, shall be delivered by said Clerk to the City Attorney, who shall file the same in the Recorder's Court, and move said Court for the drawing of a jury to determine the necessity or propriety of opening said ditch, and whether the benefits which will accrue to the owner or owners of any lands from the opening of said ditch, will or will not be equal to any damages he or they will sustain thereby.

Certified copy to be given to City Attorney by clerk.

Recorder's Court to order City Marshal, or other officer, to write the names of jurors.

SEC. 2. Said Court, upon being satisfied that the proper resolution has been filed by said Attorney, shall order the City Marshal, his assistant or other officer of said City in attendance upon said Court, to write down the names of twelve freeholders of Wayne county, who shall be approved by the Court as qualified to serve upon said jury.

Court to issue summons for jurors.

SEC. 3. Said Court shall issue a summons to the Marshal, his assistant or other officer of said City having authority to serve process in said Court, commanding him to summon said twelve freeholders to be and appear in said Court, on some day to be named in said writ, which shall not be less than seven days after the issuance thereof, and said summons shall be served at least three days before the return day thereof, and be returned in the same manner as a summons for petit jurors in said Court, and the persons thus summoned shall be bound to attend said Court and serve until discharged, and said Court shall impose upon them a fine of not more than five dollars for each day's non-attendance or neglect to serve in said Court, but they shall be exempted and excused by the Court for the same reasons that petit jurors may be exempted and excused.

Penalty for non-attendance of jurors.

City Attorney to publish notice of the ordering of jury.

SEC. 4. The City Attorney shall cause to be published in the daily newspaper printed by the contractor to print for the City, and in one other daily newspaper of said City, a notice to all whom it may concern, that said jury has been ordered, the purpose for which, and the time when and the place where they will be empanneled, which notice shall be published at least four consecutive days before said return day, and proof of publication thereof shall be filed in said Court on return day.

Persons interested may challenge jurors.

SEC. 5. Any person who shall appear upon said return day and file an affidavit in said Court, that he or she has an interest in any private land proposed to be taken, and showing to the satisfaction of said Court, that he or she has such interest, shall be allowed to challenge any person summoned to appear upon said jury for cause, in the same manner as is allowed in civil actions under the laws of the State.

Court may order talesmen.

SEC. 6. Said Court shall have power to order talesmen to be summoned to fill said jury.

Jurors to be sworn and advised by City Attorney.

SEC. 7. Said jury, when filled, shall be sworn to discharge their duties faithfully, and shall be advised by the City Attorney concerning their duties whenever they request it; they shall go upon the line of said ditch and examine the land proposed to be taken.

Jurors to report to court in writing.

SEC. 8. They shall report to said Court, in writing, which shall be signed by them, and said Court shall appoint a day upon which said report shall be received and filed.

Report to be recorded by City Clerk.

SEC. 9. A copy of the report of said jury, certified to by the Clerk of said Court, shall be recorded by the City Clerk, in the book of street opening records, and also in the records of said Court.

SEC. 10. This Ordinance shall take effect and be in force from and after five days after the passage thereof.

CHAPTER LII.

OF KEEPING A RECORD OF LOTS AND PARTS OF LOTS, SUBJECT TO ASSESSMENT FOR DRAINAGE.

[Chapter Seventy-seven of Compiled Ordinances of 1859.]

City Assessor to place on assessment rolls yearly all lots drained into private sewers.

SECTION 1. It is made the duty of the City Assessor, once in each year, to ascertain and place upon the assessment rolls all lots, premises or subdivisions thereof drained by private sewers, or drains leading into or connected with any public sewer or drain; and he shall designate on said rolls every lot, premises or subdivisions thereof, on which there is a cellar; and every lot, premises or subdivisions thereof, drained as aforesaid, on which there is no cellar; and also every lot, premises or subdivision thereof on which there is any hotel, tavern, tannery, or any kind of manufactory.

TITLE VI.

OF MARKETS AND SALES.

CHAPTER LIII.

OF RENTING STALLS AND STANDS IN PUBLIC MARKETS.

[Ordinance approved January 2, 1862.]

City Hall Market.

SECTION 1. The square of ground lying between the east end of the City Hall and the east line of Randolph street, is hereby declared to be a Public Market, and shall constitute and be known as the City Hall Market.

Common Council may establish other markets.

SEC. 2. The Common Council may, from time to time, establish, in addition to the City Hall Market, such other Public Markets as the convenience and necessities of the City may require.

Leasing of stalls and stands.

SEC. 3. The City Controller and the Committee on Markets shall, on the first Monday in April in each year, establish and grade the *minimum* rent, to be paid per month, upon all stalls and stands in the Public Markets It shall be the duty of the Controller, on the second Monday in April in each year, to lease, at public auction, to the highest responsible bidder, all stalls and stands in the Public Markets not then already leased; the stalls in the Meat Markets to be leased for not less than one nor more than three years, and the stands in the Vegetable Markets to be leased for a term of seven months: but no stall or stand shall be leased at a rent below the *minimum* established by the Controller and the Committee on Markets. Any stall or stand which shall not be rented at public auction as aforesaid, may be rented by the Controller to any responsible person, for any period not extending beyond the second Monday in April of the year following, at a rent not less than the *minimum* established by the Controller and the Committee on Markets. No person shall be allowed to rent more than two stands in the Meat Market.

SEC. 4. All persons leasing or renting stalls or stands in the Public Markets of the City, shall pay the same monthly in advance; and each lessee of a stall in the Meat Market shall, with one or more sureties, to be approved by the Controller, enter into a lease with the City of Detroit, conditioned for the payment of the rent of such stall, in the manner herein provided, and for the faithful observance of the provisions of all Ordinances relative to the Public Markets of the City. Payment of rent.

SEC. 5. The Controller shall make out and deliver to the Clerk of the Market a monthly roll of the amounts due for rents to the City from persons occupying stalls and stands in the Public Markets, and it shall be the duty of the Clerk to collect the same. Collection of rent.

SEC. 6. If the lessee of any stall or stand shall neglect, for five days after notice that the same has become due, to pay the rent thereof, such lease shall be thereby forfeited, and it shall be the duty of the Controller to enter and take possession of such stall or stand on behalf of the City; and the City Attorney or other proper officer of the City, shall at once commence legal proceedings to collect such rent. Lease forfeited by non-payment of rent.

SEC. 7. If any lessee of any stall or stand whose lease shall have been forfeited, or any other person without a lease from the City, shall hold, use or occupy any stall or stand in a Public Market, he shall forfeit and pay to the City of Detroit ten dollars for each day he shall so hold, use or occupy any such stand. Penalty for occupying under forfeited lease.

SEC. 8. No lessee of any stall or stand shall permit the same to be used or occupied by any other person, except by permission of the Controller or Committee on Markets: *Provided*, That not more than one person occupy one stall at the same time. Stands not to be occupied by persons other than lessees.

SEC. 9. The Public Markets of the City shall be kept open Market hours.

every day, Sunday excepted, for such hours as may be, from time to time, fixed by the Controller and Committee on Markets.

Rules and regulations for markets.

SEC. 10. The Committee on Markets and the City Controller shall have power, and it shall be their duty, from time to time, to make rules and regulations for the government of the Public Markets of the City; and such rules and regulations shall be printed and distributed among the persons leasing and occupying stalls and stands in the Public Markets.

Fees to be paid for market wagons, etc.

SEC. 11. The Committee on Markets and the Controller shall, from time to time, determine and establish the amount per day to be paid for each wagon, cart, and other vehicle standing in the market, and from which vegetables, fish, poultry, eggs, butter or fruits are sold, and shall also establish and determine the places to be occupied by such wagons, carts and other vehicles.

SEC 12. Chapter twenty-six, of the Revised Ordinances of 1859, and all ordinances amendatory thereof, are hereby repealed.

CHAPTER LIV.

OF PUBLIC MARKETS.

[Ordinance approved September 28, 1863.]

Where vehicles, offering provisions for sale, to stand.

SECTION 1. All persons selling or offering for sale, from wagons, carts or other vehicles, any vegetables, fish, poultry, butter or fruits in the vicinity of the City Hall Market, shall occupy and stand with their teams on that portion of Michigan Avenue embraced between the east line of the City Hall and the east line of Randolph street.

Unwholesome provisions, etc., not to be offered for sale.

SEC. 2. No butcher, forestaller, grocer, trader or other person, shall sell or offer for sale, at any place within the limits of the City of Detroit, any unsound, nauseous or unwholesome meat, poultry, fish, vegetables, fruits or other articles of food or provisions, or the flesh of any animal dying otherwise than by slaughter; nor any impure or spurious wines or spirituous liquors; nor any unwholesome bread, cake or pastry manufactured in whole or in part from unwholesome flour or meal.

SEC. 3. No person, within any of the Public Markets of this City, shall be guilty of any lewd, lascivious or disorderly conduct, or make any loud or boisterous noises, or use any profane or vulgar language, or do any act which is calculated to lead to a breach of the peace, or which tends to disturb the good order and decorum of the place.

Disorderly conduct in public markets prohibited.

SEC. 4. No person shall resist or obstruct the Clerk of the Market in the execution of his duties.

Resistance to Clerk of Market prohibited.

SEC. 5. All meat, poultry and provisions of every kind, sold in the Public Markets, shall be weighed or measured by scales, weights, or patent balances, or in measures duly tested and stamped by the City Inspector of Weights and Measures.

Provisions offered for sale to be weighed.

SEC. 6. No person shall kill or slaughter within the limits of any Public Market any beast, or gut or cleanse any fish, or lay or throw or deposit any dirt, filth, dung, garbage or offal therein.

Slaughtering, etc., prohibited.

SEC. 7. No person whose stock in trade shall exceed the sum of three hundred dollars, shall be allowed to sell or offer for sale in the Public Markets of the City, any merchandise or clothing of any description whatever, or any glass, china or earthenware, books and stationery.

Stock of sellers in public markets limited.

SEC. 8. No person shall sell at auction any goods, wares or merchandises, or furniture of any kind, within the limits of any Public Market, during market hours.

Auctions in public markets prohibited.

SEC. 9. No person shall slaughter or expose for sale the meat of any calf less than three weeks old.

Meat of calves under three weeks' old not to be offered for sale.

SEC. 10. No person shall burn, sear or cut the inner part of the mouth of any calf, or confine the mouth of any calf by rope, twine or any kind of muzzle placed over the mouth of such calf.

Calves not to be muzzled, etc.

SEC. 11. Any violation of the provisions of this Ordinance shall be punished by a fine not to exceed one hundred dollars, and costs of prosecution, and the offender may be sentenced to be confined in the Detroit House of Correction till the payment thereof: *Provided*, Such imprisonment shall not exceed the period of six months.

Penalty.

SEC. 12. Chapter thirty-one, of the Compiled Ordinances of the City of Detroit for the year 1859, is hereby repealed.

CHAPTER LV.

OF PRIVATE MEAT MARKETS.

[Ordinance approved January 14, 1862.]

Private markets not to be kept without license.

SECTION 1. No person shall keep or continue any stall, booth, or stand in the City of Detroit, for the sale of fresh meat, without a license from the Mayor, as provided in the next section. [*As amended by Ordinance approved January* 29, 1863.]

Licenses to be granted. Conditions thereof.

SEC. 2. The Mayor is hereby authorized to grant a license to any resident of the City of Detroit to keep a stall, booth or stand in the City of Detroit, for the purpose of selling fresh meat, on such person paying into the City Treasury the sum of five dollars, and executing a bond to the City of Detroit in the penal sum of two hundred dollars, with one or more sureties, conditioned that he will faithfully observe the provisions of this Ordinance. [*As amended by Ordinance approved January* 29, 1863.]

Private markets to be kept clean.

SEC. 3. It shall be the duty of any person licensed under this Ordinance, to keep his stall, booth, or stand in a clean and orderly condition. [*As amended by Ordinance approved January* 29, 1863.]

Sale of unwholesome meat prohibited, etc.

SEC. 4. No person licensed under this Ordinance shall sell, or expose for sale, any unwholesome, emaciated, blown, stuffed, tainted, bruised, putrid, unsound, or measly meat, poultry or provisions.

Penalty.

SEC. 5. Any person violating the provisions of this Ordinance shall be punished by a fine not to exceed one hundred dollars, and costs of prosecution; and the Court may sentence the offender to be imprisoned in the Detroit House of Correction until such fine and costs be paid: *Provided, however,* That the term of such imprisonment shall not exceed the period of six months.

SEC. 6. Chapter twenty-eight, of the Revised Ordinances of 1859, and all Ordinances and parts of Ordinances amendatory thereof, are hereby repealed.

SEC. 7. This Ordinance shall take immediate effect.

CHAPTER LVI.

OF THE SALE OF CALVES, SHEEP, AND LAMBS IN WAGONS.

[Ordinance approved September 28, 1863.]

SECTION 1. Persons owning, or having in charge, any vehicle loaded with or containing live calves, sheep or lambs, shall not permit the same to stand in any street, avenue, alley or public space in the City of Detroit, except in one of the Public Markets, at such place or places as the Clerk of the Market shall direct; and such persons shall strictly comply with the rules and regulations prescribed for the good order and government of the markets. *Where vehicles, containing calves, etc., to stand.*

SEC. 2. The Clerk of the Market shall be entitled to demand and receive from the owner or person having in charge any such vehicle, as referred to in section one, and such persons shall pay, before offering any such calves, sheep or lambs for sale, the sum of ten cents for each calf, and five cents for each sheep or lamb; which shall be paid over by the Clerk as other moneys secured by him. *Fees to be paid Clerk of Market.*

SEC. 3. Any violation of, or failure to comply with the provisions of this Ordinance, shall be punished by a fine not exceeding one hundred dollars and costs; and in the imposition of any such fine and costs, the Court may make a further sentence that the offender shall be committed to the Detroit House of Correction or to the County Jail, until the same be paid, for any period of time not exceeding six months. *Penalty.*

SEC. 4. This Ordinance shall take immediate effect.

CHAPTER LVII.

OF FORESTALLING.

[Ordinance approved January 2, 1862.]

SECTION 1. It shall not be lawful for any person who follows the business or occupation of a butcher, huckster, forestaller, grocer, *Forestalling defined and prohibited.*

or seller of any articles of provisions at second hand, directly or indirectly, to purchase, or cause to be purchased, from any farmer or other person, between the hours of four and ten o'clock in the forenoon, any poultry, game, eggs, butter, venison, fresh fish, fruit, or vegetable of any kind, which may have been brought into the City for sale or barter. The possession of any such article by any butcher, huckster, forestaller, grocer, or any other seller thereof, which may have been in the possession of any farmer or other person as aforesaid, within the limits of the City during said market hours, shall be *prima facie* evidence that such article was purchased contrary to the provisions of this section. [*As amended by Ordinance approved November* 24, 1862.]

Penalty.

SEC. 2. Any violation of the provisions of this Ordinance shall be punished by a fine not to exceed fifty dollars, and costs of prosecution; and the offender may be sentenced to be imprisoned in the Detroit House of Correction until such fine and costs be paid: *Provided, however,* That the term of such imprisonment shall not exceed the period of six months.

SEC. 3. Chapter twenty-seven, of the Revised Ordinances of 1859, and all Ordinances and parts of Ordinances amendatory thereof, are hereby repealed.

CHAPTER LVIII.

OF THE INSPECTION OF FLOUR.

[Ordinance approved March 31, 1860.]

Appointment of Flour Inspector.

SECTION 1. There shall be one Flour Inspector in said City, to be appointed by the Common Council, who shall have power to appoint one deputy.

Bond, oath and appointment of Deputy.

SEC. 2. Said Inspector shall file an official bond, with two sureties, in the penal sum of one thousand dollars, at the same time and in the manner provided by the Charter for other officers of the Corporation, and shall take the oath of office; he shall file in the office of the Clerk of the City a written appointment of his deputy, if he shall appoint one, and shall be subject to the general provisions of the Charter relative to appointed officers.

SEC. 3. It shall be the duty of the Flour Inspector, whenever requested, and not otherwise, to inspect, weigh and brand all wheat flour, rye flour and buckwheat flour to be used or sold in said City, or sold or offered for sale for the purpose of exportation. Duties of Flour Inspector.

SEC. 4. Each barrel of wheat flour shall be branded as follows, namely: If of a superior quality, "Superfine;" if of a second quality, "Fine;" if of a third quality, "Fine Middlings;" if of a fourth quality, "Middlings." And it shall also be branded with the weight of the flour contained therein, and with the initials of the Christian, and the whole of the surname, of the Inspector, together with the words "City Flour Inspector, Detroit, Michigan." Flour to be branded.

SEC. 5. It shall be the duty of the Inspector or deputy: first, to weigh such barrels as he shall suspect do not contain the full weight, and if they do not contain the full weight, to brand them with the word "Light;" second, to brand all barrels containing damaged flour with the word "Bad." Suspected barrels to be weighed.

SEC. 6. Said Inspector or Deputy Inspector shall be entitled to receive, in advance, from the person requesting the inspection, for weighing, inspecting, boring, plugging, and branding each barrel or half barrel, three cents. Fees.

SEC. 7. Every person who shall alter or counterfeit any brand marks of the Inspector or deputy, made under the provisions of this Ordinance, shall be punished by a fine not to exceed the sum of five dollars for each and every barrel the brand of which shall be so altered or counterfeited, or by imprisonment not to exceed ninety days. Penalty.

SEC. 8. Every person who shall put any flour into an empty barrel branded by said Inspector, and offer the same for sale in such barrel, without first cutting out the brand, shall be punished by a fine not to exceed the sum of five dollars for each and every such barrel, or by imprisonment not to exceed ninety days. Id.

SEC. 9. The Deputy Flour Inspector may do all acts and receive all fees which it is competent under this Ordinance for the Inspector to do and receive. Deputy to have power of Inspector.

CHAPTER LIX.

OF THE MANUFACTURE AND SALE OF BREAD.

[Chapter Thirty-three of Compiled Ordinances of 1859.]

Bakers to obtain permits.

SECTION 1. It shall not be lawful for any person to use or carry on the trade or business of a baker, either in person or by employing any other person to use or carry on the said trade or business, under his or her direction, or for his or her profit or benefit, within said City, without having obtained from the Common Council a permit for that purpose, under a penalty not exceeding fifty dollars.

How obtained.

SEC. 2. Every person desirous to use or carry on said trade or business, shall make application, in writing, to the Common Council, setting forth the street and house in which he or she intends to carry on said trade or business, and shall accompany such application with a recommendation, signed by at least twelve respectable householders of said City, certifying that such person is qualified to carry on said business, and that he or she is of good fame and correct and orderly deportment and behavior.

Clerk to deliver permit if granted.

SEC. 3. If the Common Council shall grant such application, the Clerk shall deliver such person a permit for the purpose aforesaid, for which he shall be entitled to receive from such person the sum of twenty-five cents; and the said permit shall be in force till the second Tuesday in March then next ensuing.

Bread to be made of good flour.

SEC. 4. All bread manufactured by the bakers of this City for sale, shall be made of good and wholesome flour or meal, into loaves of one pound and two pounds avoirdupois weight, and every loaf of such bread shall be marked with the numbers indicating the weight of such loaf, and also with the initial letters of the name of the baker thereof; and if any baker or other person shall offer or expose for sale any bread made of unwholesome materials, or any bread not so marked, except as aforesaid, every such baker or other person so offending shall forfeit and pay for each loaf, a sum not exceeding twenty-five dollars.

Penalty for selling bread under weight.

SEC. 5. If any baker shall make for sale, or shall sell or expose for sale, any bread that shall be deficient in weight, according to the requisitions prescribed in the preceding section of this chapter, he shall forfeit and pay for every such offence the sum of ten cents for every ounce that such bread shall be deficient in weight: *Provided, always,* That such deficiency in the weight of such bread shall be ascertained by the Inspector of Bread, by weighing or causing the same to be weighed in his presence, within eight hours after the same shall have been baked, sold or exposed for sale: *And provided further,* That whenever any allowance in the weight shall be claimed on account of any bread having been baked, sold or exposed for sale more than eight hours as aforesaid, the burden of proof in respect to the time when the same shall have been baked, sold or exposed for sale, shall devolve upon the defendant or baker of such bread.

Marshal to be Bread Inspector.

SEC. 6. The City Marshal shall, *ex officio,* be Inspector of Bread, and it shall be his duty, and he is hereby authorized and required, from time to time, and not less than once in each month, at all seasonable hours, to enter into, and inspect and examine every baker's shop, storehouse or other building where any bread is or shall be baked, stored or deposited, or offered for sale, and to inspect and examine all bread found therein, and also to stop, detain and examine in any part of the said City, any person or persons, wagons or other carriages carrying any loaf of bread, and weigh the same, and determine whether the same are in violation of the true intent and meaning of this chapter; and if the said Inspector shall find any bread not comformable to the directions herein contained, or any part of them, he shall make complaint thereof for the purpose of having such person prosecuted according to law.

Penalty for obstructing Marshal inspecting.

SEC. 7. Any person or persons who may obstruct or in any manner impede or wilfully delay any person legally qualified, in the execution of his duties under this act, either by refusing to him or delaying his entrance or admission into any of the places above mentioned, or by refusing or omitting to stop their wagon or carriage as aforesaid, or in any other manner whatsoever, so that the due execution of this act or any part of it may be impeded or obstructed, every such person shall, for every such offence, on conviction thereof before the Recorder's Court, forfeit and pay a sum not exceeding fifty dollars, and costs of prosecution; and, further, his, her or their license as a baker, if any has been granted to such person, shall be forfeited.

CHAPTER LX.

OF THE INSPECTION AND GAUGING OF OILS.

[Ordinance approved April 18, 1861.]

Appointment of Inspector and Gauger of Oils. Oath and bond.

SECTION 1. That there shall be one Inspector and Gauger of Oils and other Liquids in said City, to be appointed by the Common Council, who shall take the oath of office and file a bond in the sum of one thousand dollars, in the same manner as other officers of the Corporation.

Duties.

SEC. 2. It shall be the duty of said Inspector and Gauger to inspect all oils and other liquids to be used or sold in said City, or sold or offered for sale for the purpose of exportation; and for that purpose he shall provide himself with the most approved instruments for ascertaining the capacity of a barrel or other cask or vessel, and when called upon for that purpose, immediately attend with the same in any part of the City, and there inspect and ascertain the contents of any barrel or other cask or vessel of oil or liquids. He shall mark on such barrel or other cask or vessels the true quantity, in wine gallons, contained therein, with the name of such Inspector.

Fees.

SEC. 3. Said Inspector and Gauger shall, for services performed by him, be entitled to receive from the person or persons calling upon or employing him as aforesaid, compensation respectively as follows, viz: for inspecting and gauging a single barrel or other cask or vessel of oil or other liquids, ten cents; when the number of barrels or casks inspected and gauged in one parcel exceeds one and is less than five, for each barrel or other cask or vessel, seven cents; and when the number in one parcel exceeds five, for each barrel or other cask or vessel, five cents.

CHAPTER LXI.

OF THE PEDDLING OF MEAT.

[Ordinance approved January 2, 1862.]

SECTION 1. No person shall peddle, sell, or offer for sale, from any wagon, cart or vehicle, in or about the Public Markets, or in any street of the City of Detroit, any beef, pork, mutton or other meats, except venison, by the carcass or quarter, without a license from the Mayor, as hereinafter provided. This section shall not be construed to require any farmer, who shall sell or offer for sale any meat which shall have been fatted and killed by him, to take out a license, as provided in the next section.

Meat in wagons, etc., shall not be sold without license.

SEC. 2. The Mayor is hereby authorized to license any person to follow the business of a peddler or hawker of meat, on such person paying into the treasury the sum of twenty-five dollars, and executing a bond to the City of Detroit, with one or more sureties, in the penal sum of one hundred dollars, and conditioned that such person shall faithfully observe the provisions of the Charter and Ordinances of the Corporation.

Peddlers of meat may be licensed.

SEC. 3. Any violations of the provisions of this Ordinance shall be punished by a fine not to exceed one hundred dollars, and costs of prosecution; and the offender may be sentenced to be imprisoned in the Detroit House of Correction until the payment thereof: *Provided, however,* That the term of such imprisonment shall not exceed the period of six months.

Penalty.

SEC. 4. This Ordinance shall take effect from and after its passage.

CHAPTER LXII.

OF THE SALE OF WOODCOCK AND OTHER GAME.

[Chapter Twenty-nine of Compiled Ordinances of 1859.]

When woodcock, partridges, etc., shall not be sold.

SECTION 1. It shall not be lawful for any person to offer for sale, or sell within the limits of the City of Detroit, or bring into the City, for the purpose of selling the same, or for any other purpose, any woodcocks killed between the first day of February and the first day of July, in each year, or any quails, partridges or pheasants, killed between the first day of March and the first day of October, in each year.

Penalty.

SEC. 2. Any person who shall expose for sale, or sell, or have in his possession, for the purpose of selling the same, or for any other purpose, within the limits of said City, any woodcocks, quails, partridges or pheasants, killed within the periods specified in the first section of this chapter, shall forfeit and pay the sum of fifty cents for each woodcock, quail, partridge or pheasant, to be recovered in an action of debt before the Recorder's Court of said City, one-half of which sum shall be paid, upon recovery, to the Treasurer of the City of Detroit, and one-half to the person who shall sue and prosecute therefor.

CHAPTER LXIII.

OF HAWKERS AND PEDDLERS.

[Ordinance approved August 2, 1861.]

Hawkers and Peddlers must be licensed.

SECTION 1. No person shall follow the business or occupation of a hawker or peddler, within the limits of the City of Detroit, without a license from the Mayor.

Conditions of license.

SEC. 2. The Mayor is hereby authorized to license any person to follow the business or occupation of a hawker or peddler, on his paying into the City Treasury the sum prescribed in the next section, and executing a bond to the City of Detroit in the penal sum of one hundred dollars, with one or more sureties, conditioned that the person licensed will faithfully observe the provisions of the Charter and Ordinances of the Corporation, as provided in power sixty-three, of chapter five, of the City Charter.

SEC. 3. Any person soliciting a license, shall pay therefor as follows: If he intends to travel on foot, the sum of five dollars; if he intends to travel with one horse, or other animal, the sum of ten dollars; and if he intends to travel with two or more horses, or other animals, the sum of fifteen dollars. License Fees.

SEC. 4. This Ordinance is not intended to apply to any mechanic of this State, selling, or offering for sale, any article of his own manufacture or construction, nor to any person selling, or offering for sale, any vegetables, berries, fruit, butter or eggs. Ordinance not to apply to mechanics or sellers of vegetables, etc.

SEC. 5. Any person violating any of the provisions of this Ordinance, shall be punished by a fine not to exceed fifty dollars and costs; and in the imposition of any fine and costs, the Court may make a further sentence, that in default of the payment of such fine and costs, the offender be imprisoned in the Detroit House of Correction, or County Jail, for any period of time not exceeding six months. Penalty.

SEC. 6. An Ordinance entitled "An Ordinance relative to Hawkers and Peddlers," approved November 30, 1860, and all Ordinances, and parts of Ordinances, inconsistent with this Ordinance, are hereby repealed.

SEC. 7. This Ordinance shall take effect from and after its passage.

CHAPTER LXIV.

OF AUCTIONEERS.

[Ordinance approved July 24, 1861.]

SECTION 1. No person shall exercise the business or trade of an Auctioneer, or sell property at public auction or outcry, without a license from the Mayor. This section shall not apply to any person selling property by virtue of a legal process, or under a mortgage. Auctioneers must be licensed.

Mayor may grant licenses.

SEC. 2. The Mayor is authorized to grant a license to any resident of Detroit, of good character, or to any non-resident or transient person, of good character, on the conditions prescribed in the following section.

Bond and license fees.

SEC. 3. Any resident, applying for a license, shall, before the issuing thereof, pay into the City Treasury the sum of ten dollars, and execute a bond to the Corporation in the sum of five hundred dollars, with two sufficient sureties, conditioned for a faithful observance of the Charter and Ordinances of the City. If he be a non-resident, he shall, before the issuing of the license, pay the sum of ten dollars for each and every day he proposes to sell, and execute a similar bond as hereinbefore prescribed for residents.

Salesmen need not be licensed.

SEC. 4. This Ordinance shall not be construed to require any licensed Auctioneer to take out a license for any person whom he may employ as a salesman.

Bellmen prohibited.

SEC. 5. No bell or crier shall be used to collect bidders at any auction.

Not lawful to sell certain articles on wharves or on streets.

SEC. 6. It shall be lawful for any Auctioneer to sell on any wharf, or in any street, the following articles, to wit: Molasses, oils, wines, or any other liquors or liquids, the sale of which is authorized by law, contained in half barrels, barrels, casks, hogsheads, or other vessels, ship furniture and tackle, carriages, farming utensils, household furniture, and goods or merchandise, in packages or parcels, which shall weigh one hundred pounds: *Provided, however,* That such Auctioneer shall not obstruct or encumber any wharf or street, so as to interfere with travel.

Penalty.

SEC. 7. Any violation of the provisions of this Ordinance shall be punished by a fine not to exceed one hundred dollars and costs; and in the imposition of any fine and costs, the Court may make a further sentence, that in default of the payment thereof, within a time to be fixed in such sentence, the offender be imprisoned in the Detroit House of Correction, or County Jail, for any period of time not exceeding six months.

SEC. 8. Chapter thirty-two, of the Compiled Ordinances of 1859, and "An Ordinance relative to licensing Auctioneers," approved November 18, 1859, are hereby repealed.

SEC. 9. This Ordinance shall take effect from and after its passage.

CHAPTER LXV.

OF PAWNBROKERS.

[Ordinance approved December 21, 1861.]

SECTION 1. No person shall engage in the business of a Pawnbroker, in the City of Detroit, without a license from the Mayor, as hereinafter provided. Pawnbrokers must be licensed.

SEC. 2. The Mayor is hereby authorized to grant a license to any person of good character, to engage in the business of a Pawnbroker in the City of Detroit, on his paying into the City Treasury the sum of fifty dollars, and executing a bond to the City of Detroit, in the penal sum of one thousand dollars, with one or more sufficient sureties, to be approved by the Mayor, conditioned that he will faithfully observe the provisions of the Charter and Ordinances of the City, as provided in subdivision sixty-three, of chapter five, of the Charter of the City of Detroit. Conditions of license, and license fee.

SEC. 3. No person licensed as a Pawnbroker, under this Ordinance, shall, by virtue of one license, keep more than one house, shop, or place for taking goods in pawn. Not more than one shop to be kept under one license.

SEC. 4. Every person licensed under this Ordinance, shall cause his name, or the name of the firm, with the words "Licensed Pawnbroker," to be printed in large, legible characters, and placed over the outside of the door of his shop, or place of business. Pawnbrokers to keep sign.

SEC. 5. Every Pawnbroker shall keep a book, in which shall be legibly written, at the time of each loan, an accurate description of the goods, article or thing pawned, the time of pledging the same, the amount of money loaned thereon, the rate of interest to be paid on such loan, the time within which such pawn is to be redeemed, and the name and residence of the person pledging the said goods, article or thing; and when any watch is pledged with any Pawnbroker, he shall also write in such book the number and name of the maker thereof; and where jewelry, or gold or silver articles of any kind are pledged, he shall note in such book all letters or marks inscribed thereon; and whenever any goods, article, or thing of any kind, shall be sold at auction, as hereinafter provided, the date of To keep book.

such sale, the amount for which the same was sold, and the name of the purchaser thereof, shall also be entered in such book.

To deliver receipt.

SEC. 6. Every Pawnbroker shall, at the time of making any loan, and receiving any article in pledge therefor, deliver to the person from whom he received it, a memorandum, in writing, signed by him, containing the date and amount of such loan, the rate of interest to be paid thereon, the time within which such article is to be redeemed, with a description of the same, as provided in the preceding section.

Entry Book to be open to inspection of Mayor, Marshal and Chief of Police.

SEC. 7. The book provided for in section five of this Ordinance shall, at all times, be open to the inspection of the Mayor, City Marshal, or Chief of Police.

Pawnbrokers' sales to be advertised.

SEC. 8. No pawnbroker shall sell any article or thing which may have been left with him in pledge, until the same shall have remained in his possession at least two months beyond the time in which the same was to have been redeemed, and the sale of the same shall be at public auction, after being advertised for at least ten days, in two daily City papers, to be conducted by a licensed auctioneer of the City of Detroit, and not otherwise.

Surplus of proceeds of sale to be returned to pledger.

SEC. 9. The surplus money, if any, arising from any sale, as provided in the preceding section, after deducting the amount of the loan, interest and charges due on the same, shall be paid over by such Pawnbroker to the person who would have been entitled to redeem such article if no sale had taken place; and if the owner of such surplus money shall not call for the same within one month after such sale, the same shall be paid into the City Treasury.

To notify City Marshal or Chief of Police of lost or stolen articles pledged.

SEC. 10. It shall be the duty of all Pawnbrokers, licensed under this Ordinance, on receiving information that any article or thing left with them in pledge has been lost or stolen, to notify, in writing, the City Marshal, or Chief of Police, of the fact, giving the name of the person from whom they received the same, and the time when it was received.

Not to purchase articles offered for pledge.

SEC. 11. No Pawnbroker shall purchase any article or thing offered to him as a pledge.

Not to receive pledges from infants or drunkards.

SEC. 12. No Pawnbroker shall receive in pledge any article or thing from any person under sixteen years of age, or who is intoxicated, or an habitual drunkard.

SEC. 13. No Pawnbroker shall, knowingly, take from any apprentice, or servant, any article or thing offered by them in pledge, without first ascertaining that such article or thing is the property of the person so offering the same in pledge. Nor from any apprentices or servants.

SEC. 14. Any violation of, or failure to comply with the provisions of this Ordinance, shall be punished by a fine not to exceed one hundred dollars, and costs; and the offender may be sentenced to be imprisoned, until the payment thereof, in the Detroit House of Correction, for a term not exceeding six months. Penalty.

SEC. 15. An Ordinance of the City of Detroit, approved March 7th, 1861, entitled "An Ordinance to regulate and license Pawnbrokers," and all other Ordinances and parts of Ordinances inconsistent herewith, are hereby repealed.

SEC. 16. This Ordinance shall take immediate effect.

TITLE VII.

OF THE PUBLIC HEALTH.

CHAPTER LXVI.

OF THE BOARD OF HEALTH.

[Ordinance approved June 20, 1861.]

Who shall constitute the Board of Health.

SECTION 1. The Chairman of the Committee on Health, the Aldermen of each Ward, whose terms of office will soonest expire, with two of the City Physicians, and two other physicians, to be designated by a vote of the Common Council, shall be, and are hereby constituted a "Board of Health," in and for the City of Detroit, with the powers and duties hereinafter prescribed, and any five of them shall constitute a quorum for the transaction of business.

Who shall be President.

SEC. 2. The Chairman of the Committee on Health shall be the President of the Board of Health, and preside at its meetings.

Meetings to be held at City Hall. City Clerk to be Clerk of Board.

SEC. 3. The Board of Health shall meet at the City Hall at such times as they may deem proper. The City Clerk shall be the Clerk of the Board of Health, and shall keep regular minutes of their proceedings, in books to be provided for that purpose.

Powers and duties of Board of Health.

SEC. 4. The Board of Health shall have power, and it is hereby made their duty:

To make inquiry in respect to nuisances.

1st. To make, and direct to be made, diligent inquiry with respect to all nuisances, of every description, in said City, which are, or may be, injurious to the public health, and abate the same.

2d. To stop, detain and examine, or to direct to be stopped, detained and examined, every person coming from a place infected with a pestilential or infectious disease, in order to prevent the introduction of the same into this City. To stop and detain persons coming from infected places.

3d. To cause any person, not a resident of this City, who is infected with any infectious or pestilential disease, to be sent back to the place from whence he or she came, or to the pest-house or hospital. To send away infected persons who are non-residents.

4th. To cause any person, a resident of this City, who is infected with any pestilential or infectious disease, to be removed to the pest-house or hospital, if, in the opinion of any two of the City Physicians, the removal of such person is necessary for the preservation of the public health: *Provided, however,* That such removal can be effected with safety to the patient. To remove infected persons who are residents.

5th. To destroy any furniture, wearing apparel, goods, wares, or merchandise, or articles or property of any kind, which shall be exposed to, or infected with a contagious or infectious disease: *Provided, however,* That such property shall be appraised by two disinterested persons, in order that remuneration may be made therefor by the Common Council. To destroy infected furniture, clothing, etc.

6th. To appoint, with consent of the Common Council, Health Inspectors, with the power and duties hereinafter enumerated. To appoint Health Inspectors.

7th. To rent proper houses, to be used for pest-houses and hospitals. To rent pest-houses.

8th. To employ such nurses, officers, agents, servants or assistants, and provide the necessary furniture, medicines, articles and necessaries, for the use of the pest-houses or hospitals, and the persons therein confined, as may be deemed necessary. To employ nurses, etc.

9th. To require the occupant of any dwelling house, store, shop, or other building in which there shall be any person sick with small pox, or varioloid, to put up and maintain, in a conspicuous place, on the front of said dwelling house, store, shop, or other building, a card or sign, to be furnished by the Board, on which shall be written, or printed, in large letters, the words, "SMALL POX," and in case of the neglect or refusal of any person to comply with such requirement, to remove the patient therein to the pest-house or hospital. To require signs indicating "Small Pox" to be maintained.

To require steamboats, etc., to remove from harbor.

10th. To make an order requiring any steamboat, or other vessel or craft, having on board any infected or diseased person or property, not to enter the harbor, or to remove therefrom.

To exercise general sanitary supervision.

11th. To exercise a general supervision over the health of the City, and to make, from time to time, such recommendations to the Common Council as they deem proper, to promote the cleanliness and salubrity of the City.

To make rules and regulations.

12th. To make and determine the rules of its own proceedings.

To divide City into Health Districts.

13th. The Board of Health shall annually, and oftener, if they deem it necessary, divide the City into health districts.

To provide "Small Pox" signs.

14th. The Board of Health shall provide and keep on hand a supply of cards, marked "SMALL POX," to be put upon any house in which there may be a person sick of that disease or the varioloid; and such cards, upon application, shall be furnished without charge.

Keepers of taverns, etc., to report to Board of Health.

SEC. 5. The keeper of any tavern, boarding or public house, in which any inmate thereof shall be sick with small pox, varioloid, or other infectious or pestilential disease, shall forthwith report the same to the Board of Health, or to some member, or to the Clerk thereof; and the keeper or keepers aforesaid, if required by the Board, shall close such house immediately, and keep it closed against all lodgers and customers, until the patient is removed, and such house is thoroughly cleansed and ventilated.

Physicians to report.

SEC. 6 Every physician, or person acting as such, who shall have a patient sick of the small pox, varioloid, or other infectious and pestilential disease, shall forthwith report the fact, in writing, to the President of the Board of Health, together with the name, and the street and number of the house where such patient is treated; and the President shall report the same at the next meeting of the Board.

Occupants of houses where there is small pox to maintain signs.

SEC. 7. It shall be the duty of the occupant of any dwelling house, or other building, in which there shall be small pox or varioloid, to put up and maintain, in a conspicuous place, on the front of such building, a card, or sign, to be furnished by the Board of Health, on which shall be written or printed the words, "SMALL POX," and such sign or card shall be kept on such building during all the time any person so diseased shall remain therein; and no person shall take down, injure or deface such card or sign.

SEC. 8. All persons having small pox, varioloid, or other contagious or infectious disease, are hereby required to be kept closely confined within their respective dwellings, or places of abode, and no person who has been confined with such disease, shall leave his or her place of abode, and go about the City, until, in the opinion of his or her physician, it can be done without danger of communicating the disease to others. Infected persons to be confined to their dwellings.

SEC. 9. No person having the small pox, varioloid, or other contagious disease, shall go about the City. Id. not to go about City.

SEC. 10. It shall be the duty of each Health Inspector: Duties of Health Inspectors.

1st. To ascertain any nuisance which may exist in his district, and forthwith to report the same, in writing, to the Board.

2d. To enter upon the premises, and into the house of every person in his district, as often as he shall deem necessary, or the Board of Health shall order, and to examine into the health, cleanliness, and number of persons inhabiting such house, and inspect the cellars, vaults, privies and sewers on such premises.

3d. To execute the orders and resolutions of the Board of Health, in such manner as directed.

SEC. 11. Nothing in this Ordinance shall be construed to authorize the Board of Health to expend a larger sum than twenty-five dollars, without a prior resolution of the Common Council, authorizing such expenditure. Expenditure of Board of Health limited.

SEC. 12. All debts lawfully contracted by the Board of Health, shall be paid by the City, in the same manner that other claims and demands against the City are paid. Claims against Board to be paid by City.

SEC. 13. No person shall bring, or cause to be brought into the City of Detroit, any person infected with the small pox, varioloid, or any other infectious or pestilential disease. Infected persons not to be brought to City.

SEC. 14. The Board of Health, through its President, shall, on the first Tuesday in each month, and oftener, if required, make a report to the Common Council, giving any information in their power in respect to the health and salubrity of the City, and also a detailed statement of what money has been expended by them, and for what purpose the same has been expended. Board of Health to make monthly reports to Common Council.

SEC. 15. The pest-houses and hospitals of the City shall be under the control and direction of the Board of Health. To have supervision of pest-houses and hospitals.

SEC. 16. Chapter thirty-nine, of the Revised Ordinances of 1859, is hereby repealed.

Property taken by Board to be paid for by Common Council.

SEC. 17. Whenever property of any description, as enumerated in subdivision five, of section four, shall be destroyed by order of the Board of Health, the same shall be paid for by the Common Council, like other claims and demands against the Corporation.

Penalty.

SEC. 18. Any violation of, or failure to comply with the provisions of this Ordinance, or failure or neglect to comply with any of the requirements of the Board of Health, shall, on complaint to the Recorder's Court, be punished by a fine not to exceed three hundred dollars, and costs; and in the imposition of any such fine and costs, the Court may make a further sentence, that the offender be imprisoned in the County Jail, or Detroit House of Correction, until such fine and costs be paid: *Provided, however,* That the term of such imprisonment shall not exceed the period of six months.

SEC. 19. This Ordinance shall take effect immediately.

CHAPTER LXVII.

OF CEMETERIES.

[Ordinance approved July 10, 1861.]

Certain cemeteries declared public burial grounds.

SECTION 1. The Cemeteries known as Elmwood, Mount Elliott, and City Cemetery, are hereby declared to be public burial grounds; and no person or persons, societies or congregations, shall establish or locate any other burying ground within the limits of the City of Detroit.

Interments elsewhere prohibited.

SEC. 2. No interments shall be made in any other place within the City of Detroit than the Cemeteries hereinbefore named, or such other Cemetery or Cemeteries as may be hereafter established by resolution or ordinance of the Common Council.

Dimensions of graves.

SEC. 3. The grave for an adult shall be at least six feet deep; and for a child at least five feet deep. This section shall apply to all Cemeteries within the City of Detroit.

Walks, etc., in cemeteries not to be obstructed.

SEC. 4. No person shall obstruct any walk or alley in the City Cemetery.

SEC. 5. The Common Council shall designate suitable lots in the City Cemetery for the interment of deceased strangers and poor persons.

Interments of strangers and poor persons.

SEC. 6. On application to the Director of the Poor, with satisfactory proof that the deceased left no means with which to pay funeral expenses, the corpse shall be buried at the expense of the City, and the Director of the Poor shall give an order, commanding the City Sexton to dig a grave, furnish a suitable coffin, place the body in the coffin when directed, convey the body to the Cemetery in the City hearse, and decently inter it. For furnishing the coffin and performing the services herein enumerated, the Sexton shall receive the sum of eight dollars, to be paid like other claims and accounts against the City. [*As amended by Ordinance approved April* 2, 1863.]

Interments at expense of City.

SEC. 7. The City Sexton shall have charge of the City Cemetery, and it shall be his duty:

Duties of City Sexton.

1. To keep and preserve the grounds, buildings, fences, enclosures, and other property of the City Cemetery, in repair.

2. He shall report from time to time to the Common Council any repairs which he may deem necessary.

3. He shall make complaint to the Recorder's Court for any trespasses or injuries done to the tombstones, monuments, fences, enclosures, or other things, erected within said Cemetery.

4. He shall keep the alleys, walks and avenues of the Cemetery free from bushes, weeds or other obstructions.

5. The City Sexton and his employees, and by his direction alone, shall have the right to dig or open graves in the City Cemetery. [*As amended by Ordinance approved April* 2, 1863.]

SEC. 8. Any person wishing to purchase a lot, half lot, or single grave, in the Cemetery of the City, may do so by paying the Controller such sum as may be fixed by a resolution of the Council; and the Controller is hereby authorized to execute deeds for such lots under the seal of the Corporation.

Sale of lots in City Cemetery.

SEC. 9. The money received by the Controller for lots, as provided in the last section, shall be by him immediately paid over to the City Treasurer; and such money shall constitute a fund by itself, to be used, under the direction of the Council, in keeping in repair the City Cemetery.

Proceeds of such sales to be paid over to City Treasurer, etc.

Duty of City Sexton.

SEC. 10. The City Sexton shall, on application, perform any or all of the services enumerated in clause six, of section seven, of this Ordinance, and shall not improperly treat any dead body, or neglect to perform any of his duties as enumerated herein.

Salary.

SEC. 11. The Sexton shall receive a salary of two hundred dollars. He may be removed at any time by the Mayor. [*As amended by Ordinance approved April* 2, 1863.]

Sexton to keep register.

SEC. 12. The City Sexton, and the Sextons or Superintendents of Elmwood and Mount Elliott Cemeteries, shall each keep a register, to be provided by the City, of all persons buried in each of said Cemeteries, giving in alphabetical order the name of the deceased, age, color, sex, occupation, place of birth and residence, the disease or manner and time of death, and the number of the lot in which the body was buried; which register shall be kept in the office of the City Clerk. And the Sextons or Superintendents aforesaid shall, on Monday of each week, in the forenoon, record in the said register, in the manner herein provided, the burials which have been made since their last report.

Trespasses in Cemeteries prohibited.

SEC. 13. No person shall commit any trespass, by destroying, injuring or defacing any grave, vault, tombstone, monument, enclosure, building, fence, basin, fountain, bridge, seat, tree, flower, shrub, or other thing belonging to any Cemetery.

Penalty.

SEC. 14. Any violation of or failure to comply with the provisions of this Ordinance, shall be punished by a fine not to exceed one hundred dollars, and costs; and in the imposition of any such fine and costs, the Court may make a further sentence, that in default of the payment thereof, within a time to be fixed in such sentence, the offender be committed to the County Jail or Detroit House of Correction, for any period of time not exceeding six months.

Appointment and term of office of City Sexton.

SEC. 15. The City Sexton shall be appointed by the Common Council, on the nomination of the Mayor, and shall hold his office for one year, or until his successor is appointed.

SEC. 16. Chapter forty of the Revised Ordinances of 1859, and all Ordinances inconsistent herewith, are hereby repealed.

SEC. 17. This Ordinance shall take effect from and after its passage.

CHAPTER LXVIII.

OF NUISANCES.

[Ordinance approved June 22, 1861.]

SECTION 1. No person shall, himself, or by another, throw, place, deposit, or leave in any street, highway, lane, alley, public space or square, any animal or vegetable substance, dead animal, fish, shells, shavings, dirt, rubbish, excrement, filth, ordure, slops, unclean or nauseous water or liquor, hay, straw, ashes, cinders, soot, offal, garbage, swill, or any other article or substance whatever, which may cause any noisome, offensive or unwholesome smell. Nuisances in streets and public places prohibited.

SEC. 2. No distiller, soap-boiler, tallow-chandler, dyer, machinist, or other person, shall himself, or by another, discharge out of or from any still-house, soap or candle factory, dye-house, work shop, factory, machine shop, dwelling house, kitchen or other building, any foul or nauseous liquid, water or other substance, into or upon any highway, street, lane, alley, public space or square, or into any adjacent lot or ground. Discharges from still-houses, soap factories, etc., prohibited.

SEC. 3. No person shall keep, place or have, on or in any private house, lot or premises in this City, or within one mile distant therefrom, any dead carcass, putrid, offensive, or unsound beef, pork, fish, hides, skins, bones, horns, stinking or rotten soap grease, tallow, offal, garbage, or other animal or vegetable matter or substance, which may cause any unwholesome, noisome or offensive smell. Nuisances in private houses, etc., prohibited.

SEC. 4 When any dumb animal shall die within the limits of the City of Detroit, the owner, or person in possession of it, shall, within twelve hours thereafter, cause the carcass to be removed to the place provided by the Common Council, or one mile beyond the City limits. Dead animals to be removed.

SEC. 5. No owner or occupant of any grocery, cellar, tallow-chandler's shop, soap, candle, starch or glue factory, tannery, butcher shop, slaughter house, stable, barn, privy, sewer, or other building or place, shall allow any nuisance to exist or remain on his or her premises. Nuisances in groceries, etc., prohibited.

Livery stables to be kept clean.

SEC. 6. The keeper of any livery or other stable shall keep the stable and stable yard clean, and shall not permit, between the first day of June and the first day of November, more than two cart-loads of manure to accumulate in or near the same, at any one time.

Carriages not to be washed in streets, etc.

SEC. 7. No person shall, himself, or by another, wash or clean any carriage or horse, on any street, sidewalk, or other public space, nor suffer the water used for such purposes to flow over any sidewalk, street or public space.

Places for slaughtering to be paved and cleaned.

SEC. 8. Every person slaughtering beeves, sheep, or other animals, within the City limits, shall cause the house, yard or place where such killing is done, to be provided with a tight plank floor, or to be paved with brick or stone; and, if paved, the earth below shall be sufficiently solid to prevent its becoming the receptacle of the filthy or offensive matter; such floor or pavement shall be so constructed as to carry off into a tub or reservoir all blood and offal. At the end of each day, when killing has been done on the premises, the same shall be thoroughly washed and cleansed, and the tubs or vessels containing the blood and offal emptied.

Slaughter-houses to be whitewashed.

SEC. 9. Every slaughter house in this City shall be white-washed inside, at least once in each month, between the first day of April and the first day of November.

Hides not to remain in streets, etc.

SEC. 10. No person shall allow any green or salted hides to remain on any street, sidewalk, or other open place within this City, longer than one hour.

Offensive handbills, etc., not to be posted.

SEC. 11. No person shall, himself, or by another, post or put up in any conspicuous place, or on any of the lamp posts, fences, posts, hydrants, boxes, sidewalks, bridges or buildings within this City, any card or handbill, advertising the place or means of curing syphilitic or other secret diseases.

Handbills not to be posted on public buildings, etc.

SEC. 12. No person shall place, or in any manner fasten, any placard, show bill or advertisement upon or against any public building, or part thereof, or against any fence or enclosure belonging to the City of Detroit.

Hogs not to be collected, etc.

SEC. 13. No person shall collect or confine hogs, in pens or otherwise, so as to become offensive to his or her neighbor or neighbors.

Nuisances on docks and wharves prohibited.

SEC. 14. No person shall place, deposit, throw or keep, in any dock or wharf, or in the waters of the Detroit river, within the City limits, any straw, hay, green boughs, manure, cord-wood, vegetables, perishable substance, excrement, carcass, bones, horns, shells, meats, hides, offals, garbage, or any unwholesome or decayed matter or thing whatever.

SEC. 15. Every dwelling house, store, manufactory, or shop hereafter built in the City of Detroit, shall be provided with a suitable privy, the vault of which shall be walled up with two-inch plank, brick or stone, and be sunk at least four feet below the level of the earth. The inside of such vault shall be at least one foot distant from the line of every adjoining highway, street, lane, alley or lot; and when there is a public sewer within one hundred feet of such privy, it shall be so constructed as to be drained into such sewer. Privies to be maintained.

SEC. 16. The Mayor, Aldermen of the City, and members of the Board of Health, shall have the power, and it is hereby made their and each of their duty, upon being satisfied that any store, manufactory, shop, or dwelling house, as aforesaid, is not provided with a suitable privy, as provided in the last section, to notify, in writing, the owner or occupant of such dwelling to construct such a privy within twenty days from the date of the service of such notice; and if such owner or occupant neglect or refuse to comply with the requirements of such notice, within the time specified, the Common Council may cause a suitable privy to be constructed for such dwelling house, and the expense thereof shall be charged as a special tax or assessment on the dwelling house, and the ground attached thereto, to be levied and collected in the same manner as other assessments imposed by authority of the Common Council. Construction of privies.

SEC. 17. No privy shall be emptied between the fifteenth day of June and the fifteenth day of September, unless by the written permission of the Mayor, an Alderman, or a member of the Board of Health. Privies shall be emptied between the hours of 10, P. M., and 3, A. M., and at no other time. Emptying of privies.

SEC. 18. Any cart, wagon or other vehicle, used or intended to be used for the purpose of conveying swill, offal, garbage, excrement, ordure or night-soil, shall be perfectly tight and covered, so as to prevent the contents thereof from leaking or spilling; and such cart, wagon or other vehicle, when not in use, shall not be allowed to stand in any highway, street, lane, alley, public space or square. Swill-carts, etc., to be covered.

Penalty.

SEC. 19. Any violation of the provisions of this Ordinance, shall be punished by a fine not to exceed one hundred dollars, and the costs of prosecution; and in the imposition of any fine and cost, the Court may make a further sentence that the offender be imprisoned in the Wayne County Jail or the Detroit House of Correction, until the payment thereof: *Provided, however,* That the period of such imprisonment shall not exceed the term of six months.

SEC. 20. Chapter nine, of the Revised Ordinances of 1859, is hereby repealed.

SEC. 21. This Ordinance shall take effect from and after its passage.

TITLE VIII.

OF THE PUBLIC PEACE.

CHAPTER LXIX.

OF THE PUBLIC PEACE.

[Ordinance approved June 22, 1861.]

SECTION 1. Any person found lying in wait, lurking or concealed in any building or premises, with intent to do mischief, pilfer, or commit any crime or misdemeanor, shall be punished as hereinafter provided. *Lying in wait, etc., prohibited.*

SEC. 2. Any person or persons who shall make, or assist in making, any noise, disturbance, or improper diversion, or any rout, or riot, by which the peace and good order of the neighborhood are disturbed, shall be punished as hereinafter provided. *Disturbances, etc., prohibited.*

SEC. 3. All vagrants, mendicants, and drunken or disorderly persons, shall be punished as hereinafter provided. *Vagrancy, etc., prohibited.*

SEC. 4. No person shall be guilty of any indecent or immoral language, conduct or behavior, to any person, in any street, lane, alley, or elsewhere in said City. *Indecent language and behavior prohibited.*

SEC. 5. Any person who shall, by talking, laughing, or otherwise, interrupt the service in any place of Divine worship, shall be punished as hereinafter provided. *Disturbances in places of worship prohibited.*

SEC. 6. Persons shall not collect, or stand in crowds, in front of any church or place of worship, during service. *Crowds in front of churches prohibited.*

Indecent exposures prohibited.

SEC. 7. No person shall make any indecent exposure of his or her person, in the streets, lanes, alleys, markets, or public places of said City.

Sales of obscene pictures, books, etc., prohibited.

SEC. 8. No person shall show, sell, or offer for sale, or exhibit any indecent or obscene picture, drawing, engraving, book or pamphlet.

Penalty.

SEC. 9. Any violation of the provisions of this Ordinance shall be punished by a fine not to exceed three hundred dollars, and costs; and in the imposition of any fine and costs, the Court may make a further sentence, that the offender be committed to the Detroit House of Correction, or County Jail, until such fine and costs be paid: *Provided, however,* That the term of such imprisonment shall not exceed the period of six months.

SEC. 10. Chapters forty-four, forty-five, forty-six, forty-seven, forty-eight and forty-nine, of the Revised Ordinances of 1859, are hereby repealed, and, also, "An Ordinance relative to the Public Peace and Quiet," approved March 31, 1860.

SEC. 11. This Ordinance shall take effect from and after its passage.

CHAPTER LXX.

OF QUIET AND GOOD ORDER.

[Ordinance approved September 20, 1861.]

Opening of places of business, theatrical representations, etc., on Sunday, prohibited.

SECTION 1. No person shall keep open his or her store, shop, ordinary, saloon, bar-room, beer hall, restaurant, pleasure garden, victualing house, billiard room, ball alley, grocery, or other place of business, pleasure or amusement, or give or make, or be present at, or take part in, or permit, on any premises occupied by him or her, any public diversion, show, theatrical representation, ball, dance, game or play, on the first day of the week, called Sunday. This section shall not be construed to prevent druggists from furnishing medicines and prescriptions, nor to prevent the furnishing of meals and lodging to travelers and boarders. But nothing herein contained shall authorize the furnishing of intoxicating liquors to any person whatsoever.

SEC. 2. Any violation of the provisions of this Ordinance, shall be punished by a fine not to exceed five hundred dollars, and costs; and in the imposition of any such fine and costs, the Court may make a further sentence, that the offender be imprisoned in the County Jail, or Detroit House of Correction, until the payment thereof, for any period of time not exceeding six months. Penalty.

SEC. 3. Chapter sixty-four, of the Revised Ordinances of 1859, is hereby repealed.

SEC. 4. This Ordinance shall take effect from and after its passage.

CHAPTER LXXI.

OF DISORDERLY HOUSES.

[Ordinance approved December 21, 1861.]

SECTION 1. No person shall keep, within the limits of the City of Detroit, any house of ill-fame, house of assignation, or house for the resort of common prostitutes, or a disorderly saloon, bar-room, tavern, beer hall, grocery, theatre, room, ordinary, house or building of any kind. Disorderly houses prohibited.

SEC. 2. Any person who shall violate the preceding section, shall be punished by a fine not to exceed one hundred dollars, and costs of prosecution, and the offender may be sentenced to be imprisoned in the House of Correction until the payment thereof: *Provided, however,* That the term of such imprisonment shall not exceed six months. Penalty.

SEC. 3. Chapter fifty, of the Revised Ordinances of 1859, and all Ordinances, and parts of Ordinances, amendatory thereof, are hereby repealed.

SEC. 4. This Ordinance shall take immediate effect.

CHAPTER LXXII.

OF A NIGHT WATCH.

[Chapter Fifty-three of Compiled Ordinances of 1859.]

Mayor may organize a Night Watch.

SECTION 1. The Mayor of the City is hereby vested with full power and authority to establish and organize a Night Watch, in and for said City, and for that purpose he may appoint as many discreet and suitable persons as, in his opinion, the public safety may require. The persons appointed, as aforesaid, shall, before entering on the performance of their duties, take an oath or affirmation that they will faithfully and honestly discharge the duties of their office, to the best of their ability.

Duties of Watch.

SEC. 2. The members of said Watch, and each of them, are hereby authorized, and it shall be their duty, between the hours of nine o'clock at night and the dawn of the succeeding morning, to apprehend any and every person who shall be reasonably suspected of having committed any crime or misdemeanor, or who shall be detected by either of the members of said Watch in the violation of any of the Ordinances of said City, or of an intent to commit any crime or misdemeanor, and to detain such person until morning; and thereafter, it shall be the duty of such Watch to report all persons so apprehended to the Marshal of said City, who shall thereupon have the custody of all such persons, until discharged by due course of law.

Powers of Watchmen.

SEC. 3. That the said Watch, and every member thereof, shall have power and authority, on reasonable ground of suspicion, during the hours or period of watch, aforesaid, to enter in a peaceable manner, or if resisted, (after demand made,) with force, into any house, store, shop, grocery, or other building whatever, in said City, in which any person or persons may be suspected to be for unlawful purposes, and if any person or persons shall be found therein guilty of any crime or misdemeanor, or who may be reasonably suspected thereof, the said Watch to apprehend and keep in custody any such person or persons, in manner as hereinbefore prescribed.

SEC. 4. It shall be the duty of all persons in said City, when called upon by any member of said Watch, promptly to aid and assist him in the execution of his duties; and if any person shall neglect or refuse to give such aid and assistance, he shall, on conviction, forfeit a sum not exceeding one hundred dollars, and costs of prosecution. All persons to assist Watchmen, when requested.

SEC. 5 It shall be the duty of the Marshal of said City, to bring such persons, apprehended by said Watch, before the proper authority, for examination, within a reasonable time; and all persons who shall resist, or in any manner interfere with the members of said Watch in the discharge of their duties, shall, on conviction, forfeit a sum not exceeding one hundred dollars, and costs of prosecution. Duty of Marshal.

SEC. 6. The Mayor shall have power to remove from office any member of the Watch, when, in his opinion, there shall be just cause therefor. Watchmen may be removed.

SEC. 7. All persons apprehended by said Night Watch, in the performance of their aforesaid duties, shall be confined in a room in the City Hall, provided for that purpose, during the night in which said person or persons shall be apprehended, subject to the custody and control of said Marshal, whose duty it shall be to take such person or persons, for the purpose of examination, during the morning succeeding their arrest, before the Mayor or Recorder, or, in their absence, one of the Aldermen of said City, who shall, as conservator of the peace of said City, attend at the City Council room, at nine o'clock, A. M., of each and every day, except Sunday, during the continuance of said watch, for the purpose of hearing such examination: *Provided,* That persons so apprehended during any Saturday night, shall, on the following morning, be committed to the County Jail, to be examined, as aforesaid, on the Monday following. What to be done with persons arrested.

CHAPTER LXXIII.

OF INJURIES TO PUBLIC PROPERTY.

[Ordinance approved September 28, 1863.]

Injuries to public property prohibited.

Section 1. No person shall destroy, injure, or in any manner deface the City Hall, the Market Houses, water pipes, water screws, hydrants, public school buildings, fire engine houses, fire apparatus, hay scales, public pounds, public wharves, street lamps, lamp posts, or any public building or property whatsoever, in the City of Detroit, or the appurtenances, fences, trees, or fixtures, thereunto belonging or appertaining.

Injuries to reservoirs prohibited.

Sec. 2. No person shall injure any public reservoir, or break, or enter the same, or throw or deposit any substance therein, or draw off any water therefrom, except in case of fire, or for the use of the Fire Department, without authority from the Common Council, the Mayor of the City, or Chief Engineer of the Fire Department.

Injuries to shade trees, etc., prohibited.

Sec. 3. No person shall destroy, cut, or injure, or in any way deface any shade or ornamental tree, standing in any street, avenue, public space, or square, in the City of Detroit. This section shall not be construed to prohibit any person, owning or occupying any lot, in front of, or adjacent to, which there may be any shade or ornamental trees, from trimming the same.

Penalty.

Sec. 4. Any person violating any of the provisions of this Ordinance, shall be punished by a fine not to exceed the sum of five hundred dollars, and costs, and the offender may be sentenced to be imprisoned in the Detroit House of Correction until the payment thereof, for a term not exceeding six months.

Sec. 5. Chapters fifty-one and fifty-two, of the Revised Ordinances of 1857, and all Ordinances, and parts of Ordinances, inconsistent herewith, are hereby repealed.

TITLE IX.

OF THE RECORDER'S COURT, AND THE PUNISHMENT OF OFFENDERS.

CHAPTER LXXIV.

OF PROCESS AND PROCEEDINGS IN THE RECORDER'S COURT, AND THE RECOVERY OF FINES.

[Chapter Fifty-four of Compiled Ordinances of 1859.]

When process may be issued from the Recorder's Court.

SECTION 1. Upon complaint, on oath or affirmation, being made to the Clerk of the Recorder's Court, that any person has violated any of the laws or Ordinances of said City, the Clerk shall issue a *capias ad respondendum*, unless a summons be specially prescribed for the arrest of such person, and shall be returnable any day in the present or ensuing term of said Court.

When security for costs may be required.

SEC. 2. Before issuing such process, the Clerk may, if he shall deem it necessary, require the complainant to enter into a bond, with sufficient surety, to the City of Detroit, conditioned for the appearance of the complainant at the term of the Recorder's Court, at which such process shall be made returnable, to give evidence against the person or persons complained of by him; and if, upon trial, the defendant shall be discharged, that the complainant shall pay the costs of prosecution, if so ordered by the said Court. And in his discretion, said Clerk may require a sum not exceeding five dollars, to be deposited with him by the complainant, to be applied to the payment of the costs, in case the complainant is so ordered to pay the same. [*As amended by Ordinance approved October* 16, 1863.]

Who to execute process.

SEC. 3. It shall be the duty of the Marshal, or Constable, to whom the writ shall be directed, to arrest the defendant therein named, if he be found, who may give bail for his appearance, at the time such writ shall be returnable, and in default thereof, the officer shall take him before any member of the Common Council, who may commit, let to bail, or discharge the defendant, according to his discretion.

Bond upon arrest.

SEC. 4. The bail required in the preceding section, shall be by bond, payable to the City of Detroit, with at least one sufficient surety, in a sum not less than fifty dollars, and not more than double the amount of the penalty provided in the By-law or Ordinance which may be violated, and shall be conditioned for the due appearance of the defendant before the Recorder's Court, at the time such writ shall be returnable, and that the defendant shall comply with the judgment of the Recorder's Court, and not depart without leave, and, in the meantime, keep the peace towards all the good people of said City: *Provided,* That if such bail should be insufficient or irresponsible, the officer taking the same shall be liable, in an action of debt, for the amount thereof, to be recovered in the name of the Corporation.

Execution to issue against body, goods, and real estate.

SEC. 5. Executions returnable at the next term, may issue upon any judgment of the said Court, against the body, goods and chattels of the defendant, or party prosecuted, (unless such party be in actual custody, for the offence on which judgment was rendered,) for the amount of such fine, and the costs of prosecution, which execution may be levied upon the goods and chattels, or body of such party, and all goods and chattels so levied upon, shall be sold in the same manner, in all respects, that personal property is directed by the laws of this State to be sold, except that six days' previous notice of sale shall be sufficient, and the officer levying the same shall return the execution at the next term of the Recorder's Court, with his doings thereon. And if such execution be returned unsatisfied, in whole or in part, an execution may be issued against the real estate of such defendant, which shall be executed according to the laws of this State.

SEC. 6. If, in any trial, it shall appear to the Court that the complaint was willful or malicious, or without probable cause, or if the complainant does not appear and testify in the cause, the Court may order and adjudge the complainant (and if he has entered into a bond, as required by this Ordinance, then him and his surety,) to pay the costs of such prosecution, and thereupon an execution, as in other cases, shall issue for the same. But if a deposit in money has been made, such costs shall be paid therefrom, and no execution shall issue. In all cases, the surplus of any money deposited for costs, after the payment of such costs, shall be returned by said Clerk to the complainant. [*As amended by Ordinance approved October* 16, 1863.]

When complainant to pay costs.

SEC. 7. The Marshal and Constables, once in each month, and whenever it can be done, at least three days' prior to the term of the Recorder's Court, shall return to the Clerk of said Court all process issued out of said Court, with their doings in each case endorsed thereon, and shall also, at such times, pay over all moneys collected by them, in pursuance of such process, to the said Clerk. And if any such officer shall neglect or refuse to comply with the provisions of this section, or shall knowingly do any other act inconsistent with the just and faithful discharge of his duties, he shall, on conviction, be liable to pay a penalty not exceeding one hundred dollars, and costs of prosecution. [*As amended by Ordinance approved October* 16, 1863.]

Constable's and Marshal's returns.

SEC. 8. The Clerk shall receive all fines and costs that are paid without the issuing of process for collection, and he shall, once in each month, make a report to the Common Council of all the particulars and business of the Recorder's Court, the number of persons tried, and the amount of fines and costs of each term, and the amount collected and paid into his hands; and he shall immediately pay over to the City Treasurer all moneys by him received, belonging to the Corporation, together with all witness or jurors' fees, on hand, and shall take from the Treasurer a receipt therefor, which, when presented to and countersigned by the Controller, shall be a sufficient voucher to said Clerk for such payments. [*As amended by Ordinance approved October* 16, 1863.]

Clerk to report monthly to Council.

SEC. 9. If any person or persons knowingly or willfully obstruct, resist, or oppose the Marshal or any of the Constables of said City,

Penalty for obstructing officers.

or other person or persons duly authorized in serving, or attempting to serve, any writ or process, rule or order, issued out of said Recorder's Court, or while executing or carrying into effect any order, rule or determination of the Common Council of said City, or shall resist or impede any person duly authorized, or any member of the Common Council of said City, in the performance of any of their duties or powers, or if any person shall aid or assist any person legally in custody, to escape, or conceal him after the escape, every person offending in the premises, shall, on conviction before said Recorder's Court, be punished by fine not exceeding one hundred dollars, and costs.

Duty of officers when it is not convenient to bring prisoner before Recorder, Alderman, etc.

SEC. 10. If any officer shall arrest any person, at a time that may be inconvenient to bring him before any proper officer for an examination, the officer making the arrest may place such person in the custody of the Jailor of the County of Wayne, and within fifteen hours thereafter, he shall bring him before some member of the Common Council, for examination, and if such officer shall neglect to comply with the requirements of this section, he shall be liable to pay all the expenses of keeping such prisoner in jail: *Provided*, That if the said period of fifteen hours shall terminate on the Sabbath day, said examination shall be had during the forenoon of the next ensuing Monday.

Duty of jailor.

SEC. 11. The keeper of the Jail of the County of Wayne shall not permit or suffer any person committed by virtue of a process of the Recorder's Court, or other authority of said City, to leave or depart from said Jail, without the permission of some member of the Common Council, or the City Attorney, under the penalty of a sum not exceeding one hundred dollars, and costs of prosecution.

Court may require convicted persons to give recognizances for good behavior.

SEC. 12. Whenever any person is convicted, before the Recorder's Court, of any offence against the Ordinances of the City, it shall be competent for the Court to require from the party so convicted a recognizance, with sufficient surety or sureties, in such sum as the Court shall direct, conditioned for his or her good behavior, for any period not exceeding one year, and any violation of the Ordinance under which the party was convicted, shall be deemed a breach of such recognizance. The Court may also order such party to be committed to the House of Correction, till such recognizance is given. [*This section added by Ordinance approved Oct.* 16, 1863.]

CHAPTER LXXV.

OF FEES IN THE RECORDER'S COURT.

[Ordinance approved July 10, 1861.]

SECTION 1. Officers and jurors, for duties performed in the Recorder's Court, in street opening and City Ordinance cases, shall receive the following fees: Fees.

1st. For serving a warrant, or other process, for the arrest of any person, fifty cents. For serving process.

2d. For serving a subpœna, thirteen cents. For serving subpœna.

3d. For each person taken to prison, on final commitment, thirteen cents. For commitment.

4th. For each arrest made without process, provided the Court shall determine that such arrest was for probable cause, fifty cents. For arrest.

5th. For every mile actually and necessarily traveled beyond the City, in serving process, six cents. For travel.

6th. For each day's attendance, as a juror, in the trial of cases, one dollar and fifty cents, and seventy-five cents for each half day. For attendance as juror in trial of causes.

7th. For every day actually and necessarily employed, as a juror, in the matter of opening, widening, extending, or vacating streets, alleys, etc., one dollar and fifty cents; and for each half day actually and necessarily employed, seventy-five cents. For attendance as juror in street opening cases.

SEC. 2. No fees shall be paid to witnesses. No fees to witnesses.

SEC. 3. Officers serving process for a defendant, may demand and receive his fees in advance. Fees may be required in advance.

SEC. 4. The Clerk of said Court, at the end of each term thereof, shall deliver to each officer and juror a certificate, specifying the services of such officer or juror, and the amount due him. Such services shall be paid for by the City, in the same manner as other claims and demands against the Corporation: *Provided, however*, That the Clerk of said Court shall have the right to swear the foreman, or any member of the jury, in the matter of opening, widening, vacating or extending a street, alley, etc., as to the time actually and necessarily employed by such jury. Payment of fees.

SEC. 5. Chapters fifty-five and fifty-six, of the Revised Ordinances of 1859, and all Ordinances inconsistent with this Ordinance, are hereby repealed.

SEC. 6. This Ordinance shall take effect from and after its passage.

CHAPTER LXXVI.

OF THE IMPRISONMENT OF OFFENDERS.

[Chapter Eighty of Compiled Ordinances of 1859.]

Powers of Court relative to persons convicted under the City Ordinances.

SECTION 1. Whenever, by the terms of any Ordinance of said City, it is provided that any person convicted of an offence, shall be imprisoned, said person may be confined either in the County Jail of the County of Wayne, or in any Jail, Workhouse, House of Correction, or Alms House of said City, in the discretion of the Court.

TITLE X.

OF THE PREVENTION AND EXTINGUISHMENT OF FIRES.

CHAPTER LXXVII.

OF THE FIRE DEPARTMENT.

[Ordinance approved December 1, 1863.]

SECTION 1. The Fire Department of said City shall consist of a Fire Marshal, a Chief Engineer, two or more Assistant Engineers, and as many fire engine and hook and ladder companies and Fire Wardens as the Common Council shall, from time to time, prescribe. Who shall constitute Fire Department.

SEC. 2. The Chief and Assistant Engineers shall be appointed or nominated by ballot of the firemen, at the time and in the manner herein prescribed. There shall be a meeting of the firemen constituting the Fire Department of the City of Detroit, within the meaning of section one of this chapter, on the second Monday of April, in each year—the same to be held at the Council room in the City Hall in said City, or such other place as shall be designated by resolution of the Common Council of said City, for the purpose of nominating a Chief and two Assistant Engineers. Such meeting shall be called by resolution of the Common Council. The City Clerk shall publish such call in two daily papers of the City of Detroit, for at least four days immediately preceding the time of such meeting. At such meeting, the firemen shall, from their own members, choose a President, to preside over the same; also a Secretary and two Tellers, who shall keep a record of the proceedings of such Appointment of Chief and Assistant Engineers.

meeting; and the President and Secretary shall certify to the Common Council the appointment or nomination of the Chief and Assistant Engineers, thus made.

Salaries of Chief and Assistant Engineers.

SEC. 3. The Chief Engineer thus appointed and confirmed by the Common Council, shall receive an annual salary of three hundred dollars. The two Assistant Engineers shall receive an annual salary of two hundred dollars each. Said salaries payable monthly.

There shall be two Assistant Engineers.

SEC. 4. Until the Common Council shall, by resolution or ordinance, otherwise prescribe, there shall be two Assistant Engineers, to be designated as the "First Assistant Engineer," and "Second Assistant Engineer."

Duties of Chief and Assistant Engineers upon an alarm of fire.

SEC. 5. The Chief and other Engineers, upon an alarm of fire, shall immediately repair to the place where said fire is, and the Assistant Engineers shall report themselves to the Chief, or person having command of the Department for the time being, and obey his orders. Any person willfully violating the provisions of this section, may be punished by fine, not to exceed one hundred dollars, or by imprisonment, not to exceed three months.

Penalty.

Who shall be in command at fires.

SEC. 6. The Fire Marshal and Chief Engineer shall have full power, control and command over all persons whatever at fires; the Chief Engineer shall station the engines and apparatus of companies, and see to it that all persons belonging to the Fire Department do the duties prescribed by law and ordinance. And it shall be the duty of the Chief Engineer to direct at all fires all such measures as he shall deem most advisable for the extinguishment of said fires. The Chief Engineer shall be in full command at all fires, and in his absence, the Assistant Engineer, according to rank, shall command. And any person who shall obstruct, hinder or resist him in the performance of his duties, shall be punished by a fine not to exceed one hundred dollars, and costs, or by imprisonment in the Detroit House of Correction, not to exceed six months.

Penalty for obstructing Chief Engineer.

Who shall act in the absence of the Chief Engineer.

SEC. 7. In case of the absence or sickness of the Chief Engineer, the First Assistant shall act as Chief Engineer; and if the First Assistant shall be absent or sick, then the Second Assistant shall act as Chief; and in case neither the Chief or other Engineers are present at a fire, the Fire Marshal shall designate some fireman to act as Chief, who, while thus acting at a fire, shall have the same powers, and perform the same duties, and shall be, for all purposes whatever, Chief Engineer for the time being.

SEC. 8. The Chief Engineer shall wear a leather hat when on duty, with the words "Chief Engineer" painted legibly thereon, and shall carry a speaking trumpet.

Chief Engineer shall wear hat and carry trumpet.

SEC. 9. The First Assistant Engineer shall wear a leather cap with the words "Engineer No. 1" painted on the frontispiece thereof; and the Second Assistant shall wear a leather cap with the words "Engineer No. 2" painted on the frontispiece thereof; they shall also each carry a speaking trumpet.

Also, Assistant Engineers.

SEC. 10. All persons who are now, or hereafter may be, employed by the City to ring fire alarms, shall immediately on the breaking out of a fire, ring the bells, and continue so to do during ten minutes, unless the fire be sooner extinguished, under the penalty of not exceeding ten dollars for every such omission: *Provided,* That when a chimney only shall be on fire, either by day or night, said bells may not be rung.

Ringing of fire alarms.

SEC. 11. All persons who, at a fire, shall refuse to obey any order or direction given by a person duly authorized to order or direct, or who shall resist or impede any officer or other person in the discharge of his duty, shall, in the absence of sufficient excuse, be punished by a fine not exceeding fifty dollars. The Fire Marshal, the Chief Engineer, any Fire Warden, Assistant Engineer, Foreman or Assistant Foreman of a Fire Company, may arrest any such person and detain him in custody until the fire is extinguished, when the person making the arrest shall make to the City Attorney the proper complaints, under this section, against the person arrested.

Penalty for disobedience of orders at fires.

Fire Marshal, and others, may make arrests.

SEC. 12. If any person shall willfully injure, in any manner, any hose, fire engine, or other apparatus, or building containing the same, belonging to this City, the offender shall, for every such offence, forfeit and pay not to exceed the sum of five hundred dollars, or be imprisoned, not to exceed one year, or both, in the discretion of the Court; beside being liable to an action for the recovery of the damages done.

Penalty for injuring fire engines, hose, etc.

SEC. 13. It shall not be lawful for any person or persons, without reasonable cause, by outcry, or ringing the bells, or by proclaiming fire, or by any other means whatsoever, to make or circulate, or cause to be made or circulated, in any ward of the City of De-

Penalty for making or circulating false alarm of fire.

troit, any false alarm of fire; and the person or persons so offending shall be punished by fine not exceeding one hundred dollars, or by imprisonment in the County Jail not exceeding sixty days.

Fire Marshal and other officers to enforce this Ordinance.

SEC. 14. It shall be the duty of the Fire Marshal, the Chief and Assistant Engineers, and members of the Common Council, and the City Marshals and Constables of said City, to enforce the provisions of this Ordinance.

Duties of hook and ladder and axe men.

SEC. 15. The hook and ladder and axe men shall, under the direction of the Chief Engineer or Fire Marshal, or in the absence of the Chief Engineer or Fire Marshal, then under the direction of either of the Assistant Engineers, or in the absence of all the Engineers, then under the direction of three members of the Common Council, cut down and remove any building, erection or fence, for the purpose of checking the progress of the fire.

Certain Fire Companies disbanded.

SEC. 16. Fire Engine Companies Nos. 1, 2, 3, 4, 5, 6, 8 and 11 are hereby declared to be disbanded.

Fire Marshal. Appointment, term of office, oath and bond.

SEC. 17. A Fire Marshal shall be appointed by the Common Council, on the nomination of the Mayor, on the second Tuesday of January, in each year, who shall keep his office in such place as shall be provided by the Common Council. He shall, when so appointed, continue in office for the term of one year, or until a successor is duly appointed, confirmed and qualified. He shall take the oath of office prescribed by the Charter, and shall file with the Clerk of the City a bond, in the sum of two thousand dollars, conditioned for the faithful performance of his duty; which condition shall be in the language prescribed by the Charter for the official bonds of City officers.

Duties of Fire Marshal.

SEC. 18. It shall be the duty of the Fire Marshal, in all cases of supposed incendiarism, to take such steps as, in his judgment, he may deem expedient, to investigate the case and bring the offenders to judgment. The City Marshal, or his assistants, shall serve all process which shall be issued by the Fire Marshal, and for such service shall receive the same fees as for serving similar process from the Recorder's Court.

Id.

SEC. 19. The Fire Marshal shall, once in every week, examine the condition of the fire engines and other apparatus, together with the engine houses belonging to the Corporation, and report the same to the Common Council, on the first Tuesday of each month. He shall keep a record in his office of all accidents by fire, which may happen in the City, with the causes thereof, as well as can be ascertained, and the number and description of the buildings injured, together with the names of the owners or occupants; and once in each year shall report the same to the Council. He shall also report to the Council, once in each year, the names and number of all the members of the Fire Department, and the respective companies to which they belong.

SEC. 20. At all fires, the City Marshal, Assistant Marshals, Constables and Policemen, shall act as a Fire Guard, under the control and direction of the Fire Marshal. It shall be the duty of the Fire Guard to take charge and possession of all property removed from buildings at fires, and to deliver the same to the Fire Marshal, or, in his absence, to the Chief Engineer, to store or otherwise protect the same until it is claimed by the owner or owners, and upon such claim to deliver up to the owner or owners, upon the payment to the Fire Marshal of all expenses necessarily and actually incurred in and about the care and protection of such property, and for which a receipt shall be given by the Fire Marshal. And the said Fire Guard are hereby invested with all necessary authority for the purpose of taking charge and possession of such property; and it shall be the further duty of said Fire Guard to prevent the hose from being trodden on, and to keep all idle and suspected persons from the fire and its vicinity, and also to use all proper exertions within their power for the preservation of property endangered at fires; and all citizens are hereby enjoined and required to comply with the directions of any of said Fire Guard: *Provided*, Such directions be not in opposition to the orders of the person having supreme control at said fire.

Care of property at fires

SEC. 21. The Fire Marshal shall be subject to be suspended temporarily by the Mayor, who, on making any such suspension, shall forthwith report the same to the Council, with the reason for such suspension; and the Council, thereupon, may either remove or retain said Marshal, as to them shall seem best, upon a vote of a majority of all the Aldermen elected.

Fire Marshal may be suspended.

SEC. 22. It shall be the duty of the Fire Marshal to report to the Council all repairs, alterations or improvements, that will cost a sum exceeding ten dollars, that may be needed at any time to any of the fire apparatus or engine houses, walks or fences surrounding

Further duties of Fire Marshal.

the same; and when any repairs to the same are ordered by the Council, it shall be his duty to cause the same to be repaired, and shall superintend the same; and it shall also be his duty to superintend the erection of all engine houses that may be ordered by the Council; it shall also be his duty to purchase all supplies required for the use of the different Fire and Hook and Ladder and Hose Companies of the City, when a requisition is made upon him by the Foreman of the Company, and shall keep an accurate account of all such supplies, in the name of each Company, and shall report the total amount of the same to the Council, on the first Tuesday of each month.

Fire Marshal shall wear badge.

SEC. 23. The Fire Marshal shall wear a badge when on duty, indicating his official character.

SEC. 24. Chapter thirty-six, of the Compiled Ordinances of 1859, and all other Ordinances or parts of Ordinances inconsistent herewith, are hereby repealed.

CHAPTER LXXVIII.

OF STEAM FIRE ENGINE COMPANIES.

[Ordinance approved November 22, 1861.]

Common Council may establish Steam Fire Engine Companies by resolution.

SECTION 1. Whenever, in the opinion of the Common Council, it is necessary to establish a Steam Fire Engine Company, it shall so declare by resolution.

Who shall constitute a Steam Fire Engine Company.

SEC. 2. Each company shall consist of a Foreman, an Engineer, two Drivers, five Hosemen and one Fireman, to be appointed by the Common Council, on the recommendation of the Mayor and Chairman of the Committee on the Fire Department, and to hold their offices during good behavior.

Salaries.

SEC. 3. The officers and men shall receive the following annual salaries, payable monthly: the Foreman, one hundred and fifty dollars; the Engineers, seven hundred and thirty dollars; the Drivers, five hundred and forty-seven dollars and fifty cents; the Hosemen, one hundred and twenty dollars; the Firemen five hundred and forty-seven dollars and fifty cents. [*As amended by Ordinance approved January* 29, 1863.]

SEC. 4. On an alarm of fire, the Foreman shall immediately repair to the scene of the same, and, under the direction of the Chief or Assistant Engineer of the Fire Department, get his engine into service, and remain with his company as long as his services are required. He shall preserve order in his company. Duties of Foreman.

SEC. 5. The Engineer shall be, *ex officio*, Secretary of the company, and shall record, in a legible hand, in a book to be provided by the City for the purpose, the name, age, time of admission and discharge, of each member of the company ; he shall keep an accurate account of all public property in charge of the Company, and note the absence of members from fires. On the last day of each month, and oftener if required, he shall make a written report to the Fire Marshal, setting forth the names of the members of the Company, the number of times each of them has been absent from fires, and the condition of the engine, apparatus and other property in charge of the Company. He shall see that the engine house and stables are kept clean, and that the Drivers keep their horses and harness in good condition, and that the engine, hose cart and horses are always ready for instant service, and that proper order is preserved in and about the engine house. At night, all members of the Company shall be at the engine house, or a distance not to exceed one block therefrom. No person, other than those belonging to or authorized to be there, shall be allowed to sleep in or lounge in or about said engine house. Duties of Engineer.

SEC. 6. The Engineer and Fireman shall be at all times at or in the immediate vicinity of their engine house, except when absent on duty, and shall devote their entire time and attention to the duties of their office. They shall accompany their engines to all fires, and, under the direction of the Foreman, discharge their respective duties. The Engineer shall be a practical mechanic, and with the Fireman shall keep their engine clean and always ready for instant service. Id.

SEC. 7. The Drivers shall have the care and charge of the horses, harness and hose, and keep the same in good condition, repair, and ready for instant service. They shall be under the direction of the Engineer, and when not at fires, shall be at or near their engine house. Duties of Drivers.

Watch for fires to be kept.

SEC. 8. There shall be a look-out at or near the engine house; the Drivers and Fireman shall take turns in keeping a regular and constant watch for fires.

Duties of Hosemen and extra men.

SEC. 9. The Hosemen and extra men, on an alarm of fire, shall immediately repair to the scene of the same, report themselves to the Foreman, and perform such duties as shall be required of them.

Spirituous liquors not to be allowed in engine houses.

SEC. 10. No spirituous liquors shall be allowed in the engine house or stable; and any member having or bringing any such liquor into any such stable or engine house, or who shall be intoxicated in or about the same, or at any fire, shall be discharged by the Mayor, on complaint. Any member against whom charges may be preferred to the Mayor, may be by him suspended from duty and pay, until such charges are disposed of.

Disorderly conduct in engine houses prohibited.

SEC. 11. No person shall tipple, riot, or be guilty of any lewd, lascivious or disorderly conduct, in or about any Steam Fire or Hand Engine House. Complaints for a violation of any of the provisions of this Ordinance, shall be made by the Engineer of the company to the Fire Marshal, who shall investigate the same and report, with his opinion, to the Mayor, who is hereby authorized to remove any member for cause. [*As amended by Ordinance approved October* 16, 1863.]

Penalties for absence from fires.

SEC. 12. Officers and men absent from a fire without a good excuse, shall be fined as follows: The Foreman, two dollars; the Engineer, ten dollars; a Driver, five dollars; the Fireman, five dollars; a Hoseman, one dollar, an extra man fifty cents; to be deducted from their pay at the end of the month.

SEC. 13. An Ordinance approved October twenty-fifth, A. D. 1860, "relative to Steam Fire Engine Companies," is hereby repealed.

SEC. 14. This Ordinance shall take immediate effect.

CHAPTER LXXIX.

OF PAID HAND ENGINE COMPANIES.

[Ordinance approved June 27, 1861.]

SECTION 1. Whenever, in the opinion of the Common Council, it is necessary to organize a Paid Hand Engine Company, it shall so declare by resolution. Common Council may establish Paid Hand Engine Companies by resolution.

SEC. 2. Each Company shall consist of a Foreman, a Steward, and twenty-three men, to be appointed by the Common Council, on the recommendation of the Mayor and the Chairman of the Committee on Fire Department, and to hold their offices during good behavior. Who shall constitute a Paid Hand Engine Company.

SEC. 3 No person shall be a member of any such company who is under twenty-one or over forty-five years of age, and who does not reside in the fire district to which his engine is assigned. Qualifications for membership.

SEC. 4. The Foreman and Steward shall each receive an annual salary of one hundred dollars, and the men an annual salary of fifty dollars each, the same to be paid quarterly. [*As amended by Ordinance approved October* 16, 1863.] Salaries.

SEC. 5. On an alarm of fire, they shall immediately repair to their engine house, and with the engine and apparatus proceed to the scene of the fire, and, through their Foreman, report to the Chief or Assistant Engineer, whose orders they shall obey. Company to repair to fires on alarm thereof.

SEC. 6. The Foreman shall be Secretary, and perform the following duties: He shall record, in a legible hand, in a book to be provided by the Fire Marshal, the name, age, time of admission and discharge of each member. He shall keep an account of all public property in charge of the Company. He shall call the roll after each alarm, and note the absentees; and when the engine has been in service the roll shall be called before the Company starts for home, and the absentees noted. He shall, once in each month, and oftener if required, make a report, in writing, to the Fire Marshal, in which he shall give the names of the members, the number of times each has been absent from roll call, and the cause therefor, and the condition of the engine, hose cart, hose and other public property in charge of Duties of Foreman.

the Company. He shall cause the engine house, engine, and all apparatus connected therewith, to be kept clean and ready for service. He shall be responsible for the behavior of his men when on duty. He shall have the command of his Company, and the control of all public property which his Company may have in charge, and shall also assign to each man the duty he is to perform at fires, and in taking care of the engine and apparatus.

Members may be removed for cause.

SEC. 7. If any member of the Company refuses or neglects to perform any duty assigned him by the Foreman, or is guilty of any disorderly or improper conduct, he may, on complaint, be removed from office by the Mayor.

Companies may make rules.

SEC. 8. Each Company may make rules for its own government, not inconsistent with this Ordinance, subject to the approval of the Common Council.

Supplies to be furnished by Fire Marshal.

SEC. 9. All needful supplies for the Company shall be furnished by the Fire Marshal, on the written order of the Foreman.

Duties of Steward.

SEC. 10. The Steward shall keep the engine, hose and hose cart in good running and working order, and shall be assisted, from time to time, by the members of the Company, who shall be regularly detailed for that service.

Penalties for absence from fires.

SEC. 11. Any Foreman or Steward who is absent from roll call without a good excuse, shall forfeit for each absence the sum of three dollars, to be deducted from his pay at the end of each quarter; and any member who is absent from roll call without a good excuse, shall forfeit for each absence the sum of two dollars, to be deducted from his pay at the end of each quarter. It shall be the duty of the Foreman, or acting Foreman, at the end of each quarter, to make a full and accurate report (verified by his affidavit) to the Fire Marshal, and the Fire Marshal shall make out the company roll from such report. [*As amended by Ordinance approved October* 16, 1863.]

Assistant Foreman to be elected.

SEC. 12. The Company shall elect an Assistant, who, in the absence of the Foreman, shall perform his duties.

Foreman to have powers of policeman.

SEC. 13. The Foreman shall possess and exercise the powers and duties of a Policeman, for the preservation of the peace at fires, and in and about his engine house.

Disorderly conduct in engine houses prohibited.

SEC. 14. No person shall play at cards, tipple, riot, or be guilty of any lewd or lascivious conduct, in or about any engine house.

SEC. 15. On the complaint, in writing, of any three members of a company against the Foreman thereof, the Fire Marshal shall investigate the charges preferred, and report the evidence, with his opinion thereon, to the Mayor.

Fire Marshal to investigate charges against Foreman.

SEC. 16. The officers and men of Paid Hand Engine Companies may be removed at any time by the Mayor or Common Council.

Officers and men may be removed.

SEC. 17. In going to and returning from fires, the members of Companies shall make as little noise as possible, and, where there are paved streets, shall not use the sidewalks.

Noise in streets prohibited.

SEC. 18 All Ordinances or parts of Ordinances in conflict with this Ordinance, are hereby repealed.

SEC. 19. This Ordinance shall take effect from and after its passage.

CHAPTER LXXX.

OF PAID HOOK AND LADDER COMPANIES.

[Ordinance approved June 27, 1861.]

SECTION 1. Whenever, in the opinion of the Common Council, it is necessary to organize a Horse Hook and Ladder Company, it shall so declare by resolution.

Common Council may establish Hook and Ladder Companies by resolution.

SEC. 2. Each Company shall consist of a Foreman, a Steersman, and six Hook and Ladder men, to be appointed by the Common Council, on the recommendation of the Mayor and the Chairman of the Committee on Fire Department, and to hold their offices during good behavior.

Who shall constitute a Paid Hook and Ladder Company.

SEC. 3. No person shall be a member of any such Company, who is under twenty-one, or over forty-five years of age.

Qualification for membership.

SEC. 4. The following annual salaries shall be paid: The Foreman, five hundred and forty-seven dollars and fifty cents; the Steersman, five hundred dollars; the Hook and Ladder men, each one hundred and twenty dollars. The said salaries shall be paid monthly. [*As amended by Ordinance approved April* 10, 1863.]

Salaries.

SEC. 5. The Foreman shall be the Secretary of his company, and keep its books and records. He shall record, in a legible hand,

Duties of Foreman.

in a book to be provided by the Fire Marshal, the name, age, time of admission, and discharge of each member. He shall devote his entire time to the business of the City, and be ready for service at all times, with his horses and apparatus. On the breaking out of a fire, he shall at once proceed with his Company to the scene of the same, and aid in its extinguishment, under the orders of the Chief or Assistant Engineer. He shall record the absence of any member from duty, and, at the end of each month, report to the Fire Marshal, giving an account of all public property under his control, its condition, the names of the members absent from fires, and the number of times they were so absent, with their excuses.

Duties of Steersman.

SEC. 6. The Steersman shall act under the direction of the Foreman, and shall keep his truck and truck house in good order.

Steersman to take turn in keeping watch.

SEC. 7. If there be a watch-tower adjoining any truck house, the Steersman shall take his turn in keeping a regular watch.

Company to repair to fires on alarm thereof.

SEC. 8. On an alarm of fire, the members shall repair at once to the truck house, and report to the Foreman for duty.

Penalties for absence from fires.

SEC. 9. Any Foreman or Steersman who is absent from any fire, without good cause, shall forfeit the sum of five dollars, to be deducted from his pay at the end of each month; and any member who is absent, without good cause, shall forfeit the sum of fifty cents, to be deducted from his pay at the end of each month.

Foreman to make report to Controller.

SEC. 10. The Foreman shall make a report, at the end of each quarter, to the City Controller, giving the names of the members of his Company, and the number of times each has been absent from roll call, and their excuse therefor, and the Controller shall make his pay roll therefrom.

Assistant Foreman to be elected.

SEC. 11. The Company shall elect an Assistant, who, in the absence of the Foreman, shall perform his duties.

Foreman to have powers of policeman.

SEC. 12 The Foreman shall possess and exercise the powers and duties of a Policeman, for the preservation of the peace at fires, and in and about his truck house.

Disorderly conduct in truck houses prohibited.

SEC. 13. No person shall play at cards, tipple, riot, or be guilty of any lewd or lascivious conduct, in or about any truck house.

Fire Marshal to investigate charges against Foreman.

SEC. 14. On the complaint, in writing, of any member of a Hook and Ladder Company, against the Foreman, the Fire Marshal and the Chairman of the Committee on Fire Department, shall investigate the charge contained in such complaint, and report the evidence to the Mayor, with their opinion thereon.

SEC. 15. The officers and members of any Hook and Ladder Company, may be removed at any time by the Mayor or Common Council. Officers and men may be removed.

SEC. 16. In going to and returning from fires, the members of Hook and Ladder Companies shall make as little noise as possible, and, where there are paved streets, shall not use the sidewalks. Noise in streets prohibited.

SEC. 17. Each company may make rules for its own government, not inconsistent with this Ordinance, subject to the approval of the Common Council Companies may make rules.

SEC. 18. All Ordinances, or parts of Ordinances, in conflict with this Ordinance, are hereby repealed.

SEC. 19. This Ordinance shall take effect from and after its passage.

CHAPTER LXXXI.

OF THE PREVENTION OF FIRES.

[Ordinance approved December 2, 1861.]

SECTION 1. The following boundaries shall constitute and be known as the Fire Limits of the City of Detroit, to wit: Beginning at the channel bank of the Detroit river, on the easterly line of the Rivard Farm (so called); thence northerly, on said easterly line, to a point within one hundred (100) feet of the south line of Jefferson avenue; thence easterly, parallel with said avenue, and one hundred (100) feet therefrom, to the west line of Dequindre street; thence northerly, across Jefferson avenue, on the west line of Dequindre street, to a point one hundred and thirty (130) feet north of the north line of Larned street; thence west, parallel with said Larned street, and one hundred and thirty (130) feet therefrom, to the easterly line of Rivard farm; thence northerly, on said easterly line, to an alley between Fort and Lafayette streets; thence west, on a line with the centre of said alley, to the easterly side line of lot No. 113, Lambert Beaubien Farm (so called); thence northerly, along the easterly side lines of lots Nos. 113, 124, 129, 140, F. L. 145 and Fire Limits.

156, on the Lambert Beaubien Farm, to the northerly side line of the alley between Clinton and Gratiot streets; thence easterly, along said northerly side line, and along the rear lines of all lots fronting on, or touching the southerly line of Gratiot street, to the centre of Russell street; thence northerly, on the centre of Russell street, to a point one hundred (100) feet distant, at right angles from the northerly line of Gratiot street; thence south-westerly, and parallel with Gratiot street, one hundred (100) feet therefrom, to the easterly side line of lot No. 172, on the corner of Gratiot and Prospect streets; thence northerly, on the side line of said lot, to the rear line of the same; thence south-westerly, along the rear lines of all lots fronting on, or touching the northerly line of Gratiot street, to a point one hundred (100) feet east of Brush street; thence north, parallel with said Brush street, and one hundred (100) feet distant therefrom, to an alley between Adams avenue and Elizabeth street; thence west, on a line with the centre of said alley, to a point one hundred feet distant from the easterly line of Woodward avenue; thence northerly, parallel with said Woodward avenue, and one hundred (100) feet distant therefrom, to a point one hundred (100) feet beyond Charlotte street; thence across Woodward avenue, parallel with Charlotte street, to a point one hundred (100) feet west of the westerly line of Woodward avenue; thence southerly, parallel with said avenue, one hundred (100) feet distant therefrom, to the centre of an alley between Adams avenue and Elizabeth street; thence westerly, on the centre of said alley, to the centre of Clifford street; thence southerly, to the northerly line of Middle street; thence westerly, to the northerly line of the Grand River road; thence north-westerly, to the westerly line of Cass avenue; thence northerly, to the rear line of the lots fronting on Grand River road; thence north-westerly, along the rear lines of all lots fronting on said Grand River road, to a point one hundred (100) feet north-west to the west line of Third street; thence south, parallel with Third street, to the rear line of the lot fronting on the south line of the Grand River road; thence south-easterly, along the rear lines of all lots fronting on said road, to a point one hundred (100) feet west of the west line of Cass street; thence southerly, in the alley in rear of Cass street, to the southerly line of lot No. 2, block 54; thence easterly, between said lot 2 and lot 3, to the westerly side line of

Cass street; thence in a straight line across Cass street, to the middle of an alley between lots 72 and 34; thence through said alley, to the easterly side line of lot 34; thence southerly, between lots 33 and 34, in block 12, to Macomb avenue; thence across said avenue, to the dividing line between lots 33 and 34, block 10; thence southerly, between said lots 33 and 34, and between 72 and 73, to Palmer street; thence across Palmer street and Park street, to the dividing line between lots 60 and 61, in said block 10; thence on the dividing line between said lots 60 and 61, to the alley between Park street and Washington avenue; thence southerly, in said alley, to an alley eighty (80) feet northerly from Michigan avenue; thence along said alley, adjoining the lots fronting on Michigan avenue, to an alley one hundred (100) feet westerly from Cass street; thence west, along the rear lines of all lots fronting on said avenue, to the easterly line of the Woodbridge farm (so called); thence southerly, to the rear line of lots fronting on the south line of Michigan avenue; thence along said rear line of all lots fronting on Michigan avenue, to a point one hundred (100) feet west of the westerly line of Third street; thence southerly, parallel with Third street, and one hundred (100) feet therefrom, to the rear line of lots fronting on Fort street; thence westerly, along the rear lines of all lots fronting on Fort street, to a point one hundred (100) feet west of Thompson street; thence south, and parallel with Thompson street, to a point one hundred and thirty-eight (138) feet south of the southerly line of Fort street; thence easterly, and parallel with Fort street, one hundred and thirty-eight (138) feet therefrom, to the easterly side line of the Forsyth farm (so called); thence southerly, to the channel bank of the Detroit river. It is to be understood, that in all reference to the lines of lots, that those shown on Munro's City Map, are those referred to. [*As amended by Ordinance approved May* 1, 1863,]

Buildings erected within Fire Limits must be of stone or brick, etc.

SEC. 2. No person shall erect or place any building, or part of any building, within said fire limits, unless the same shall be constructed of stone, brick or iron, roofs covered with slate, tile, metal, gravel and composition, or shingles laid on not less than five-eighths inches of mortar, and cornices of stone, brick, metal or wood; and if wood, the same shall be painted with three coats of paint, and heavily sanded; the gutters shall be of metal. And in all buildings erected of stone, brick or iron, in blocks of two or more buildings, within said Fire Limits, there shall be erected partition walls of stone or brick, at least one foot in thickness, where such building is over two stories in height, and not less than eight inches in thickness where such building is two stories, or less, in height; and all party and side walls, in such blocks, shall extend at least twenty inches above the roof.

SEC. 3. [*Repealed by Ordinance approved April* 10, 1863.]

Common Council may authorize erection of wooden buildings within Fire Limits.

SEC. 4. The Common Council may, by resolution, authorize the erection of wooden buildings within said Fire Limits, under such restrictions, and upon such conditions, as they may prescribe by resolution: *Provided*, That the erection of such wooden building will not increase the fire risk of any building adjacent thereto.

Wooden buildings within Fire Limits not to be repaired without permission of Common Council.

SEC. 5. No person shall, within said Fire Limits, except as provided in section six, repair any wooden building which has been partially destroyed by fire, or otherwise, nor elevate from the ground, or in any way increase the height of, nor remove any such building from one lot to another lot, or to any part of the same lot, without being first authorized to do so by the Common Council.

Fire Marshal to give permits for repairs of buildings.

SEC. 6. When any wooden building within the Fire Limits shall be partially destroyed by fire, or otherwise, and the damage thereto shall not exceed one-third its value, to be ascertained in the manner hereinafter provided, such building may be repaired, and not otherwise; and the Fire Marshal shall give a written permit to such owner, to repair such building, and shall keep a record of the same in his office.

Fire Marshal, with others, to make estimate of damage to buildings partially destroyed by fire.

SEC. 7. In case of the partial destruction by fire, or otherwise, of any wooden building in said Fire Limits, the Fire Marshal, and in case of his absence or inability to act, then the City Controller, with a master builder, to be selected by the owner of such building; and if the building be insured, a third party, to be selected by the Insurance Company, or its agent; and if there be more than one Insurance Company having risks upon such building, then such Insurance Companies, or their agents, shall, together, select such third person, who shall proceed at once to estimate the amount of the damage to such building. But if the Insurance Companies, or their agents, shall neglect or refuse to act, or if there be no insurance on such building, and the Fire Marshal, and the person selected by the owner of such building, cannot agree as to the amount of such damage, they shall call in a third disinterested person, and the estimate of any two of the parties hereinbefore named, shall be binding on the City, as well as on the owner, and all other persons interested in such building.

How estimate shall be made.

SEC. 8. In estimating the value of any building partially destroyed by fire, or otherwise, the sum of money it would cost to build the same new, from the bottom of the sills, shall be taken as its value; and in estimating the damage to such building, the same shall be assumed to be the sum of money it would require to restore such building to the condition in which it was before its partial destruction.

Common Council may extend Fire Limits by resolution.

SEC. 9. On the application, in writing, of the owner or owners of two-thirds of the ground in any block not included within the Fire Limits, the Common Council may, by resolution, passed by a two-thirds vote of the Aldermen present, extend to such block the provisions of this Ordinance. A block shall be construed to mean a space bounded by three or more streets.

Such resolution shall be published.

SEC. 10. Every resolution for the extension of the Fire Limits, as provided in the last section, shall be published for six successive days in the official newspaper of the City, and in one other daily newspaper published in said City.

Offenses against this Ordinance.

SEC. 11. For each and every week which a building erected, placed, removed, or repaired, contrary to the provisions of this Ordinance, shall be allowed to remain, the owner of such building may be complained of as for a distinct offense, and punished as hereinafter provided.

Buildings not to be occupied for manufacture of inflammable substances without permission of Common Council.

SEC. 12. No person shall, without permission of the Common Council, use or occupy, within the limits of the City of Detroit, any building for the manufacture of turpentine, camphene, lime, fire works, or other dangerous or easily inflammable or explosive substances, or for the storage of gunpowder, in larger quantities than twenty-eight pounds.

Hay, shavings, etc., to be enclosed.

SEC. 13. No person shall have, put or keep any hay, straw, cotton, hemp or wood shavings, in stack or pile, without having the same securely enclosed, so as to protect them from flying sparks of fire.

Lamps in stables, etc., to be secured in lanterns.

SEC. 14. No lighted candle or lamp shall be used in any stable, building, or other place where hay, straw, hemp, cotton, flax, rushes, shavings, gunpowder, or other combustible materials shall be stowed or lodged, unless the same is well secured in a lantern.

Construction of chimneys.

SEC. 15. Every chimney hereafter erected within the limits of the City, shall be so constructed as to admit of being scraped, brushed or cleansed.

Construction of stove pipes, etc.

SEC. 16. No pipe of any stove, chimney or fireplace, shall be put up or used, unless the same be conducted into a chimney of stone or brick; and in all cases where a stove pipe passes through the woodwork of a building, it shall be separated from such woodwork at least six inches, by metal or other incombustible material; and all pipes from stoves or fire places, over fifteen feet in length, shall be riveted together at each joint, and, when necessary for safety, shall be supported and stayed by wires.

Chimneys to be swept.

SEC. 17. Every chimney and pipe from a stove or fire place, in use in this City, shall be swept, scraped, or burnt out, once in every three months; and if burnt out, the same shall be done between the hours of nine A. M. and three P. M., on a wet or rainy day, or when the roof is covered with snow.

Fire carried in streets, etc., to be covered.

SEC. 18. No person shall carry fire in or through any street, alley or lot in this City, unless the same be placed in some covered pan or vessel.

Ashes to be covered.

SEC. 19. No ashes shall be kept or deposited in any part of this City, unless the same be kept or deposited in a close iron or earthen vessel, or brick or stone ash house, thoroughly secured.

Fires not to be kindled in streets, etc.

SEC. 20. No person shall kindle any fire, or furnish the materials for any fire, to be made or kindled in any street, alley or vacant place, within the thickly populated portions of this City, unless for the purpose of boiling tar, pitch or oil, to be used in the construction or repair of some building or vessel.

Explosions in streets prohibited.

SEC. 21. No person shall fire or set off any squib, cracker, gunpowder or fireworks, or fire any cannon, gun or pistol, in any street, lane or alley, or in any yard, public or private, within the limits of the City, unless by a written permission from the Mayor, and such permission shall specify the object, and limit the time of such firing. This section shall not be extended to the prohibition of the usual demonstrations on the fourth of July, the twenty-second of

February, the first of January, and seventeenth day of March ; but no such permission from the Mayor shall be construed to incur on the part of the City, any liability for damages, by reason of any accident caused by such firing.

Buildings to have scuttles.

SEC. 22. Every building hereafter erected, more than one story in height, shall have a scuttle through the roof, and a convenient stairway leading to the same.

Gunpowder kept in buildings to be secured.

SEC. 23. There shall not be kept in any house, or its appurtenances, within the limits of the City, except in a magazine, to be approved by the Fire Marshal, at any one time, more than twenty-eight pounds of gunpowder, which shall be secured in metal canisters, with metal stoppers or covers ; and no one canister shall contain more than seven pounds. Any gunpowder kept contrary to this section, shall be seized by the Fire Marshal, and on conviction, before the Recorder's Court, of the party so keeping the same, it shall be forfeited to the use and benefit of the City, to be sold under the direction of the Mayor, and the offender shall be punished as hereinafter provided.

Gunpowder carried in streets to be secured.

SEC. 24. Persons carrying gunpowder through the City, to or from the magazine, shall secure the casks in which the same is contained, by good canvas, tow cloth, or leathern bags.

Fire Marshal may enter and examine buildings.

SEC. 25. The Fire Marshal shall have the right and power, and it is hereby made his duty, at such times as he may deem it necessary, between sunrise and sunset, to enter any and all buildings and enclosures, to discover whether the same are in a dangerous state, and if they are, to cause such to be put in a safe condition; he shall also have the power, and it is hereby made his duty, to see that all chimneys, hearths, fire-places, fire-arches, ovens, stove-pipes, boilers, kettles, or any structure or apparatus that may be dangerous in causing or promoting fires, are constructed in such a manner as to secure the greatest protection against fire; he shall also have power, and it is hereby made his duty, to require of the owner or occupant of any blacksmith's shop, furnace, foundry, or other manufactory, to erect, alter, or reconstruct his chimney, so as to prevent sparks from passing into the open air; every person who shall neglect, for forty-eight hours after being notified, in writing, or otherwise, by the Fire Marshal, to comply with the requirements provided herein, shall be punished as hereinafter provided.

Fire Marshal, Marshal, and Constables, to make complaints.

SEC. 26. It shall be the duty of the Fire Marshal, Marshal, and Constables of the City, to make complaint for any violation of the provisions of this Ordinance, and their neglect or refusal to do so, shall be sufficient cause for their removal from office.

Penalty.

SEC. 27. Any violation of, or failure to comply with the provisions or requirements of this Ordinance, shall be punished by a fine not to exceed three hundred dollars, and costs; and in the imposition of any such fine and costs, the Court may make a further sentence, that the offender be imprisoned in the Detroit House of Correction, or the County Jail, until such fine and cost be paid: *Provided, however,* That the term of such imprisonment shall not exceed the period of six months.

SEC. 28. Chapters thirty-seven and thirty-eight, of the Revised Ordinances of 1859, are hereby repealed.

SEC. 29. This Ordinance shall take effect from and after its passage.

RESOLUTION FOR THE EXTENSION OF THE FIRE LIMITS.

[Approved December 20, 1862.]

Fire Limits extended over certain lots of Williams' subdivision of Park Lot No. 4.

Resolved, That the provisions of the Ordinance relative to the preventing of fires, approved December 2d, 1861, be, and the same is hereby extended over the following lots: Lots from and including lot No. 158, to and including No. 180; also, over all lots from and including lot No. 197, to and including lot No. 221, of Williams' subdivision of Park lot No. 4, being all lots on the north and south sides of Montcalm street, west of John R street, and east of the alley running along said lots Nos. 158 and 221.

[Adopted by the Council December 16, 1862, together with the amendment of Alderman Hoek, "That contracts for building already made, should not be affected by the adoption of the above resolution."]

TITLE XI.

OF RESTRAINING ANIMALS.

CHAPTER LXXXII.

OF POUNDS AND POUND MASTERS.

[Ordinance approved September 20, 1861.]

SECTION 1. There shall be two or more public Pounds in the City of Detroit, to be located in such places as may be designated by the Common Council, and which shall be kept open between the first day of April and the first day of December, in each year. Number and location of Public Pounds.

SEC. 2. Pound Masters shall be appointed by the Common Council, on the first Tuesday in March, and shall enter upon the duties of their offices on the first day of April, and shall hold their offices for the period of eight months, and shall receive for their services the sum of forty-five dollars per month, but the present incumbents shall hold their offices till the second Tuesday in January, 1862. Appointment, term of office, and salary of Pound Master.

SEC. 3. Before entering upon the duties of their respective offices, the Pound Masters shall execute a bond to the City of Detroit, in the penal sum of five hundred dollars, with two sureties, conditioned as prescribed in sections twenty-eight and twenty-nine, of chapter two, of the Revised Charter of 1861, and subscribe the oath of office prescribed in section fifteen, of the same chapter. The bond and oath shall be filed in the office of the City Clerk. Bond and oath.

Horses, etc., shall not run at large.

SEC. 4. No horse, ass, mule, swine, sheep, goat, or other cattle, and no geese or domestic fowls, shall run at large within the limits of the City of Detroit.

Who may take up stray animals.

SEC. 5. It is hereby made the duty of the Pound Masters, Marshals, Assistant Marshals, Policemen, Constables, and Public Watchmen, and it shall be lawful for any other person above the age of eighteen years, to take up and convey to one of the public Pounds, any animal or domestic fowl which may be found running at large within the City limits; and for such service, the person performing it shall receive from the City Treasury the following compensation:

Fees for taking up animals.

For taking to a Pound any horse, ass, mule or swine, one dollar a head; any cattle, fifty cents a head; for any sheep or goat, twenty-five cents; for any goose, or other domestic fowl, ten cents. [*As amended by Ordinance approved April* 23, 1863.]

Pound Masters to receive stray animals.

SEC. 6. The Pound Masters shall receive, keep, and feed any animal or fowl which may be brought to the Pound.

Pound Masters to keep record.

SEC. 7. The Pound Masters shall record, in a book to be kept for that purpose, and which shall at all times be open for public inspection, the time when any animal or fowl was received. He shall also keep a record of all sales, and the amount for which each animal and fowl was sold, and the amounts paid for bringing animals or fowls to the Pound.

Sale of impounded animals.

SEC. 8. The Pound Masters shall, on Saturday of each week, at the public Pounds, sell at public auction any horse, ass, ox, or cow, which has been impounded therein for a period of six days, and all other animals and fowls which have been impounded therein for a period of three days, and are unclaimed, or whose owners refuse to pay the fees hereinafter provided. Notice of such sale shall be given at least three days prior thereto, and shall contain a description, as near as may be, of the animal or fowl to be sold, and shall be posted in conspicuous positions in the three following places, to wit: At the City Hall, the County Court House, and the Pound where such sale is to be held.

Proceeds of sales to be paid into City Treasury.

SEC. 9. The proceeds arising from the sale of any animal or fowl, and all fees received by the Pound Masters, shall, on Saturday of each week, be paid into the City Treasury, and shall constitute a separate fund, to be disposed of as provided in section ten.

SEC. 10. After deducting all lawful fees and costs, the money paid into the Treasury, as provided in the last section, shall be delivered to the former owner of such animal or fowl, on satisfactory proof to the Treasurer that he or she was such owner: *Provided, however,* That all money deposited, as aforesaid, which may remain unclaimed for the period of one year, shall be transferred and credited by the Treasurer to the Sinking Fund.

Surplus to be paid to owners of animals.

SEC. 11. Pound Masters shall demand and receive the following fees for the benefit of the City of Detroit: For receiving and discharging, or selling any horse, ass, mule, swine or ox, two dollars; any calf, cow, sheep or goat, one dollar; for keeping and feeding any horse, ass, mule, swine or ox, one dollar a day; any sheep, goat, cow or calf, twenty-five cents a day; for receiving and discharging any goose or fowl, ten cents, and for keeping any domestic fowl, ten cents a day: *Provided,* When animals or fowls are redeemed the same day on which they are impounded, the Pound Master shall demand and receive the compensation for one day's keeping and feeding. The Controller shall purchase all necessary supplies for the sustenance of all animals and fowls impounded, upon the order of the Pound Master. [*As amended by Ordinance approved April* 23, 1863.]

Fees of Pound Masters.

SEC. 12. The Pound Masters shall, on Saturday of each week, report, under oath, in writing, to the City Controller, giving a detailed statement of the animals and fowls impounded since their last report, the number of animals and fowls claimed and sold, and the amount of money received by reason of fees and sales, and the quantity of grain and hay used for the Pound, and the amount paid into the City Treasury, since their last report.

Pound Masters to make report.

SEC. 13. No person shall hinder, delay, or interfere with any one who is driving or carrying any animal or fowl to the public Pound.

Resistance to persons taking up animals prohibited.

SEC. 14. No person shall break, or attempt to break, or assist in breaking, into any Pound.

Breaking into Pounds prohibited.

SEC. 15. Pound keepers shall possess and exercise the powers and duties of Policemen, for the preservation of the public peace.

Pound Keepers to have powers of policemen.

SEC. 16. No person shall take up, drive or carry to the public Pound, any animal or fowl not legally liable to be impounded therein.

Illegal impounding prohibited.

Complaints against Pound Masters.

Sec. 17. All complaints against the Pound Masters shall be in writing, and be investigated by the Committee on Pounds. The complaint, and the testimony taken before the Committee, with their opinion thereon, shall be reported to the Mayor, who shall take such action as the facts warrant.

Pound Masters may be removed.

Sec. 18. The Pound Masters shall not receive any other compensation than that herein provided. They may be removed at any time by the Mayor.

Animals escaping from Pounds may be retaken.

Sec. 19. If any animal or fowl, that may have been lawfully impounded, shall escape, or be rescued, any Pound Master, Marshal, Assistant Marshal, Constable, or Policeman, may, within seven days thereafter, retake such animal or fowl, and the same may be held and sold, as if no escape or rescue had taken place.

Penalty.

Sec. 20. Any violation of the provisions of this Ordinance, shall be punished by a fine not to exceed one hundred dollars, and costs; and in the imposition of any fine and costs, the Court may make a further sentence, that the offender be committed to the County Jail, or Detroit House of Correction, until the payment thereof, for any period of time not exceeding six months.

Sec. 21. Chapter fifty-seven, of the Revised Ordinances of 1859, and all Ordinances amendatory thereof, are hereby repealed.

Sec. 22. This Ordinance shall take effect from and after its passage.

CHAPTER LXXXIII.

OF POUND KEEPERS, FENCE VIEWERS, ETC.

[Chapter Fifty-eight of Compiled Ordinances of 1859.]

Duties of Pound Keepers.

Section 1. Pound Keepers shall have and exercise the same powers, duties and privileges, and be subject to the same restrictions, so far as the said powers, duties, privileges and restrictions are consistent with chapter fifty-seven of these Ordinances, and the laws of the State prescribe, relative to the keeper of a Public Pound.

Fence Viewers.

Sec. 2. The Overseers of Highways of said City shall have and exercise the same powers, duties and privileges, and be subject to the same restrictions and penalties, as the laws of this State prescribe relative to Fence Viewers.

SEC. 3. Every provision of the law of this State relative to Pound Keepers thereof, Fence Viewers, stray cattle or beasts in the Pound, is hereby adopted, and all violations of the same shall be prosecuted in the Recorder's Court of said City. Laws of this State applicable to Pounds may be enforced in Recorder's Court.

CHAPTER LXXXIV.

OF DOGS.

[Ordinance approved December 30, 1861.]

SECTION 1. Upon each dog in this City a tax of two dollars per annum shall be paid by its owner or possessor, to be levied and collected in the same manner as other City taxes, upon personal property. Tax on dogs.

SEC. 2. The owner or possessor of any dog, shall put around the neck of the same a collar, upon which shall be engraved, or marked, the name of the owner or possessor. Collars to be placed on dogs.

SEC. 3. Any person who shall suffer to be, or remain in or about the premises occupied by him or her, or to run at large, any dog not having a collar thereon, as required by section two of this Ordinance, may be punished as hereinafter provided. Dogs not to run at large without collars.

SEC. 4. Any dog found at large, not having a collar thereon, as herein required, may be impounded, as hereinafter provided. Dogs without collars may be impounded.

SEC. 5. It shall be the duty of the Marshal, Assistant Marshal, Constables, and such person or persons as may be authorized by the Common Council, and it shall be lawful for any persons, to take up and impound any dog found at large without a collar. Who shall take up and impound dogs without collars.

SEC. 6. Any person who shall permit or suffer his or her dog to be at large between the first day of May and the first day of October, without a good and sufficient muzzle, rendering it impossible for such dog to bite or snap, shall be punished as hereinafter provided. Dogs not to run at large without muzzles.

SEC. 7. It shall be the duty of the Marshal, Assistant Marshal, Constables, and such person or persons as may be authorized Who shall take up and impound dogs without muzzles.

by the Common Council, and it shall be lawful for any person, to take up and impound any dog found at large between the first day of May and the first day of October, without a good and sufficient muzzle, rendering it impossible for such dog to bite or snap.

Dog-pound.

SEC. 8. The Common Council shall provide a suitable place to be used as a dog pound, in which all dogs found running at large, contrary to the provisions of this Ordinance, shall be impounded. Such pound shall be provided with a suitable vat or basin, in which all dogs unreclaimed, as provided in the next section, shall be drowned.

Unclaimed dogs to be drowned.

SEC. 9. At the setting of the sun, on each day, all dogs which have been twenty-four hours impounded, under the provisions of this Ordinance, and unreclaimed, shall be drowned, and their bodies buried by the City Scavenger, at the expense of the City.

Pound Master to have control of Dog-pound.

Dogs may be reclaimed on payment of fee.

SEC. 10. The Pound Master of the Pound where the dog pound is located, shall have charge and control of the same; and the owner may reclaim any dog impounded, on paying to said Pound Master, for the benefit of the City, the sum of one dollar.

Pound Master to make report and pay over moneys.

SEC. 11. The Pound Master shall, on Saturday in each week, pay into the City Treasury all moneys by him received under this Ordinance, and shall at the same time report, under oath, to the City Collector, the number of dogs impounded since his last report, the number reclaimed, the number drowned, and the amount of fees received.

Vicious dogs to be muzzled.

SEC. 12. If any owner or possessor of a fierce or vicious dog shall permit the same to go at large, without being provided with a good and sufficient muzzle, rendering it impossible for such dog to bite or snap, he or she shall be punished as hereinafter provided.

Female dogs shall not run at large.

SEC. 13. Any owner or possessor of a female dog, who shall allow the same to run at large while in heat, shall be punished as hereinafter provided, and it shall be the duty of the Marshal and his assistants to cause any female dog, so running at large, to be slain.

Penalty.

SEC. 14. Any person violating or failing to comply with the provisions of this Ordinance, shall be punished by a fine not to exceed one hundred dollars, and costs; and in the imposition of any such fine and costs, the Court may make a further sentence, that the offenders be imprisoned in the Detroit House of Correction until the payment thereof, for any term not exceeding six months.

SEC. 15. Chapter fifty-nine, of the Revised Ordinances of 1859, is hereby repealed, and all other Ordinances, with provisions inconsistent with the provisions of this, are hereby repealed.

SEC. 16. This Ordinance shall take effect from and after its passage.

TITLE XII.

OF HACKS, DRAYS, AND PORTERS.

CHAPTER LXXXV.

OF PUBLIC CARRIAGES.

[Ordinance approved August 2, 1861.]

Carriages, etc., not to be kept without license.

SECTION 1. No person shall keep for hire, within the limits of the City of Detroit, any public carriage, cab, hackney coach, omnibus, or other vehicle, without a license therefor from the Mayor.

Conditions of license.

SEC. 2. The Mayor is hereby authorized to grant licenses, for the purpose aforesaid, to any resident of the City of Detroit, and a citizen of the United States, of the age of twenty-one years or upwards, of good moral character, upon his paying into the City Treasury the sum of five dollars, for each carriage, cab, hackney coach, omnibus, or other vehicle, to be kept, as aforesaid, for a public conveyance, and executing a bond to the City of Detroit, in the penal sum of one hundred dollars, with sureties, conditioned as provided in power sixty-three, of chapter five, of the City Charter. [*As amended by Ordinance approved November* 24, 1862.]

Carriage drivers must be licensed.

SEC. 3. No person shall drive, or be permitted to drive, any public carriage, cab, hackney coach, omnibus, or other public vehicle, without being licensed as a public driver by the Mayor.

Conditions of license. Fee and bond.

SEC. 4. The Mayor is hereby authorized to grant licenses to residents of Detroit, of the age of twenty-one years and upwards, of good moral character, to act as drivers of public carriages, cabs, hackney coaches, omnibuses, or other vehicles, on the person applying for such license paying into the City Treasury the sum of one dollar, and executing a bond to the City of Detroit, in the penal sum of fifty dollars, with sureties, conditioned as prescribed in power sixty-three, of chapter five, of the City Charter.

Carriages to be provided with lamps and numbered.

SEC. 5. Every conveyance licensed under this Ordinance, when driven or used at night, shall be provided with two lighted lamps, with plain glass fronts and sides, and having the number of the license of each conveyance painted in legible characters thereon, to be placed in conspicuous places on the outside of such conveyance, in such a manner that the same may be distinctly seen and read when the conveyance is standing or in motion.

Persons licensed, to keep a good carriage and horses.

SEC. 6. Every person licensed under this Ordinance to keep a public conveyance, shall, at all times, keep a good and sufficient carriage and horses.

Carriage drivers shall not direct and safe route, etc.

Carriages to be driven by most quick and direct route, etc.

SEC. 7. No owner or driver of any public conveyance, while waiting for employment, shall refuse or neglect, when applied to, to convey any person or persons to any place or places within the City of Detroit; and on the person or persons being placed in such conveyance, the same shall be driven by the most direct and safe route, to the place to which such person or persons wish to go, and not elsewhere; and no driver or owner of any conveyance, except omnibusses, shall, without the consent of the person or persons therein, or of the person who first engaged such conveyance, place therein any other person or persons.

Public conveyances not to stand in streets.

Disorderly conduct prohibited.

SEC. 8. No owner or driver of any public conveyance shall suffer the same to remain in any street, square, lane or alley, without some proper person to take care of the same. And no owner or driver of any public conveyance, while waiting for employment on any street or dock, shall snap or flourish his whip, or be guilty of any rude or boisterous conduct or language.

Travel on streets, etc., not to be obstructed.

SEC. 9. Every driver of any public conveyance, while the same is waiting for employment, shall remain on or near to the same, and shall so keep his carriage and horses, as that the same shall not obstruct the travel on any street, avenue or cross-walk.

Unlicensed persons shall not procure passengers, etc.

SEC. 10. No person, unless licensed as an owner or driver, as herein provided, shall procure passengers for, or charge or receive any fare for any public conveyance; and not more than one licensed person shall take charge of, or ride on or in any such conveyance.

Rates of carriage hire.

SEC. 11. The drivers or owners of public conveyances may demand and receive, for conveying passengers, the following rates or prices of fare, and no more, to-wit:

Where the time occupied does not exceed half an hour, twenty-five cents per ride for each passenger; and where the time occupied is more than half, and less than one hour, fifty cents per ride for each passenger.

Children between two and ten years of age, when accompanied by their parents or guardians, shall be charged half fare; and children under two years of age, shall be carried free of charge.

For the use of any public conveyance by the hour, for not more than four persons, and with the privilege of going from place to place, and stopping as often as required, one dollar per hour for the first hour, and seventy-five cents for each additional hour, and for fractional hours, at the rate of seventy-five cents per hour; and for each additional passenger, twenty-five cents. For the use, by the day, of such conveyance, five dollars per day. For each trunk, ten cents; but no charge shall be made for any bag, valise or bundle, weighing less than fifty pounds.

When a public conveyance is used between the hours of 11 P. M. and 5 A. M., it shall be lawful to demand and receive, for the same services, one-half more than the rates prescribed above. Any disagreement as to time and rates, shall be determined by the Mayor.

Name of owner and number of license to be posted in public carriages.

SEC. 12. There shall be fixed in every conveyance, licensed under this Ordinance, and in such a manner as to be conveniently read by any person in the same, a card containing the name of the owner of such conveyance, the number of his license, and the whole of section eleven of this Ordinance, printed in plain, legible characters. The said card shall be furnished by the City of Detroit, and be given to any licensed owner or driver who may apply for the same. Any driver who shall drive a conveyance, without such a card being placed therein, and any owner who shall neglect to place such a card in his conveyance, shall be punished as hereinafter provided.

SEC. 13. This Ordinance shall apply to any carriage which may at any time be placed on a public stand, for public hire, and to all omnibuses or carriages kept by hotel keepers, for the purpose of conveying passengers, for hire, to and from steamboats and railroad depots, or other places, in said City. Ordinance to apply to hotel carriages, omnibuses, etc.

SEC. 14. Any violation of, or failure to comply with the provisions of this Ordinance, shall be punished by a fine not to exceed one hundred dollars, and costs; and in the imposition of any such fine and costs, the Court may make a further sentence, that in default of the payment thereof, within a time to be fixed in such sentence, the offender be committed to the County Jail, or Detroit House of Correction, for any period of time not exceeding six months. Penalty.

SEC. 15. This Ordinance shall take effect from and after its passage.

CHAPTER LXXXVI.

OF DRAYS.

[Ordinance approved September 5, 1861.]

SECTION 1. Every cart, truck, wagon, dray, or other vehicle having two or more wheels, and drawn by one or more horses or other animals, which shall be kept, used, driven or employed for the transportation or conveyance of anything whatsoever, from place to place, within the City of Detroit, for hire, shall be deemed a "public dray," within the meaning of this Ordinance; and no person shall hire or keep for hire any such public dray, without a license therefor from the Mayor, as hereinafter provided. Drays, etc., to be licensed.

SEC. 2. The Mayor is hereby authorized to grant licenses to any resident of the City of Detroit, and who is a citizen of the United States, to keep a public dray, on his paying into the City treasury the sum specified in section three of this Ordinance, and his executing a bond to the City of Detroit, in the penal sum of fifty dollars, with one or more sureties, conditioned for a faithful observance of the Charter and Ordinances of the City. [*As amended by Ordinance approved September* 28, 1863.] Conditions of license. Bond.

SEC. 3. The person applying for a license for a dray designed License fee.

24

to carry twenty-five hundred pounds or over, shall pay the sum of ten dollars; and for all other drays, the sum of one dollar.

Drays to be numbered.

SEC. 4. Every person, licensed as herein provided, shall cause the number of his license to be painted and kept conspicuously, in plain, legible figures, at least two inches long, upon each side of his dray.

Compensation for drayage.

SEC. 5. The owner or driver of a licensed dray, shall be entitled to demand and receive the following compensation, and no more: For removing or transporting furniture a distance of not exceeding one mile, fifty cents per load, and ten cents for each additional mile; for conveying any article a distance not exceeding one mile, twenty-five cents, and ten cents for each additional mile. All disputes and disagreements as to distance or rates of compensation, between draymen and persons employing them, shall be determined by the Mayor. [*As amended by Ordinance approved April* 2, 1863.]

Deceit or misrepresentation by draymen prohibited.

SEC. 6. No drayman shall be guilty of any deceit or misrepresentation in the execution of his duties.

Cruelty to dray-horses prohibited.

SEC. 7. No drayman shall cruelly beat or torture any horse or other animal, whether belonging to himself or another.

Tire of drays.

SEC. 8. The iron tire around the wheel of a dray designed to carry twenty-five hundred pounds or more, shall not be less than three inches in breadth, and the nails with which the tire is nailed or fastened to the wheel, shall be sunk into the iron or tire, so that the nails shall not project beyond the surface thereof.

Draymen shall not refuse employment.

SEC. 9. No public drayman shall refuse to be employed, unless otherwise actually engaged; nor shall any public drayman neglect or refuse to carry such a load as can be safely and conveniently stored on his dray, and drawn by his horse or horses, mule or mules.

Compensation to be paid immediately.

SEC. 10. A drayman shall be entitled to receive the compensation provided in this Ordinance immediately on the transportation of his load, and, unless so paid, he may retain the articles or things so transported until the matter is determined by the Mayor, whose decision shall be binding on both parties.

Drays not to be driven on sidewalks, etc.

SEC. 11. No drayman or person having a dray in charge, shall drive or back the same on any sidewalk, or stop the same on any cross-walk, so as to obstruct or hinder travel, or place the same crosswise of any street, except in loading and unloading, and not then for a greater length of time than is necessary for such purpose.

SEC. 12. It shall not be lawful for any drayman or other person having charge of a dray, to be away from such dray while the same is moving or passing along any street or avenue; and draymen and persons having charge of drays, shall, while waiting for employment, be on or near their drays; and they shall not snap or flourish their whips, or use any rude or boisterous talk or conversation, so as to be an annoyance to persons passing the street.

Draymen to be near their drays.

Disorderly conduct prohibited.

SEC. 13. It shall be the duty of the Marshal and his Assistant to make complaint for any violation of the provisions of this Ordinance.

Complaints against draymen.

SEC. 14. Chapter sixty-three, of the Revised Ordinances of 1859, and all Ordinances and parts of Ordinances amendatory thereof, are hereby repealed.

SEC. 15. Any violation of, or failure to comply with the provisions of this Ordinance, shall be punished by a fine not to exceed one hundred dollars, and costs; and in the imposition of any such fine and costs, the Court may make a further sentence, that the offender be committed to the County Jail or Detroit House of Correction until the payment thereof, for any period of time not exceeding six months.

Penalty.

SEC. 16. This Ordinance shall take effect from and after its passage.

CHAPTER LXXXVII.

OF STANDS OF PUBLIC CARRIAGES, DRAYS, ETC.

[Chapter Sixty-two of Compiled Ordinances of 1859.]

SECTION 1. Hereafter all hackney coaches, carriages, cabs, and other vehicles used for carrying passengers, plying for hire within the limits of the City, shall, while waiting for employment, occupy the following stands and no others, that is to say: The centre of Jefferson avenue, from a point fifteen feet easterly of the east line of Woodward avenue, to a point fifteen feet westerly of the west line of Bates street; the centre of Jefferson avenue, from a point fifteen feet westerly of the west line of Woodward avenue, to a point fifteen feet easterly of the east line of Griswold street; the centre of Wood-

Places where cabs, etc., to stand.

ward avenue, from a point fifteen feet northerly of the north line of Jefferson avenue, to a point fifteen feet southerly of the south line of Larned street; the centre of Woodward avenue, from a point fifteen feet southerly of the south line of Jefferson avenue, to a point fifteen feet northerly of the north line of Woodbridge street.

Stands for drays, etc.

SEC. 2. All drays, carts, wagons, and other vehicles used for the transportation of goods, merchandise and other wares, plying for hire within the limits of the City, shall, while waiting for employment, occupy the following stands and no others, that is to say: The centre of Jefferson avenue, between Griswold street and Third street; the centre of Jefferson avenue, between Bates street and Brush street; the centre of Woodward avenue, between Larned street and the Campus Martius; the centre of Woodward avenue, between Woodbridge street and the River: *Provided*, That none of the said vehicles shall stand within fifteen feet of any cross street.

Driver to remain on his vehicle.

SEC. 3. The driver of any carriage, cart or other vehicle mentioned in this Ordinance, shall, while waiting for employment as aforesaid, remain upon his said vehicle.

Vehicles to occupy centre of streets.

SEC. 4. The said vehicles, while occupying the stands aforesaid, shall stand in the centre of said streets, and in a line parallel with the course of said streets.

Penalty.

SEC. 5. Any person violating any of the provisions of this Ordinance, shall, for each offence, upon conviction before the Recorder's Court, forfeit and pay a fine of not more than fifty dollars, and costs of prosecution.

CHAPTER LXXXVIII.

OF PORTERS AND RUNNERS.

[Chapter Seventy of Compiled Ordinances of 1859.]

Porters and runners to be licensed.

SECTION 1. The Mayor of the City of Detroit, for the time being, shall have power, from time to time, to issue licenses, under his hand and seal, to so many and to such persons as he shall think proper, to carry on the business of public porters or runners for hotels, and all omnibus agents, omnibus drivers, and drivers of baggage, and all other persons when acting as porters or runners for hotels; and the Mayor or Recorder, or any three Aldermen of the City, shall have power to revoke all or any of such licenses.

SEC. 2. All such licenses shall expire on the first day of August next after the date thereof, and may be renewed on application of the holders thereof. When license to expire.

SEC. 3. For every such license shall be paid, by the person applying for the same, the sum of one dollar, and for every renewal, the same sum. Fees for license.

SEC. 4. No person shall act or engage in the business of a public porter or runner for any hotel, or as an omnibus agent, omnibus driver, or driver of baggage, acting as porters or runners for hotels, without being duly licensed as such by the Mayor, under a penalty not exceeding five dollars, in the discretion of the Court, and costs of prosecution, for every such offence. Persons not to act without license.

SEC. 5. Every public porter or runner, omnibus agent, omnibus driver and baggage driver, and every other person acting as runner for hotels, shall wear a badge on his hat, and in a conspicuous place on his body, on which shall be legibly and plainly engraved or printed, his name and the number of his license, under a penalty not to exceed five dollars, in the discretion of the Court, and the costs of prosecution, for each neglect of the provisions of this section. Porters and runners, etc., to wear a badge.

SEC. 6. Every public porter or runner, omnibus agent, omnibus driver or baggage driver, and every other person acting as porter or runner for hotels, shall have, on a card or a plate, printed or engraved, his name and the number of his license, and also the prices or rates of fare allowed by law for omnibuses, hackney coaches, etc., in legible characters, which shall be nailed on a conspicuous part of his carriage, omnibus, wagon, sleigh, wheelbarrow or hand cart, under a penalty not to exceed five dollars, in the discretion of the Court, and the costs of prosecution, for every violation of the provisions of this section. Porters, runners, etc., to have a card containing his name, etc., in carriage.

SEC. 7. Every person to whom such licenses shall be granted, shall first execute to the City of Detroit, a bond, with one or more sufficient sureties, to be approved by the Mayor, in the penalty of five hundred dollars, conditioned that he will conduct himself in a decent and orderly manner while acting as such porter, runner, omnibus agent, omnibus driver, or driver of baggage, when acting as porter or runner for hotels, and in all respects comply with the provisions of this Porters and runners to execute bonds.

Ordinance: *Provided, however,* That it shall be lawful for such sureties, or either of them, to vacate such bond by giving ten days notice, in writing, to the Mayor; and in such case, the said license shall be annulled and made void, unless other sureties are furnished as above provided.

Not to approach within twenty feet of boats and cars, when.

SEC. 8. No porter, runner, hackmen, draymen, City expressmen, omnibus agent, omnibus driver, driver of baggage, or other persons acting as porters or runners for hotels, so licensed as aforesaid, shall, on the arrival of any steamboat or railroad cars in the City of Detroit, for a period of fifteen minutes thereafter, go upon or approach within twenty feet of the wharf or depot where such steamboat or railroad cars have made fast or stopped running, or are about to make fast or stop running, unless such porter, runner, hackmen, draymen, City expressmen, omnibus agent, omnibus driver, or driver of baggage, be requested by a passenger to remove some trunk or other baggage from said wharf or depot, in which case it shall be lawful to go near, in or upon such steamboat or depot for such purpose, under a penalty not to exceed five dollars, in the discretion of the Court, and costs of prosecution, for every such offence. [*As amended by Ordinance approved July* 16, 1860.]

Punishment for acting without license.

SEC. 9. No person shall act as porter or runner, or omnibus agent, omnibus driver or baggage driver, when acting as runner or porter for any public house or hotel in the City of Detroit, without being duly licensed, according to the provisions of this Ordinance, under a penalty not to exceed twenty-five dollars, in the discretion of the Court, for every such offence.

When license forfeited.

SEC. 10. On conviction of any porter, runner, omnibus agent, omnibus driver, or baggage driver, or other person acting as porter or runner for any hotel or public house, licensed as aforesaid, before the Recorder's Court, of any violation of the provisions of this Ordinance, the Mayor or Recorder shall, in his discretion, be authorized, in addition to the fines hereinbefore provided, to vacate and annul any such license that may then be held by any such porter, runner, omnibus agent, omnibus driver or driver of baggage, and to declare the bond of such person forfeited.

When City Attorney to put bond in suit.

SEC. 11. On the forfeiture of the bond of any such porter, runner, omnibus agent, omnibus driver, driver of baggage or other person, as provided in the preceding section, it shall be the duty of the City Attorney to prosecute the principal and sureties named in such bond, for the benefit of the City.

TITLE XIII.

OF PLACES OF AMUSEMENT AND RECREATION.

CHAPTER LXXXIX.

OF BALL ALLEYS, BILLIARD TABLES, ETC.

[Ordinance approved July 3, 1861.]

Keepers of billiard tables and ball alleys must be licensed.

SECTION 1. No person shall keep a billiard table, nine or ten pin alley, without a license from the Mayor.

Who are deemed keepers of billiard tables.

SEC. 2. A keeper of a billiard table is one who owns, possesses or keeps a billiard table whereon others are permitted to play, and for which any money or its equivalent, or any check or counter in lieu of money, is paid or received.

Who are keepers of ball alleys.

SEC. 3. A keeper of a nine or ten pin alley is one who owns, possesses or keeps a ball alley on which persons are permitted to play, and for which money or its equivalent, or any check or counter in lieu of money, is paid or received.

License fee and bond.

SEC. 4. The Mayor is hereby authorized to grant a license to any person to keep a billiard table, nine or ten pin alley, on the payment of five dollars for each table or alley proposed to be kept by such person, and his executing a bond to the Corporation, in the sum of one hundred dollars, with one or more sufficient sureties, conditioned that such person will faithfully observe the Charter and Ordinances of the City.

Penalty.

SEC. 5. Any violation of the provisions of this Ordinance, shall be punished by a fine not to exceed one hundred dollars, and costs; and in the imposition of any such fine and costs, the Court may make a further sentence, that in default of the payment thereof, within a time to be fixed in such sentence, the offender be committed to the County Jail or Detroit House of Correction, for any period of time not exceeding six months.

SEC. 6. An Ordinance "relative to Ball Alleys, Billiard and other Tables," approved April 26, 1861, and all Ordinances and parts of Ordinances inconsistent with this Ordinance, are hereby repealed.

SEC. 7. This Ordinance shall take effect from and after its passage.

CHAPTER XC.

OF GAMING.

[Ordinance approved July 24, 1861.]

SECTION 1. No person shall manage, use or practice any game or device whatsoever, with intent to cheat or defraud another. Fraudulent gaming prohibited.

SEC. 2. No person shall play for money or other valuable thing, with cards, dice, tables, wheels of fortune, machines, billiards, nine or ten pins, or other instruments or devices whatsoever, in any hotel, grocery, eating or victualing house, store, boat, shop, tavern, saloon, beer hall, bar room, or other public or private building, or in any highway, street, lane, alley, public space or square, or elsewhere, within the City of Detroit. Gaming in hotels, streets etc., prohibited.

SEC. 3. No person shall let or rent any building to be used for gaming purposes. Renting buildings for gaming prohibited.

SEC. 4. No person shall keep any building, instrument, or means for gaming. Keeping buildings or instruments for gaming prohibited.

SEC. 5. Any instrument kept for the purpose of gaming for money, or other valuable thing, shall be destroyed by the Marshal or any Policeman of the City, under the direction of the Chief of Police, and the neglect or refusal to obey such an order, shall be deemed sufficient cause for removal from office. Instruments for gaming to be destroyed.

SEC. 6. No person shall keep, maintain, direct, or manage, or aid in the keeping, maintaining, directing, or managing, any lottery for the drawing or disposing of money, or any other property whatsoever. Lotteries prohibited.

25

SEC. 7. Chapters sixty-six, sixty-seven and sixty-eight, of the Revised Ordinances of 1859, are hereby repealed.

Penalty.

SEC. 8. Any violation of, or failure to comply with the provisions of this Ordinance, shall be punished by a fine not to exceed one hundred dollars, and costs; and in the imposition of any such fine and costs, the Court may make a further sentence, that in default of the payment thereof, within a time to be fixed in such sentence, the offender shall be committed to the County Jail, or Detroit House of Correction, for any period of time not exceeding six months.

SEC. 9. This Ordinance shall take effect from and after its passage.

CHAPTER XCI.

OF SHOWS.

[Ordinance approved June 12, 1861.]

Shows must be licensed.

SECTION 1. No person or persons, company or companies, shall make or exhibit, in said City, any circus, menagerie, play, game, or theatrical exhibition; or give any concert, vocal or instrumental; or exhibit any natural or artificial curiosity; or give any public entertainment or amusement of any kind, for which pay is demanded or received, without a license from the Mayor.

Mayor may grant licenses.

SEC. 2. The Mayor is hereby authorized to grant licenses for the purposes aforesaid, on the payment of such sum of money as may be previously determined upon by himself and the Committee on Licenses.

Ordinance not to apply to exhibitions of schools, paintings, etc.

SEC. 3. This Ordinance shall not extend to any exhibition by the pupils of any private or public school, or to any exhibition of painting, engraving, sculpture or fine art, executed by a citizen of Detroit, or to any concert or musical entertainment for the benefit of any Church or benevolent object.

Good order to be maintained in licensed shows.

SEC. 4. It shall be the duty of any person or company receiving a license, to keep good order in and about his or their place of amusement or exhibition; and for that purpose, to keep at his or their expense a sufficient Police force thereat.

SEC. 5. Any violation of this Ordinance, shall be punished by a fine not to exceed the sum of two hundred dollars, and by imprisonment in the County Jail or Detroit House of Correction, for a period not exceeding six months, or either, in the discretion of the Court; and in the imposition of a fine only, the Court may make a farther sentence, that the offender be imprisoned until such fine be paid; but for a time not exceeding that provided herein. Penalty.

SEC. 6. This Ordinance shall take effect immediately.

TITLE XIV.

OF THE SUPPORT OF THE POOR.

CHAPTER XCII.

OF PAUPERS AND THEIR SUPPORT.

[Chapter Seventy-two of Compiled Ordinances of 1859.]

Vessels not to land paupers.

SECTION 1. If any owner, captain, or master of a vessel, or other person, shall, by land or water, bring and leave within the limits of this City, any person or persons, poor, and unable to maintain themselves, they shall forthwith, or as soon as may be thereafter, transport the same back to the place whence they were taken, and shall provide all the necessary means of comfort and subsistence for such paupers, if requested by them, or by any citizen, until so transported.

Persons bringing paupers to support them.

SEC. 2. In case of refusal or neglect to provide for such paupers the necessary means of comfort and subsistence, according to the foregoing section, and any member of the Common Council, or Director of the Poor, shall make such provision, the same may be recovered back, and may form part of the judgment in a prosecution for a violation of this chapter.

Penalty.

SEC. 3. Any violation of the two preceding sections of this chapter, may be punished with a fine not exceeding fifty dollars, and costs of prosecution.

SEC. 4. The Director of the Poor for said City, shall have and exercise the same powers and duties, and be subject to the same liabilities and restrictions as the laws of this State prescribe relative to Directors of the Poor, in any township of this State; and the laws of this State relative to Township and County paupers, shall be observed with respect to such paupers in said City, and all suits and prosecutions, for violations of such laws, may be brought in the Recorder's Court of said City.

Powers and duties of Director of Poor.

TITLE XV.

OF STREET RAILWAYS.

CHAPTER XCIII.

ORDINANCE GRANTING PERMISSION TO CERTAIN PERSONS TO ESTABLISH AND LOCATE STREET RAILWAYS.

[Ordinance approved November 24, 1862.]

Preamble.

Whereas, CORNELIUS S. BUSHNELL, JOHN A. GRISWOLD, NEHEMIAH D. SPERRY, EBEN N. WILLCOX, their associates, successors and assigns, propose to organize, as a body politic and corporate, under a Charter from the Legislature of Michigan, or under the "Act to provide for the construction of Train Railways," approved February 13th, 1855, laws of 1855, page 338, and act or acts amendatory thereto, for the purpose of constructing and operating in and through the streets of the City of Detroit, City or Street Railways ; therefore,

Be it ordained by the Common Council of the City of Detroit:

Grant of Franchise to Eben N. Willcox and associates.

SECTION 1. That consent, permission and authority is hereby given, granted, and duly vested in EBEN N. WILLCOX, and his associates, who may be approved by the Council, their successors and assigns, organized into a Corporation, under the laws of the State of Michigan, as aforesaid, to lay a single or double track for a Railway, with all the necessary and convenient tracks for turnouts, side tracks and switches, in and along the course of the streets of, and bridges in, the City of Detroit, hereinafter mentioned, and the same to keep, maintain and use, and to operate thereon Railway Cars and Carriages, during all the term hereinafter specified and prescribed, and in the manner, and upon the conditions set forth in this Ordinance. [*As amended by Ordinance approved December* 27, 1862.]

SEC. 2. The said grantees are, by the provisions of this Ordinance, exclusively authorized to construct and operate Railways, as herein provided, on and through Jefferson, Michigan and Woodward avenues, Witherell, Gratiot, Grand River, and Brush or Beaubien streets; and from Jefferson avenue, through Brush or Beaubien streets, to Atwater street; and from Jefferson avenue, at its intersection with Woodbridge street, to Third street; up Third street, to Fort street; and through Fort street, to the western limits of the City; and through such other streets and avenues, in said City, as may, from time to time, be fixed and determined by vote of the Common Council of the said City of Detroit, and assented to, in writing, by said Corporation, organized as provided in section first of this Ordinance: *And provided,* The Corporation does not assent, in writing, within thirty days after the passage of said resolution of the Council, ordering the formation of new routes, then the Common Council may give the privilege to any other Company to build such route, and such other Company shall have the right to cross any track of rails already laid, at their own cost and expense: *Provided, always,* That the Railways on Grand River street, Gratiot street, and Michigan avenue, shall each run into and connect with the Woodward avenue Railways, in such direction that said Railways shall be continued down to, and form, each of them, one continuous route to Jefferson avenue: *Provided, always,* That said railroad down Gratiot street may be continued to Woodward avenue, through State street, or through Randolph street, and Monroe avenue and the Campus Martius, as the grantees or their assigns, under this Ordinance, may elect. [*As amended by Ordinance approved January* 12, 1863.] Routes.

SEC. 3. The Railways through all the streets shall be laid in the centre thereof, if on a single track, and if on a double track, the inside rail of each track shall be laid a sufficient distance from the centre of the street, to enable two cars to pass on opposite tracks, and leave a space between of at least eighteen inches, and the gauge of the track shall be at least four feet eight and one-half inches, and so as to accommodate the most common width of carriage wheels: Construction of Railway Tracks.

Provided, however, That where a double track shall not be laid in the first instance, and a second track shall afterwards be required, such second track may be laid upon either side of the first: *And provided further,* That in all streets which are not paved, or where plank roads are laid, the tracks of said Railways may be laid elsewhere than in the centre thereof, as may be most convenient, under the direction of the Common Council, and shall least obstruct the public travel thereon. When the grantees shall complete one track of the said railway, and place cars thereon for public use, they may at any time thereafter, within five years, build a second track, so that they do not interrupt the running of their cars on the first completed track: *Provided,* The consent of the Common Council is first obtained. [*As amended by Ordinance approved January* 12, 1863.]

Construction of Railway Tracks.

SEC. 4. The track of said Railways shall be laid of such rails as shall least obstruct the free passage of vehicles or carriages over the same; and the upper surface of the rails shall be laid flush with the surface of the streets, and shall conform to the grades thereof, as now established, or as they shall, from time to time, be re-established or altered; and in case of grading, paving, or otherwise, if it be necessary to relay said rails, the same shall be done at the expense of the grantees; and in all streets, or parts of streets, which are not paved, the rails shall be laid in such manner as shall least interfere with the public travel thereon, and as shall be authorized and approved by the City Surveyor. The grantees, and their assigns, shall be required to keep the surface of the streets, inside the rails, and for two feet four inches outside thereof, in good order and repair, and all snow, ice, dirt and filth, cleared and removed from the same, at the expense of the grantees: *Provided, however,* That upon the paved portions of said streets, the materials for re-paving shall be supplied at the expense of the City. [*As amended by Ordinance approved January* 12, 1863.]

Routes to commence at Campus Martius, etc,

SEC. 5. The routes of all said Railways shall commence in the Woodward avenue road, at Campus Martius; from thence, running on their several courses, to the outer limits of the City: *Provided,* That in collecting fare, those portions between Atwater, through Brush or Beaubien streets, and through Woodward avenue to Jefferson avenue, and between Brush or Beaubien and Third streets, on Jefferson avenue and Woodbridge street, shall be respectively deemed to belong to either of the above routes, any portion of which is then being traveled continuously by any one passenger at the same time, and shall pay only one fare. [*As amended by Ordinance approved January* 12, 1863.]

SEC. 6. Said Railway on Woodward avenue, or Witherell street, to Park lot sixty-two (62,) through Jefferson avenue to the eastern limits, and through Jefferson avenue to Woodbridge, through Woodbridge to Third, and up Third to Fort, and through Fort street to the western limits of the City, shall be completed within six months from the thirty-first day of March, A. D. 1863, and through Gratiot street to the easterly line of the B. Chapaton Farm, shall be completed within three years from and after the thirty-first day of March, A. D. 1863; and through Grand River to the easterly line of the Woodbridge Farm; through Michigan avenue to Thompson street, shall be completed within two years from and after the thirty-first of March, A. D. 1863; and the remainder thereof, at such times as the public necessity may require: *Provided,* That no such Railway shall be required to be laid through any part of such routes, which shall not be worked up to the established grade thereof, until the City shall have completed such work **Railway, on certain routes, to be completed within a limited time.**

SEC. 7. The cars to be used on said Railways shall be drawn by animals only, at a speed not exceeding the rate of six miles per hour, and shall be run as often as public convenience shall require, and the Common Council shall prescribe: *Provided, always,* That said Council will not require them to run regular cars oftener than once in twenty minutes during fourteen hours every day, from the fifteenth day of April to the fifteenth day of October, and twelve hours every day from the fifteenth day of October to the fifteenth day of April, and the cars in use upon said Railways shall be run for no other purpose than to transport passengers and their ordinary baggage, and the cars and carriages for that purpose shall be of the best style in use on such Railways: *Provided,* That other cars and carriages may be used for cleaning said railway tracks from obstructions by snow, or otherwise. **Cars and speed**

SEC. 8. The rate of fare for any distance shall not exceed five cents in any one car, or on any one route named in this Ordinance, except where cars or carriages shall be chartered for specific pur- **Rates of Fare.**

poses: *Provided*, Cars so chartered shall not be considered regular cars, within the meaning of the preceding section.

Cars, drawn in same direction, not to approach each other within 100 feet.

SEC. 9. Cars drawn in the same direction shall not approach each other within a distance of one hundred feet, except in cases of accident or at stations, or for the purpose of connecting two cars together.

Cars not to stop on cross-walks, etc.

SEC. 10. No car shall be allowed to stop on a cross-walk, or in front of any intersecting street, except to avoid collision or prevent danger to persons or property in the street

Manner of stopping cars.

SEC. 11. When the Conductor of any car is required to stop at the intersection of streets, to receive or leave passengers, the cars shall be stopped so as to leave the rear platform slightly over the crossing.

Qualifications and duties of Conductors, Agents and Drivers.

SEC. 12. The grantees, or their assigns, shall employ careful, sober, and prudent Agents, Conductors and Drivers, to take charge of their cars while on the road, and it shall be the duty of all such Agents, Conductors, and Drivers, to keep vigilant watch for all trains, carriages, or persons on foot, and especially children, either upon the track or moving towards it; at the first appearance of danger to such teams, carriages, footmen, or children, or other obstructions, the cars shall be stopped in the shortest time and space possible.

Persons not to leave cars while in motion.

SEC. 13. Conductors shall not allow ladies or children to enter or leave the cars while in motion.

Names of principal squares and streets to be announced by Conductors.

SEC. 14. Conductors shall announce to the passengers the names of the principal squares and streets, as the cars reach them.

Cars to be entitled to the track.

SEC. 15. The cars shall, at all times, be entitled to the track, and any vehicles upon the track of said Railways, shall turn out when any car comes up, so as to leave the track unobstructed, and the drivers of any vehicle refusing to do so, shall be liable to a fine not exceeding five dollars, on conviction before the Recorder's Court, of said City of Detroit, and costs of prosecution shall not be at the expense of the City.

Penalty for obstructing cars.

Signal lights.

SEC. 16. The cars, after sunset, shall be provided with colored signal lights, a red light in front, and a green light in rear.

Railways to be subject to rights to lay down gas and water pipes.

SEC. 17. Wherever gas or water pipes, or sewers, are now laid in the streets herein specified, and through which Railways are to pass, the said Railways must be laid down and maintained subject to the right now in the City, and the Gas Company, and the Sewer and Water Commissioners, to take up or remove said pipes or sewers, in such a manner as not unnecessarily to damage or injure said Railways or their use, without claim against said City, Gas Company, or Water or Sewer Commissioners; and the Common Council expressly reserves to itself the right hereafter to lay down, or to permit to be laid down, and repaired, in said streets, gas or water pipes, and sewers, whenever the public or private convenience may require; the said gas or water companies, or private individuals, who shall take up pavement for the purposes aforesaid, being always required, as by the present City Ordinance, to restore the pavement in the streets to its former condition.

Franchise forfeited by neglect to complete Railways.

SEC. 18. If said grantees, or their assigns, shall fail to complete any of the aforesaid Railways, within the time prescribed by this Ordinance, then the rights and privileges herein granted shall be forfeited as to any and every route herein established, which is not commenced and completed in the time herein prescribed, and the City shall be entitled to take possession thereof, provided the Council does not extend the time: *Provided,* That if said grantees shall be delayed by the order or injunction of any Court, and said order or injunction shall not be obtained at the instance, or by the contrivance of said grantees, then the time of such delay shall be excluded from the time of completion prescribed in this Ordinance. [*As amended by Ordinance approved December* 27, 1862.]

Common Council may make rules and regulations.

SEC. 19. It is hereby reserved to the Common Council of the City of Detroit, the right to make such further rules, orders or regulations, as may, from time to time, be deemed necessary to protect the interests, safety, welfare, or accommodation of the public, in relation to said Railways.

Franchise limited to thirty years.

SEC. 20. The powers and privileges conferred by the provisions of this Ordinance, shall be limited to thirty years from and after the date of its passage.

Deposit of forfeit.

SEC. 21. Said grantees shall, on or before the tenth day of January, A. D. 1863, deposit with the Controller of said City the sum of five thousand dollars in money, or in United States stocks, or in Treasury notes, bearing seven and three-tenths per cent. interest, which deposit shall be security for the completion, by said grantees, of the lines of Railway which they are required to construct and complete, on or before the first day of October, A. D. 1863; and if these said Railways shall not then be completed, the sum so deposited shall be forfeited to the City: *Provided, however*, That if said grantees, or their assigns, cannot procure the requisite amount of rail of the Philadelphia, or other suitable pattern, to build said Railways, within the time specified, with a suitable and competent force, then the time shall be extended until such rail can be obtained, and laid with a suitable and competent force: *And provided further*, That the time for the completion of said roads be extended not to exceed nine months, upon good and sufficient reasons being given, that the iron rail cannot be procured. [*As amended by Ordinance approved January* 12, 1863.]

Tax on cars.

SEC. 22. The said grantees, and their assigns, shall pay to the Treasurer of the City of Detroit, annually, fifteen dollars on each and every passenger, or other car, excepting only those cars used for cleaning the track on said roads, to be collected as a license, for the use of the City, after the term of five years from and after this date.

When franchise shall be vested in grantees.

SEC. 23. Whenever the said grantees, their successors or assigns, shall have organized themselves into a body politic and corporate, under the said act of the Legislature of the State of Michigan, or Charter thereof, all the powers and privileges granted and conferred to and upon them, by this Ordinance, shall be given, granted and duly vested in said Corporation, without any further action, consent, permission or authority of the Common Council, whatever.

SEC. 24. All Ordinances, or parts of Ordinances, heretofore made, ordained and passed, inconsistent with the provisions of this Ordinance, are hereby repealed.

CHAPTER XCIV.

ORDINANCE REGULATING THE CONSTRUCTION AND USE OF THE TRACKS OF THE DETROIT CITY RAILWAY.

[Ordinance approved August 19, 1863.]

Permission to build Railway on Michigan avenue, instead of Third street and Fort street.

SECTION 1. Permission is hereby given to the Detroit Railway to build its road and track on Michigan avenue, from Woodward avenue to Fourth street, and on Gratiot street, from Woodward avenue to Russell street, instead and in lieu of upon Third street and Fort street, as provided by the Ordinance approved November 24, 1862, and the amendments thereto, (and such building on Michigan avenue and Gratiot street, together with Jefferson and Woodward avenues, shall be deemed a compliance with the condition of deposit mentioned in section twenty-one, of said Ordinance.)

Railway on Fort street to be completed in limited time.

SEC. 2. As a condition of the acceptance of this permission, the said Detroit City Railway may and shall complete its road and track on Fort street, Michigan avenue, and Gratiot street, as provided by the aforesaid Ordinances, by the first day of October, 1864; and a failure to complete the same by that time, shall be regarded as a forfeiture of the route or routes not so completed.

Construction of track on Woodward avenue, etc.

SEC. 3. On Woodward avenue, Gratiot street and Michigan avenue, beyond the pavement, the said Railway may build its track a sufficient distance from the plank road in those streets, respectively, to leave the grade track of said plank road clear, and allow teams and vehicles to pass between said track and said plank road; and upon Michigan avenue and Gratiot street, beyond the pavement, said Railway may construct its track with the "T" rail, which is used for street railways, and weighs not less than thirty-three pounds to the yard.

Id. on Third street.

SEC. 4. The said Railway is hereby authorized to extend its track, and run its cars, through Third street, southerly from Woodbridge street, to the dock, and to lay the said track on such part of said street, westerly of the center, as they shall agree upon with the Michigan Central Railroad Company.

Routes.

SEC. 5. The tracks upon Jefferson avenue, Woodward avenue, Michigan avenue and Gratiot street, shall each be considered and run as one route, and subject its passengers to the payment of a single fare each: *Provided, however,* That all cars running north of Jefferson avenue shall run to and from Jefferson avenue, and that portion of Woodward avenue between Jefferson avenue and the routes intersecting Woodward avenue, shall be considered as making a portion of each of said routes, respectively.

Permission to build Railway on Elmwood avenue and Mount Elliott avenue.

SEC. 6. The Detroit City Railway, upon obtaining the consent of the owners of real estate on Elmwood avenue, or such real estate owners as are affected thereby, may, and is hereby authorized to build a track, from its present track on Jefferson avenue, to Elmwood Cemetery, and run its cars thereon at such times as will accommodate the public: *Provided, however,* No person shall be charged more than one cent either way, on this track; and said Railway are also authorized to run a track and their cars to Mount Elliott Cemetery, along Mount Elliott avenue, and charge the same rate of fare as to the said Elmwood Cemetery.

CHAPTER XCV.

ORDINANCE IN REGARD TO THE DETROIT CITY RAILWAY.

[Ordinance approved October 7, 1863.]

Permission to build Railway on Randolph street.

SECTION 1. The Detroit City Railway is hereby authorized to build its track, and run its cars, from its track on Jefferson avenue, upon and along Randolph street southerly to Atwater street, and thence along Atwater street easterly to Brush street; and, as said track approaches the Detroit and Milwaukee depot, the said Railway may turn the same on to the southerly side of said Atwater street, so as to run said cars up to the sidewalk in front of the office buildings of the Detroit and Milwaukee Railway Company.

TITLE XVI.

MISCELLANEOUS.

CHAPTER XCVI.

EXTENDING THE LIMITS OF THE THIRD WARD.

[Chapter Eighty-three of Compiled Ordinances of 1859.]

SECTION 1. The limits of the Third Ward of said City shall be, and hereby are extended to Gratiot street, by adding to said Third Ward, and incorporating as part of the same, all that portion of the Sixth Ward in said City bounded as follows, to wit: On the south by Croghan street, on the west by Randolph street, on the north by Gratiot street, and on the east by St. Antoine street, and by a line on the course of St. Antoine street, if extended from Clinton street to Gratiot street. Boundaries.

SEC. 2. Nothing in this Ordinance contained shall be construed to affect the basis of taxation in the Sixth or in the Third Ward, aforesaid, during the present year, or to affect or remove from office any officer continued in office by the Revised Charter of the present year, during the time for which said person is so continued in office. Ordinance not to affect basis of taxation.

CHAPTER XCVII.

OF LICENSES.

[Ordinance approved July 24, 1861.]

Licenses to be for one year, unless otherwise provided, and to expire on the first of August.

SECTION 1. In all cases, unless otherwise provided, where, by Ordinance or Resolution of the Common Council, a sum of money is fixed for the payment of a license, it shall be understood to be for the period of one year, and, except as provided in the next section, all licenses shall expire on the first day of August next after the date thereof.

Mayor may grant licenses for three months.

SEC 2. For good cause shown, the Mayor is hereby authorized to grant licenses, in all cases where the price of the licenses amounts to five dollars or more, for any period not less than three months, on the payment of a sum proportioned to the time for which any such license is granted. The amount required to be paid for any license so issued, shall be paid to and collected by the City Collector, and the receipt of such Collector shall be taken and received by the Mayor as evidence of the payment of the same. [*As amended by Ordinance approved October* 10, 1863.]

Licenses revocable, but not assignable.

SEC. 3. All licenses shall be revocable at the pleasure of the Mayor or Common Council, but no license granted under any Ordinance or Resolution of the Common Council, shall be assignable; but for the promotion of the ends of justice, the Mayor is hereby authorized, with the consent of the parties, to transfer a license from one person to another, on the transferee executing a bond to the Corporation, as provided in the Charter and Ordinances of the City for persons receiving licenses.

Mayor may transfer licenses.

Licenses to be signed by Mayor, and countersigned by City Clerk.

SEC. 4. All licenses granted under any Resolution or Ordinance of the Common Council, shall be signed by the Mayor and countersigned by the Clerk of the City, who shall keep, in books to be provided therefor, full minutes of the same, and of all transfers thereof, and, as near as may be, shall be in the following form:

Form of transfer.

"CITY OF DETROIT:—I, ——, Mayor of the City of Detroit. To all who shall see these presents—Greeting:

"Know ye, that ——— has paid into the Treasury of the City

the sum of —— dollars, and otherwise complied with the provisions of the Charter and Ordinances of the City in this behalf; therefore, the said ——— is hereby authorized and empowered to —— for the period of —— months from the date hereof.

"In witness whereof, I have hereunto set my hand, and caused the seal of the City to be affixed, at the City Hall in said City, this —— day of ——, A. D. 18—.

[L. S.]

———, *Mayor.*

"Countersigned, ———, *City Clerk.*"

SEC. 5. Chapter sixty-nine, of the Compiled Ordinances of 1859, and an Ordinance "to amend Chapter seventy, of the Compiled Ordinances of 1859," approved March 31, 1860, and all Ordinances and parts of Ordinances inconsistent with this Ordinance, are hereby repealed.

SEC. 6. This Ordinance shall take effect from and after its passage.

CHAPTER XCVIII.

OF THE PAYMENT OF CLAIMS AND DEMANDS AGAINST THE CITY OF DETROIT.

[Ordinance approved January 14, 1862.]

SECTION 1. All claims and demands, of every name and nature whatsoever, against the City of Detroit, shall, in the first instance, be presented and filed with the City Controller, who shall present the same to the Common Council, at its next session, or as soon thereafter as practicable, with a communication, in writing, setting forth the facts in relation to such claims and demands and his opinion in relation to the payment thereof. Claims to be presented to City Controller, and, by him, presented to the Common Council.

SEC. 2. Any unliquidated claim or demand against the City, when presented to the Controller, shall be accompanied with an affidavit of the person rendering it, as provided in section twenty-five, of chapter four, of the Charter of the City of Detroit. Unliquidated claims must be accompanied by affidavit.

SEC. 3. Any person presenting a claim or demand against the City, for supplies furnished for the use of the Corporation, or any Board thereof, shall accompany the same with a bill of the items Claims for supplies to be accompanied by bill of items.

thereof, with the name or names of the person or persons upon whose order the same were furnished.

Claims for work and labor, etc., to be accompanied by a written and sworn statement.

SEC. 4. All claims and demands against the City, for work or labor performed for the Corporation, under any contract for paving any street, lane or alley, or for the construction or repair of any sewer, drain, side or cross-walk, bridge or culvert, shall be accompanied with a written statement, under oath, of the amount of work or labor performed, and the precise locality where such work was performed, and the extent of the same. And before any such claim or demand is presented for allowance to the Common Council, it shall be the duty of the Controller to refer the same to the City Surveyor to ascertain whether such work has been performed agreeably to contract, and in the manner and to the extent set forth in the statement accompanying such claim or demand, and has been performed in other respects in a good, substantial and workmanlike manner.

And to be referred to City Surveyor.

Claims to be paid out of funds raised by special assessment.

SEC. 5. In the allowance of any claim or demand for the payment of which a special assessment has been levied, the Common Council shall not appropriate any money for the payment thereof, except such as shall have been paid into the City treasury in payment of the assessment levied upon the lot or lots in front of or adjacent to which such work has been performed.

Warrants not to be drawn when fund is exhausted.

SEC. 6. The Common Council shall not order any warrant to be drawn on the City Treasurer, when the fund out of which such warrant is to be paid has been exhausted.

Controller to take and file receipts.

SEC. 7. It shall be the duty of the Controller, when any claim or demand against the City has been paid, to take a receipt therefor and file the same in his office.

Claims not to be paid until allowed by Common Council.

SEC. 8. No claim or demand against the City of Detroit shall be paid until the same has been audited and allowed by the Common Council.

SEC. 9. This Ordinance shall take immediate effect.

CHAPTER XCIX.

OF CANCELING THE ORDERS, WARRANTS AND DUE-BILLS OF THE CITY OF DETROIT.

[Chapter Seventy-three of Compiled Ordinances of 1859.]

Treasurer to cancel warrants, etc.

SECTION 1. The City Treasurer shall, without delay, procure a proper canceling hammer, such as is ordinarily used by banking institutions, with which he shall immediately cut, mark and cancel every order, due-bill, warrant or other evidence of debt, issued by the City of Detroit, or by the Common Council of said City, or under their direction, which now are in the City treasury; and hereafter the said Treasurer shall, as soon as any order, due-bill or warrant, or other evidence of debt heretofore issued, or which hereafter shall or may at any time or times be issued by said City of Detroit, or by said Common Council, or by or under their direction or authority, shall come or be paid into the treasury of said City, cut, mark and cancel the same with said canceling hammer.

To keep canceled warrants.

SEC. 2. After the City Treasurer shall have so cut, marked and canceled said orders, warrants, due-bills or other evidences of debt, as aforesaid, he shall carefully and safely file and keep the same until the further order or action of said Common Council.

To record the same.

SEC. 3. It shall be the duty of the City Treasurer, from and after the passage of this chapter, to keep a book or record, in which he shall enter, as soon as he receives the same, the number, date and amount of each and every warrant, order, due-bill and evidence of debt, as aforesaid, received into the City treasury; and whenever the City Treasurer shall report to said Common Council any amount of warrants, orders, due-bills or other evidences of debt, as hereinafter provided for, he shall accompany his report with a schedule or list of said warrants, orders, due-bills or other evidences of debt so reported, with the number, date and amount of each.

Warrants, etc., to be returned to Council and destroyed.

SEC. 4. Whenever the City Treasurer shall have in his possession one thousand dollars of cut, marked and canceled warrants, orders, due-bills or other evidences of debt, issued or hereafter to be issued, as aforesaid, he shall report the fact to the said Common

Council, whilst in session, and thereupon, at the same session of said Council, or at the next regular meeting, said Council shall cause said orders, due-bills, warrants or other evidences of debt aforesaid, to be carefully examined and checked on the warrant book, in presence of the Council, by a committee of three, to be appointed, from time to time, by the Mayor, of whom the Clerk shall be one ; and the same having been so counted, examined and checked, shall be forthwith burned, or otherwise destroyed, in the presence of the Council, and the amount so destroyed, with the number or other suitable designation of each, shall be entered on the Journal of the Council.

CHAPTER C.

OF THE SALE OF LOTS HELD BY THE CITY UNDER TAX TITLES, AND CANCELING DEFECTIVE TAX TITLES.

[Ordinance approved December 24, 1863.]

Treasurer authorized to sell interest of City in lands held under tax titles.

SECTION 1. The Treasurer is authorized to advertise and sell and convey all the right, title and interest of the City in and to the several lots and premises held through tax titles by the City, giving three months' notice of the time and place of sale, in two or more newspapers published in the City, and by publishing a list or description of said lands in handbill form, for general distribution through the several wards ; the expense thereof to be added to the sum fixed as a minimum price for said lots. The City Marshal shall cause said handbills to be posted in ten public places in each ward, thirty days before said sale. Any lot or parcel of land not sold and paid for at said sale, may, at any time thereafter, be sold and disposed of at private sale, at the minimum price.

In cases of erroneous assessment, etc., Treasurer may compromise the claim of the City.

SEC. 2. The City Treasurer shall, in all cases wherein satisfactory evidence shall be presented to him of erroneous assessment or return or sale, of any lot or premises, be authorized to receive the original tax, with interest at seven per cent., from the day of sale, in compromise of the claims of the City for its tax title to any such lot or premises: *Provided,* The same shall be approved by the Controller.

Where tax has been paid, premises to be discharged, etc.

SEC. 3. It shall be the duty of the City Treasurer, whenever satisfactory evidence is presented to him of the payment of any tax on any lot or parcel of land, to discharge said premises from said tax, if the same has not been sold; and if the same has been sold to the City, he shall cancel or quit-claim to the owner the tax title thus acquired; and if the tax thus paid has not been accounted for and paid over by the officer receiving said tax, the Treasurer shall immediately cause proceedings to be taken for the collection of the same.

If tax has been twice paid Treasurer may refund amount.

SEC. 4. If any tax upon any lot or parcel of land shall be twice paid, the City Treasurer may, with the approval of the Common Council and the Controller, refund one of said payments to the party entitled thereto.

SEC. 5. This Ordinance shall take immediate effect.

AN ORDINANCE

TO GIVE EFFECT TO THE REVISED ORDINANCE OF EIGHTEEN HUNDRED AND SIXTY-THREE.

It is hereby Ordained by the Common Council of the City of Detroit:

SECTION 1. That the edition of the Ordinances of the City of Detroit, compiled and published under the direction of the Controller, in accordance with the resolution of the Common Council adopted July 21, 1863, shall be called "The Revised Ordinance of the City of Detroit for the year 1863," and the same, together with this Ordinance, shall take effect and go into operation from and after the twenty-second day of December, A. D. 1863.

SEC. 2. All by-laws and Ordinances, or parts of By-Laws and Ordinances, repugnant to, or in any manner inconsistent with, the edition of Ordinances so arranged and published as aforesaid, shall be repealed from and after the taking effect of the said Revised Ordinance so arranged and published.

SEC. 3. The repeal provided for in the preceding section, shall not affect any act done, or any right accruing or accrued, or established, or any suit had or commenced for any purpose whatever, before the time when such repeal shall take effect; nor shall any offence committed, or penalty or forfeiture incurred, under any of the Ordinances or By-Laws repealed by the preceding section, and before the time when such repeal shall take effect, be affected by such repeal.

SEC. 4. No suit or prosecution pending at the time of the said repeal, for any offence committed, or for the recovery of any penalty or forfeiture incurred, under any of the Ordinances or By-Laws repealed as provided for in section three, shall be affected by such repeal, except that the proceedings in such suit or prosecution shall be conformed, when necessary, to the provisions of said Revised Ordinances.

SEC. 5. All persons who, at the time when the said repeal shall take effect, shall hold any office under any of the Ordinances or By-Laws so as aforesaid repealed, shall continue to hold the same according to the tenure thereof.

SEC. 6. No Ordinance or By-Law which has heretofore been repealed, shall be revived by the repeal provided for in section three.

SEC. 7. Whenever an Ordinance or By-Law, or any part thereof, shall be repealed by a subsequent Ordinance or By-Law, such Ordinance or By-Law, or any part thereof, so repealed, shall not be revived by the repeal of such subsequent repealing Ordinance or By-Law.

SEC. 8. All Ordinances and By-Laws hereafter to be passed by the Common Council, shall be promulgated by being printed in such manner as the Charter directs.

SEC. 9. This Ordinance shall take effect and be in force from and after the twenty-second day of December, A. D. 1863.

Ordained and dated in Common Council, the twenty-second day of December, A. D. 1863.

Approved December 24, 1863.

WM. C. DUNCAN, *Mayor.*

Attest: FRANCIS PRAMSTALLER, *City Clerk.*

INDEX.

ERRATUM.

On page 18, in beginning of form of affidavit, for "Controller" read "Collector."

www.ingramcontent.com/pod-product-compliance
Lightning Source LLC
LaVergne TN
LVHW050524100826
845148LV00002B/429

* 9 7 8 1 4 2 5 5 2 0 4 0 3 *